The Saltwater Angler's Guide
to Florida's Big Bend and Emerald Coast

WILD FLORIDA

UNIVERSITY PRESS OF FLORIDA

Florida A&M University, Tallahassee
Florida Atlantic University, Boca Raton
Florida Gulf Coast University, Ft. Myers
Florida International University, Miami
Florida State University, Tallahassee
New College of Florida, Sarasota
University of Central Florida, Orlando
University of Florida, Gainesville
University of North Florida, Jacksonville
University of South Florida, Tampa
University of West Florida, Pensacola

The Saltwater Angler's Guide to Florida's Big Bend and Emerald Coast

Tommy L. Thompson

Foreword by M. Timothy O'Keefe

University Press of Florida

Gainesville

Tallahassee

Tampa

Boca Raton

Pensacola

Orlando

Miami

Jacksonville

Ft. Myers

Sarasota

Library of Congress Cataloging-in-Publication Data
Thompson, Tommy L.
The saltwater angler's guide to Florida's Big Bend and Emerald Coast / Tommy L.
Thompson.
p. cm.—(Wild Florida)
Includes bibliographical references and index.
ISBN 978-0-8130-3338-9 (alk. paper)
1. Saltwater fishing—Florida—Big Bend Region—Guidebooks. 2. Saltwater fishing—
Florida—Emerald Coast—Guidebooks. 3. Big Bend Region (Fla.)—Guidebooks.
4. Emerald Coast (Fla.)—Guidebooks. I. Title.
SH457.T54 2009
799.16'0916364—dc22   2008040307

The University Press of Florida is the scholarly publishing agency for the State
University System of Florida, comprising Florida A&M University, Florida Atlantic
University, Florida Gulf Coast University, Florida International University, Florida
State University, New College of Florida, University of Central Florida, University
of Florida, University of North Florida, University of South Florida, and University
of West Florida.

University Press of Florida
15 Northwest 15th Street
Gainesville, FL 32611-2079
http://www.upf.com

WILD FLORIDA

Edited by M. Timothy O'Keefe

Books in this series are written for the many people who visit and/or move to Florida to participate in our remarkable outdoors, an environment rich in birds, animals and activities, many exclusive to this state. Books in the series will offer readers a variety of formats: Natural history guides, historical outdoor guides, guides to some of Florida's most popular pastimes and activities, and memoirs of outdoors folk and their unique lifestyles.

Contents

Part 2. Practical Matters

Foreword

Already ranked as one of the most populous states, Florida absorbs hundreds of thousands of new residents every year. It seems impossible that truly wild places can remain anywhere in such a densely inhabited region. In spite of the tremendous influx of people wanting to enjoy the Sunshine State's warm climate and active outdoors lifestyle, significant sections of the original natural Florida do still endure.

The University Press of Florida in its broad-ranging series *Wild Florida* takes you to one of the lesser-known and more pristine regions with *The Saltwater Angler's Guide to Florida's Big Bend and Emerald Coast*. There could be no better guide than Florida native Tommy Thompson of Gainesville who knows the area thoroughly after fishing it regularly for decades.

Because Tommy Thompson's name is a common one, he should not be confused with who he is not. For instance, he is not Tommy Thompson, the former Wisconsin governor who later was Secretary of the U.S. Department of Health and Human Services. Nor is he the Tommy Thompson who was a one-time Republican presidential hopeful from New York. No, this is Florida's fish 'n' grits Tommy Thompson, licensed captain, fishing guide, noted photographer and—as you're about to appreciate—unusually engaging writer.

As those of us who know Tommy expected, his Big Bend and Emerald Coast angler's guide is anything but the ordinary how-to, where-to fishing book salted with colorful personal anecdotes but offering relatively few useful information nuggets. Tommy, who I've always considered something of a perfectionist, isn't content to limit himself to coaching lessons on how-where to catch upper Gulf Coast game fish. He has moved beyond the typical fishing guide to provide the variety of detailed information every first-time angler wants: where to stay, where to dine, where to buy bait, where to launch a boat. And all without the influence of advertising.

Another unexpected bonus is here. Although you may never intend to fish the entire upper Gulf Coast from the Chassahowitzka River north of Tampa to the Alabama state line, once you start reading you will want to finish, compelled onward by Tommy's honesty and wry wit. Here's why, with one opening paragraph I particularly like: "Horseshoe Beach has no beach, unless you count the twenty-foot strip of white sand next to the county boat ramp. You *will* find horseshoe crabs there."

No hype, hyperbole or pretense. Just honest information. Maybe in this age of glossing over almost everything, that's what makes Tommy's writing so refreshing. More importantly, you know you can trust him because he is something of a throwback: a no-nonsense tell-it-like-it-is writer.

This is a very complete book but there's more information beyond these time-bound pages. You'll continue to enjoy more coaching and travel tips at Tommy's Web site www.saltwateranglersguide.com. I consider this the angler's version of *The Neverending Story*, and it's about time!

This makes *The Saltwater Angler's Guide to Florida's Big Bend and Emerald Coast* unique, a much overused term I dislike but is decidedly apt in this instance. Anglers today rely on GPS coordinates, weather satellites, and cell phones, so it's only fitting that fishing guidebooks become part of the Internet age. Not only will this allow a continuing relationship with the author, the information within these pages need never go out of date. As long as Tommy keeps fishing—and we all expect a few more decades from him—his advice will be as timely as the day's weather forecast but probably much more accurate. For those without this book as a reference, his updates will be gibberish.

In a state developing as fast as Florida, updating the outdoors is critical. As Tommy notes, too much of Florida continually is lost "in the wake of 'progress'" yet you'll be hard-pressed to find another Florida fishing guide offering timely online information.

You can trust Tommy Thompson's opinions and recommendations—and, most important, his facts—both now and in the future. He is too much of a perfectionist to expect otherwise.

M. Timothy O'Keefe
Series editor

Before You Leave Home

Be sure to check this guide's companion Web site,
www.saltwateranglersguide.com, for updates to local information.

Introduction

We are anglers, and this is a guidebook just for us. My goal is to outline the essentials of fishing Florida's Gulf of Mexico coast from Chassahowitzka to Florida's western border while providing valuable information regarding lodging, meals, and fishing-related amenities. I hope you'll enjoy reading the entire book and not just the chapter that deals with your destination. As there are no real physical boundaries between the locations I've chosen to describe, a certain overlap of information is inevitable. There are also chapters dealing with universal fishing and boating knowledge that I hope you'll enjoy. I make no promises that spouses or children with interests other than fishing will find its recommendations interesting and suggest you consult more general travel guides for non-fishing possibilities. However, if you're a visitor or just a resident needing some practical information, please read on.

Anglers have special needs. We eat, we sleep, and we fish. If you're like me, fishing comes first, but after a hard day on the water, it's nice to come back to a good meal and a nice bed. It's also nice to start the day in a strange or seldom-fished territory with good advance information as to where to launch your boat, where to buy gas and supplies, and where and how to start fishing. This book is about those details.

A brief explanation of the conventions used in the book will be helpful. First, I use *gulf* to simplify any reference to the Gulf of Mexico. There are plenty of bays, harbors, and inlets located within the geographic scope of this guide—but only one gulf. There is no ocean on the western side of Florida. Second, I assume that everyone can get to US Highway 98, the highway that forms the spine of the Big Bend and Emerald Coast. It makes a northerly turn at Chassahowitzka and runs north to Perry, where it makes a turn westward past Pensacola. Authoritative map resources exist, and a visit to your local American Automobile Association office or bookstore will provide you the necessary tools to get to a jumping-off spot from the big roads. Don't overlook owning a copy of DeLorme's *Florida Atlas & Gazetteer*, a terrific resource showing roads and trails in very fine detail. Third, although this is a fishing guide and I list GPS coordinates (in Latitude/Longitude format) for some fishing spots, space for elaborate detailed fishing maps is limited. I have checked my GPS coordinates and they are reasonably *correct*, but I don't guarantee that they are absolutely accurate. Use them with some care, as you would any navigational directions. NOAA charts, available from most marine suppliers, are essential. Even if you carry a sophisticated GPS unit loaded with digital charts, you'll still need paper charts to plan your trip. Good commercial interpretations of United States Government NOAA charts are also available, and take accurate navigation one step further. I highly recommend the portable and convenient fishing charts produced by Waterproof Charts, Inc. Maptech's *Chartkit* books are complete volumes of enhanced NOAA charts that offer a wealth of information not found on the basic NOAA charts, such as GPS grids and a companion CD that allows viewing of charts on a computer. Maptech's Region 8 set, *Florida West Coast and the Keys* is a great investment for any gulf angler, particularly if you plan to fish from a boat. Another good, albeit slightly outdated, reference is the series of *Boater's Guides*, produced by the Florida Department of Environmental Protection's Marine Research Institute. These valuable guides are available for free and cover Citrus County, Apalachicola Bay, St. Joseph Bay, St. Andrew Bay, Choctawhatchee Bay, and Pensacola Bay. Find them at many tackle shops and visitors' bureaus.

While I don't aim to go into tremendous detail about each species of fish found in the gulf, I will mention some good references and mention their food value. While many sport fishermen, including myself, practice catch-and-release fishing, those of you planning to keep and eat seafood should be aware of safe storage practices. The basic rule is to ice your catch quickly and use more ice than you think you need.

Finally, I will make references to fishing tackle and fishing-related gear. I recommend things that I've personally used or that come highly recommended by guides and serious anglers I know. And, if it's an obscure or hard-to-get item, I'll mention where it can be found. This guide's "Part Two—Practical Matters" will also help you understand certain general terms and techniques mentioned in the first sixteen chapters.

Even though this guidebook is based on my knowledge of and visits to all the locations covered, time can be a factor. Hurricanes and real-estate developers have, in recent years, overrun Florida. Not only do marinas and boat ramps disappear in the wake of "progress," but also entire navigable channels may be redirected and grass flats scrubbed clean by Mother Nature. Local, state, and federal authorities frequently update rules and regulations too. This guide's companion Web site, www.saltwateranglersguide.com, will have regular updates to the information included herein. Please check it before you head out, just to be sure. I'd love your input too. Let me know if you've had a good or bad experience, noticed a change about a location, or simply that you've discovered the best lure ever made. My contact information is on the Web site.

I've fished Florida's Gulf Coast all my life and despite the proclamation, "It's fishing, not catching," made by many anglers after a slow day on the water, I'm still disappointed coming home after catching nothing. Certainly, factors such as equipment failure and weather are insurmountable and make for some forgettable days. But I'm hopeful this guide will provide enough local knowledge to get you started fishing a new location, making *catching* a reality.

1

The Destinations

1

Florida's Big Bend and Emerald Coast

What's in a name? In the case of Florida's upper Gulf Coast, some confusion exists. Names such as Big Bend, Forgotten Coast, Suncoast, and Emerald Coast are primarily slogans created by local chambers of commerce, convention and visitors bureaus, and advertising agencies. From an angler's point-of-view, these names are not mere slogans but real places, and there are fewer places he'd rather be.

Beginning at the Hernando County–Citrus County line on the central western coast, proceeding north then west toward Cape San Blas beyond Apalachicola, the close-in water depths are relatively shallow and mostly rocky. Many locals at the southern end of the Big Bend remark that you've got to travel a mile offshore to notice a one-foot increase in water depth.

From St. George Island westward to Pensacola, the water deepens quickly just off the white-sand beaches. It's not uncommon to find depths to 60-feet within a quarter-mile of shore on the Emerald Coast. This is not to say that there are no nearshore shallows west of the St. Joe Peninsula, but it's pretty safe to say that most inshore fishing along this stretch is within bays and coves. Beach fishing is the exception—just don't wade out too far!

Taken as a whole, this entire stretch offers some of the finest inshore and offshore fishing to be found on the planet. Whether you're fishing for marlin from a 47-foot boat in the upper reaches of the Florida Middle Grounds out from Destin or stalking redfish along the shallow Taylor County flats north of Steinhatchee, know that no matter how far you've traveled, you're in some of the world's best angling water.

Warm tropical currents push baitfish and game fish northward along the western edge of Florida's peninsula. Some fish are stopped and redirected by natural prominences, including the Cedar Keys and the St. Joseph's Peninsula, while others make home in outflows of major rivers: the Crystal, Withlacoochee, Suwannee, Apalachicola, and Perdido. These river systems also affect local fishing patterns with their input of fresh water and silt into the Gulf of Mexico. Inshore anglers should take care not to disregard smaller rivers, or even creeks, that influence local fishing conditions. And, offshore anglers using sophisticated depth-sounding gear will realize that estuarine systems of major rivers reach far offshore.

Fishing options vary all along this coastline. Offshore anglers don't really have as many options as their inshore and nearshore brethren, but there's still plenty to keep them busy. If you fish offshore, you will need to either take your own craft or charter a party, or head, boat. A boat's not necessary for successful inshore angling. Great opportunities to catch fish from bridges and piers, or by wading, abound all up and down the gulf.

The chapters that follow discuss specific angling locations and address topics of interest to fishermen. If you have a boat, there's information on marinas, launching, fueling, and basic navigation. If you need bait, food, or lodging, you'll find that information, too. If you don't know where to go to catch a few fish, I'll pass along some inshore and offshore suggestions with GPS coordinates. And, if you want to fish a specific location without doing lots of research or without getting your own boat wet, a list of eager, professional fishing guides is included.

2

Homosassa, Chassahowitzka, and the Southern Suncoast Keys

I'll take the liberty of proclaiming that Florida's Big Bend starts at the mouth of the Chassahowitzka River, about 80 miles west of Orlando and 65 miles north of St. Petersburg. Heavy urban populations bring overcrowded waterways and highways, but most of that crowding ends near the Citrus County–Hernando County line, which also serves as the lower boundary of the Chassahowitzka National Wildlife Refuge.

Chassahowitzka, pronounced *chess-a-whisky* by locals, is a small settlement at the headwaters of the river bearing its name. The main waterway and town, however, in southern Citrus County is at Homosassa.

The Chassahowitzka is a small gin-clear spring-fed river that's extremely shallow and should be navigated with caution. In fact, as in the case of many smaller Big Bend rivers, there's no appreciable increase in depth for several miles outside the river's entrance at the gulf. The Homosassa River, on the other hand, while rocky and tricky to navigate, is deep enough for larger boats to use and has a marked channel to the gulf. Like the Chaz, the Homosassa is spring-fed but by springs with greater capacity, and it pumps huge volumes of 72-degree water into the gulf. Both rivers feed into a nearshore mixture of shallow rocks, oyster beds, and mangrove islands known as the Suncoast Keys. Shallow relatively warm water affects fishing all year,

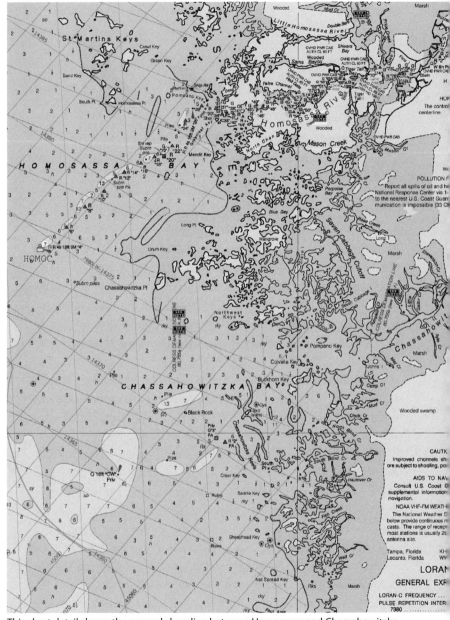

This chart detail shows the rugged shoreline between Homosassa and Chassahowitzka.

particularly in the winter, when many fish species are attracted by the river's springs.

Departing either river will get you to excellent fishing, and the surrounding communities offer plenty of amenities for anglers.

Inshore and Nearshore Fishing at Homosassa and Chassahowitzka

The inshore and nearshore waters from the Chassahowitzka River north to the St. Martins River offer something for every angler. Anglers wishing to fish the ultra-shallow backwaters, including Mason Creek, the Salt River, and the Chassahowitzka River, will find abundant stocks of redfish, sea trout, and in recent years, snook. Less fearless types or those with deeper-draft boats will find plenty of trout and redfish action in the Homosassa River near the mangrove-lined gulf shoreline or on the grass flats, which extend several miles offshore. Sheepshead, Spanish mackerel, jack crevalle, and ladyfish round out the inshore species list. Did I mention tarpon? Homosassa and Chaz are legendary tarpon fisheries, and many fly-rod world records have come from these shallow flats.

If you're able to access the backwaters, you'll find rocky "Swiss cheese" bottom that's not very friendly to many types of boats. Many local anglers and guides use specially designed tunnel-hull boats to weave through the maze of rocks and mangrove islands; others use kayaks and canoes.

During the warmer months, redfish rule this area while trout and snook move toward cooler deeper waters. Reds seem to be much more tolerant of warm water than are other species.

In cooler months, all these species seek comfort on the sun-drenched shallow rocky bottom, in holes, or the numerous springs, including those at the headwaters of each river. Find a spring, a deeper bay, or a south-facing rocky shore and you'll find fish in the wintertime.

These backwater fish are finicky and spooky. Some days they'll eat any lure or natural bait tossed at them, including live shrimp or jigs; other days they turn up their noses at all baits. Some days they'll spook if you pole your boat within 100 yards and other days they let you approach within ten feet via trolling motor. Stealth and accurate long casts will usually pay off.

Shallow-water fish are excellent targets for topwater lures (Mirr-Olure Top Dogs, for example), in any season. While live bait (shrimp, pinfish, mud minnows, or crabs) is popular here, there's nothing like the jolt of a big trout, red, or snook striking a surface lure.

It's not a bad trip from the public launching ramp in Homosassa to some nice ultra-shallow water north of Tiger Tail Bay (in the Homosassa River) or in the Salt River, which flows northward to Ozello and then on to the Crystal River. You can also reach the same backwaters by launching at the John Brown ramp east of Ozello. The county ramp at Chassahowitzka and the primitive ramp at Mason Creek, south of Homosassa, are options that put you right in the middle of the backwaters. In this skinny water, look for signs of moving fish or bait and act accordingly. Don't hesitate to try different baits, as predators here may be hiding amongst mullet but not eating them. Schools of big mullet stir up the bottom, revealing crustaceans that are easier prey for game fish. Of course, if the mullet are small, throw a look-alike, for ex-

Anglers fishing Homosassa and Chassahowitzka backwaters often use boats specially built for navigating the extreme shallows.

The backwaters of the Suncoast Keys to the north and south of Homosassa are known for an abundance of redfish.

ample the Rapala Skitterwalk. This is also excellent water for fly fishermen, and the crystal-clear water offers great sight-fishing for redfish.

Super-shallow water fishing is intriguing, but many anglers here prefer to say in more comfortable depths. The natural rocky shoreline of the Homosassa River usually provides excellent year-round fishing. Anchor up just outside the channel and try fishing jigs (D.O.A. CAL tails on ¼-ounce red jig heads) or live shrimp near the rocky edges. A low-tide scouting trip or family boat ride on this river can be an invaluable learning exercise. Note the potential hot spots on low water, and fish them on the higher tides when predators forage along the channel edges.

The Chassahowitzka River is shallower than the Homosassa but still offers access to moderate-draft boats and is structurally the same. Leaving either river or backwater you'll find miles of healthy grass flats mixed with sandy patches. On very cold days, you won't do well in these four- to five-foot depths for trout, so move shallower with the fish to the limits of your boat. A few reds are caught on the flats, but remember that reds don't usually venture too far offshore unless they've reached mature lengths of thirty inches or more. Good starter spots for drifting flats are south of Homosassa markers #6 and #8 and off the St. Martins Keys. Live shrimp, pinfish, or jigs under noisy popping corks are popular flats baits in this area, but slow-sinking plugs and shrimp imitations work well, too.

Other species of game fish are not to be forgotten. Expect to see sheepshead all year, but the big spawners show up during late winter and are easy prey around channel markers and deeper rock piles. Try using small shrimp or fiddler crabs on ⅜-ounce jig heads for sheepshead. Anglers fishing the flats will occasionally have their lure and leader ripped away by the teeth of a Spanish mackerel. Marauding schools of jack crevalle, bluefish, and ladyfish are usually found on the flats feeding under flocks of wheeling sea birds. Mackerel, blues, ladyfish, and jacks all love flashy baits moved rapidly through schools of baitfish. And, if you'll take a look in the rod holders of experienced local anglers, you'll find a big spinning outfit rigged with a jig or plug for the occasional tarpon or cobia swimming within casting distance on the flats.

Tarpon fishing at Homosassa and Chassahowitzka is some of the best in the world. While resident fish are found in the Homosassa River all year long, it's the big, pre-spawning fish that migrate through the flats that get all the press. In May and June of each year, the flats are host to many world-class fly fishermen. A word of caution, though, to visiting anglers: The fly-fishing guides working the flats south of Chassahowitzka Point to Bayport are an irritable and sensitive bunch. Fly fishing for these big tarpon is exacting work, and weekenders, live-baiters, and plug-tossers are best served if they fish other areas. The standing rule on the shallows to the south of Homosassa, known locally as the Oklahoma Flats, is that if you can tell the color of the angler's shirt, you're too close to his boat! For the fishermen who are less serious than these intent fly anglers, there are plenty of tarpon closer to the mouth of the Homosassa River, just offshore of the St. Martins Keys, and near the northern end of the Wildlife Refuge boundary markers south of Homosassa marker #14 (N28 45.073 W82 43.984).

Homosassa attracts world-class fly fishermen in the spring. Several world records have been broken here.

Offshore Fishing at Homosassa and Chassahowitzka

On close inspection of NOAA chart #11409, you'll notice that shallow water extends much farther off southern Citrus County than almost any other place on the Gulf Coast. That being the case, it's no surprise that Homosassa and Chassahowitzka are better known for their inshore waters than for what's conveniently reached offshore. However, a number of good artificial reefs exist nearby. Although south of Chassahowitzka, the Champion Reef (N28 36.440, W82 56.470), and the Bendickson Reefs (N28 31.660, W82 58.720 and N28 30.030, W82 58.700) all lie in twenty to thirty feet of water and have been good areas for grouper, sheepshead, cobia, and king mackerel for years. To the north, off Crystal River, the water deepens more rapidly and many anglers from Homosassa head to the deeper troughs and rocky spots near the confluence of the Progress Energy channel and the Cross Florida Barge Canal channel to troll for gag grouper and king mackerel. The Citrus County reefs (N28 55.300 W82 52.501 and N28 54.900 W82 52.301) are also good but older manmade sites just south of the Progress Energy channel.

Southern Citrus County is known for its shallow-water grouper fishery. There are literally hundreds of natural limestone rock outcroppings scattered in the coastal shallows, and many reach to within a foot of the water's surface. Good areas to begin your search for shallow rocks are the five- to twelve-foot depths northwest of St. Martins Keys (N28 49.935 W82 49.700) and the vast area of rocks to the southwest of Chassahowitzka off Bayport. (Try N28 35.581 W82 51.472 as a central starting point for a search of this area.) While these big rocks are scattered, they are numerous and hold grouper most of the year. In the colder winter months, the grouper are not as enthusiastic about feeding as they are in spring and fall. Late spring brings sharks to the rocks, making the summer a difficult time—unless you're fishing for sharks—to present baits to these grouper.

Nevertheless, in any season, it's worth throwing a diving plug or live bait over a chum line you've set up next to a big shallow rock. Use the chum to bring the fish away from the rocks and you'll have a better chance of getting him to the boat once he hooks up. A word of warning is in order: Motor slowly on your search for grouper among shallow rocks—they've been known to jump up and eat the lower units right off of outboard motors!

In the warmer months, the close-in rocky bottom off Homosassa and Chassahowitzka affords a shallow refuge for large schools of migratory baitfish, generically termed *white bait*. These schools are followed by king mackerel and offer good targets for fisherman who hunt these skyrocketing acrobats. Slow-trolling live baits at one to two knots or simply drifting live bait rigged on a stinger rig are popular methods used by local fishermen to target kings. Warm water also brings an influx of cobia, which roam the shallows and sometimes linger near rock piles or markers. A jig, rigged with a long eel-like tail, is handy to keep on a pre-rigged rod just in case a cobia swims by, but a small silver-dollar size crab is real cobia candy.

Getting Around

The town of Homosassa Springs is located at the intersection of US Highway 19/98 and County Road 490. Traveling west from the in-

This aerial view shows the upper Homosassa River and Old Homosassa, looking westward to the Gulf of Mexico.

tersection, you'll have a choice of continuing straight on Halls River Road or turning left onto Fishbowl Drive. Take the left, and Fishbowl Drive joins with Yulee Drive, leading to Homosassa proper.

Chassahowitzka is located just west of the intersection of US 98 and US 19. Follow West Miss Maggie Drive westward to the settlement and the county boat ramp.

Where to Stay

Chassahowitzka

The Chassahowitzka Hotel, 8551 W. Miss Maggie Dr., (352) 382-2075, 1-877-807-7783. Lodging.

Chassahowitzka River Lodge, 8501 W. Miss Maggie Dr., (352) 382-2081. Cabins, RV park, bait, and tackle.

Homosassa Area

Homosassa Riverside Resort, 5297 S. Cherokee Way, Homosassa, (352) 628-2474, 1-800-442-2040, www.riversideresorts.com. Lodging, food, bar, dockage, launching ramp for guests, boat rentals, bait, and tackle. This comfortable complex is located on the river in Old Homosassa. The facilities are excellent and include a first-rate restaurant and bar.

MacRae's of Homosassa, 5300 S. Cherokee Way, Homosassa, (352) 628-2602. Lodging, public launching ramp, dockage, boat rentals, bait and tackle, and outdoor bar. The motel rooms are above average, and the location is excellent. On the Homosassa River next to the public boat ramp, MacRae's is an Old Homosassa institution. Smoking is allowed in all rooms.

Riversport Kayaks, 5297 S. Cherokee Way, Homosassa, (352) 621-4972, 1-877-660-0929, www.flakayak.com. Kayak sales, rentals, and guide service.

Blue Moon B&B, 10137 W. Fishbowl Dr., Homosassa, (352) 621-1960, www.thebluemoonbb.com. Lodging.

Seagrass River Resort, 10386 W. Halls River Rd., Homosassa, (352) 628-2551, 1-866-732-4727, www.seagrasspub.com. Lodging, food, and dockage.

Rod 'n' Nod B&B, (352) 628-5986, www.rodnnod.com. Lodging.

River Safaris, 10823 W. Yulee Dr., Homosassa, (352) 628-5222, 1-800-758-3474, www.riversafaris.com. Lodging and boat rentals.

Where to Eat

Riverside Crab House, Homosassa Riverside Resort, Homosassa. Lunch, dinner, bar, and dockage. Excellent food and bar service. Don't miss the Seafood Feast.

Downtown Diner, US 19/98, Homosassa Springs. Breakfast and lunch. Excellent breakfasts and sandwiches. Box lunches are available here for fishing trips.

Dan's Clam Shack, Grover Cleveland Blvd., Homosassa Springs. Seafood, lunch, and dinner. Worth the trip to the eastern side of Homosassa for the fresh fried seafood.

Yulee Café, W. Yulee Dr., Homosassa. Breakfast and lunch.

Misty River Seafood, US 19/98, Homosassa Springs. Lunch and dinner.

Marinas, Marine Supplies and Service, Bait-and-Tackle Shops, and Launching Ramps

Chassahowitzka

Chassahowitzka River Campground (County Ramp), W. Miss Maggie Dr., (352) 382-2200. Public ramp with ample parking, frozen bait, some tackle, camping, restrooms, and boat rentals.

Homosassa Area

MacRae's of Homosassa, 5300 S. Cherokee Way, Homosassa, (352) 628-2602. Lodging adjacent to free public launching ramp with good parking, dockage, boat rentals, bait and tackle, outdoor bar, and gas. The staff at MacRae's is always willing to give free, up-to-the-minute fishing reports.

Homosassa Riverside Resort, 5297 S. Cherokee Way, Homosassa, (352) 628-2474, 1-800-442-2040, www.riversideresorts.com. Lodging, food, bar, dockage, launching ramp for guests, boat rentals, trailer parking, gas, and bait and tackle.

River Haven Marina, Halls River Road, Homosassa, (352) 628-5545. Ten-dollar launching ramp, frozen bait, clean restrooms, and Mercury, Honda, and Yamaha service.

Magic Manatee Marina, Halls River Road, Homosassa, (352) 628-7334. Gas, launching ramp, boat rentals, dry storage.

Homosassa Marine, US 19/98, Homosassa Springs, (352) 628-2991. Yamaha and Evinrude sales and service.

Gulf Coast Marine Service, W Yulee Drive, Homosassa, (352) 628-5885. Mercury, MerCruiser, Detroit, and Volvo diesel sales and service.

Quality Marine Service, Grover Cleveland Blvd, Homosassa Springs, (352) 628-7678. New and recycled marine hardware and supplies. This place is fun to visit on a rainy day. You never know what you'll find!

Outcast Fly Shop, Capt. Cade Burgdorf, US 19/98, Homosassa Springs, (352) 621-3474, www.homosassaflyfishing.com. Kayaks and extensive fly, spin, and offshore gear. There are usually a few locals hanging around the shop, willing to impart fishing advice or consolation. And Cade almost always has a new tarpon fly to show off.

Back Country Concepts, Capt. Earl Waters, W Yulee Dr., Homosassa, (352) 628-0359, www.backcountryconcepts.com. Extensive fly and light tackle, and custom flats boat rigging. Earl is the person to see if you're interested in air switches for your flats boat's trolling motor, a new PowerPole, or a trolling motor repair. His custom flies are also very impressive.

Blue Water Tackle, US 19/98, Homosassa Springs, (352) 628-0414. Live and frozen bait, and block ice. Known locally for excellent fishing-reel repairs.

Public Launching Ramp, Old Homosassa, between MacRae's and Homosassa Riverside Resort. Paved ramp, and adequate parking. Practice your trailer-backing skills before you try this ramp; it's a long back-up.

Mason Creek Boat Ramp, Mason Creek Road, Homosassa. This ramp, located on the backwaters of Mason Creek, offers good access to the southern Suncoast Keys, but it's shallow with limited roadside parking and no security.

John Brown Boat Ramp, Ozello. Located six miles from US 19/98 on County Road 494, this is a free shallow ramp with adequate parking but no security. The John Brown ramp offers excellent access for smaller boats, canoes, and kayaks to the Salt River.

Local Fishing Guides

Homosassa Guides Association, www.homosassaguidesassociation. com

Capt. Mike Locklear, (352) 422-1927, www.homosassafishing.com, captmike@homosassafishing.com. Fly fishing for tarpon, spin fishing, flats fishing, and shallow-water grouper fishing.

Capt. Jimmy Long, (352) 628-0383, www.homosassaoutfitters.com, cjl@homosassaoutfitters.com. Fly fishing for tarpon, spin fishing, and shallow-water grouper fishing.

Capt. Earl Waters, (352) 302-0359, www.backcountryconcepts.com, bccinfo@earthlink.net. Fly-fishing for tarpon, spin fishing, and shallow-water grouper fishing.

Capt. John Bazo, (352) 895-7811, www.hightidecharters.com. Fly-fishing for tarpon, spin fishing, and shallow-water grouper fishing.

Capt. William Toney, (352) 621-9284, www.homosassainshorefishing. com. Light-tackle and fly fishing, tarpon fishing, scalloping, flats fishing, shallow-water grouper fishing.

Capt. Dan Clymer, (352) 382-1313. Light-tackle inshore and backwater fishing, and shallow-water grouper fishing.

Capt. Rick Spratt, (352) 302-1606, www.captrickspratt.com, rick@captrickspratt.com. Inshore and offshore fishing.

Capt. J. W. Romish, (352) 302-2597. Inshore and backwater fishing.

Capt. Cade Burgdorf, (352) 621-3474, www.homosassaflyfishing.com. Fly fishing only.

Capt. Billy Henderson, (352) 257-6999, bhender5@tampabay.rr.com, www.plugsandslugs.com. Spin fishing and shallow-water grouper fishing.

Capt. Charlie Harris, (352) 634-4309, www.homosassaredfishing.com. Light-tackle flats fishing.

Capt. Glen Touchton, (352) 422-6838, www.southernfishingguide.net. Light-tackle fishing, eco- and sunset tours, and scalloping trips.

Capt. Gary Cox, (352) 634-3679, www.slapstikcharters.com. Light-tackle and fly fishing.

Capt. Leo Riddle, (352) 636-4466, captainleoriddle@aol.com. Inshore flats fishing.

Capt. Don Franklin, Florida River Tours, (352) 601-2480, www.floridarivertours.com. Homosassa River fishing trips for families with wheelchair needs.

Many guides from Crystal River are familiar with the waters at Homosassa and Chassahowitzka, and vice-versa. Please consult the guide listings for Crystal River, if necessary. Also, the Web site of the Florida Guides Association (www.florida-guides.com) has a complete listing of United States Coast Guard licensed-and-insured fishing guides.

3

Crystal River, Ozello, and the Northern Suncoast Keys

The town of Crystal River lies toward the northern end of Citrus County, about ten miles from Homosassa. It surrounds a large harbor, Kings Bay, where large springs form the Crystal River.

This is an aerial view of Kings Bay and the headwaters of the Crystal River, which is a popular wintertime fishing area.

This aerial view shows the backwaters between the Salt River and Ozello, in the northern Suncoast Keys.

The Crystal River is about seven miles long and feeds into the Gulf of Mexico. The river follows a well-marked and well-maintained channel from Kings Bay to deep water well offshore of the river's mouth. The vast array of oyster bars, shell bars, and lush grass flats near the river's mouth provide good habitat for many inshore species.

Ozello is a small settlement between Crystal River and Homosassa located several miles into the interior of the Suncoast Keys. In fact, it looks landlocked if viewed on a low-resolution map, but in reality, it is surrounded by an immense network of small channels and rocky mangrove islands. Some of Citrus County's best inshore fishing begins here, but only for those with boats able to handle the shallow depths.

Facilities for anglers at Crystal River are very good. Marine services are convenient, while lodging and other amenities cover a broad range of price and value.

Inshore and Nearshore Fishing at Crystal River and Ozello

Anglers who wish to fish inshore or nearshore in the northern areas of Citrus County will find a variety of opportunities. From the extremely shallow and rocky areas toward the south, including Ozello, to the deep channels formed by the dredging of the Crystal River Energy Complex intake and delivery channel, the area has something for every fisherman.

Popular local inshore species include sea trout, redfish, tarpon, flounder, Spanish mackerel, and a few snook. Of course, schools of jack crevalle, bluefish, and ladyfish abound year-round—on the flats in warmer months and in the river's relatively warm fresh water during the winter.

The major springs in Kings Bay pump a steady flow of fresh 72-degree water into the headwaters of Crystal River. During the winter you will find trout, reds, and schools of large jack crevalle near the manatee-area buoys around the springs on the southern side of

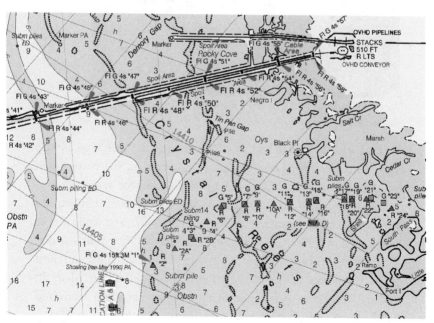

Crystal Bay, south of the power-plant and barge-canal channels, is known for its many oyster bars and lush grass flats.

A day of fishing near Crystal River is marked a success with a top-of-slot redfish in hand.

Banana Island. Tarpon and snook are seen near this spring as well. Other smaller springs, some found in canals on the eastern and southeastern edges of Kings Bay provide shelter for game fish, primarily redfish, and in recent years, snook. All of these fish move into the river's temperate waters during the coldest days, and while they're warm, you may not be. For anglers, it seems that the colder the day, the better the fishing. Winter fish also tend to be lethargic, and most probably bite out of annoyance rather than actual hunger. Many an angler comes home weary after tossing every combination of lure and bait he owns at big tarpon and snook seen swimming in Kings Bay.

Slow-moving slow-sinking lures such as the Corky Mullet and MirrOlure's Catch 2000 series are favorite artificial lures here. If live shrimp are available, they also work well, rigged tail-first on ⅛-ounce jig heads and fished very slowly across the bottom. Freshly cut mullet is also used as bait by local anglers. Residential boat docks are popular spots to fish in the headwaters of the Crystal River in winter, particularly on sunny days. The sun warms the pilings more quickly than it does the water, and game fish will nudge up to the pilings in search of a warm place to hide and feed. Another good wintertime spot is Bagley Cove, just upriver from marker #21. This spot has saved the reputations of many professional fishing guides on bitter-cold days, as it's known to hold schools of big ladyfish year-round. It's also an excellent place to practice your fly-fishing techniques, as ladyfish, referred to by many as the "poor-man's tarpon," are great fighting and jumping fish.

A few wintertime reds and trout are found along the river's rocky banks west of the Crystal River's confluence with the shallow Salt River, but it takes a few weeks of warm sunny days, usually as spring approaches, to get the fish really active along the shoreline.

In the winter months, snook, trout and reds warm themselves in the relatively deep holes in the backwaters of the Suncoast Keys and the Salt River. If your powerboat has shallow-water capabilities or you fish from a canoe or kayak, don't hesitate to try launching at one of the Ozello boat ramps or the county ramp at Fort Island near the end of County Road (CR) 44. From these ramps, it's an easy trip into the super-shallow backwaters and some great wintertime fishing. Try fishing with tail-rigged live shrimp or slow-sinking lures, both good cold-weather favorites. Be prepared, however, to lose some tackle and to snag the craggy bottom frequently.

Another popular wintertime fishery is the hot-water discharge at the Crystal River Energy Complex. Reaching the area from the Crystal River channel can be a chore, because there is no longer a shortcut through the spoil banks. The long run to the end of the spoils can be rough—and cold. An alternative is to launch at the Marine Patrol Ramp in the Cross Florida Barge Canal and approach the power-plant area from the north. Run westward in the Barge Canal channel to marker #31, steer a course (about 140 degrees) through the islands to waypoint N28 57.289 W82 46.990, then run *slowly* toward

North of Crystal River, the hot-water discharge at the Crystal River Energy Complex is a popular fishing spot on cold winter days.

During winter low tides, game fish gather in the power plant's deep channel, which is warmed by the facility's hot-water discharge.

the tall stacks. There is a large spoil island between the turn and the hot-water discharge. Pass to the left of the island and steer to N28 57.530 W82 44.571, Rocky Point, which is the end of the jetty on the southern side of the discharge. Fish the entire channel with jigs, live shrimp, or trolled MirrOlure 52M lures. It abounds with trout, reds, and even a few snook and cobia. The colder the weather and the lower the tide, the better the fishing.

Toward the gulf from Kings Bay or the backwaters of the St. Martins Keys, the fishing becomes better as the weather warms. Fish begin to move onto the grass flats and away from the warm sun-lit shores of the mangrove islands. As is typical all along the Gulf Coast, the warmer the day, the deeper onto the flats the fish venture. Redfish are caught closer to mangrove islands than are trout, but both are found year-round near the Crystal Reefs, which stretch from the Energy Complex spoil banks southward to Mangrove Point, at the northern end of the Suncoast Keys. These bars are mostly shell-covered and the cuts between them attract all varieties of bait during warmer months. The ones north of the Crystal River channel make for good wade-fishing late on summer afternoons, while the deeper bars to the south seem to attract greater numbers of baitfish. These bars and the grass flats that surround them are a popular summertime destination for anglers using topwater lures, jigs, or live shrimp and pinfish. The rocky bottom near Gomez Rocks (N28 52.180 W82 45.314) is also an easy drift for nice sea trout on warm days, but boaters should be careful of the area's larger rocks. Avoid a falling tide here! Big cobia and tarpon also cruise all of Crystal Bay in search of prey, and keeping a few small blue crabs in your live well is not a bad idea. Crabs, free-lined on 30-pound-class spinning tackle to tarpon or cobia can make a memorable day for those aboard your boat.

Spring and fall also bring an influx of larger redfish to the area. While they're found along the outer edges of the Suncoast Keys in Grey Mare Pass, Shark Point, and Fish Creek Bay, this area may be too shallow for your boat. Another option is to fish the cuts and points of the Energy Complex spoil banks to the north. Live pinfish, big shrimp, or mullet imitations, such as D.O.A. Lures' Bait Buster,

Snorkeling for bay scallops is a popular summertime activity on the grass flats to the south of Crystal River.

do very well tossed toward the rocks and then worked slowly across the bottom. Boats typically anchor stern-first into the current, and care must be taken not to take waves over the transom. Occasional schools of Spanish mackerel and the stray pompano or two are also caught here, but mainly by anglers tossing jigs sweetened with pieces of shrimp or FishBites artificial bait. In recent years, the best spots on the spoil banks have been Long Point (N28 55.996 W82 49.326) and Short Point (N28 56.030 W82 48.414). On most tides, you can safely run from marker #2 (N28 54.724 W82 44.860) in the Crystal River channel directly to the spoil banks.

Offshore Fishing at Crystal River

Crystal River has a moderate reputation as a jumping-off point for offshore fishing. The facts that the length of the river represents some extra running time for bigger boats docked or launched closer to the headwaters, and that the channel to the gulf extends at least two miles beyond the shoreline, make it less appealing to many offshore anglers. However, there are only two slow-speed or manatee zones outside of

Kings Bay, and this allows fast offshore boats relatively quick access to the open gulf. One zone is at the entrance to the Salt River, and the other is a short section of the channel next to Shell Island at the river's mouth. The Fort Island boat ramp at the end of CR 44 is adequate for bay boats and light offshore rigs, but mainly at higher tides. The ramp at Fort Island Trail Park, off CR 44 near the Salt River, is good, but there's hardly maneuvering room in the ramp area for boats much longer than 24 feet. The best ramps for anglers with larger boats are the city ramp at Pete's Pier or the Florida Marine Patrol ramp, located where US Highway 19/98 passes over the Cross Florida Barge Canal. However, both are several miles from the gulf—and then it's many more miles to deep water.

For anglers who run offshore out of Crystal River, popular species include gag and red grouper, cobia, sheepshead, and king mackerel. Gag grouper are found year-round here in depths ranging from ten to fifty feet. Many shallow rocks are found southwest of Crystal River and hold grouper throughout the winter months. Making them bite can be a chore, but large subsurface plugs such as the Bomber Long-A can sometimes entice fish from their lairs. During the warmer months, these shallow grouper feed better, but so do the sharks. Gags are also found in areas of deeper water, but the trip to either The Pit (N28 52.317 W83 07.713) or the Grouper Grounds (N28 49.590 W83 11.581) is almost thirty miles from the main channel entrance of the Crystal River.

For anglers who wish to fish in closer waters, possibilities include the areas between waypoints N28 47.259 W83 03.570 and N28 55.938 W83 05.354 where depths run between twenty to thirty feet. Red grouper are usually found on large expanses of live or grass bottom rather than always over rocks, ledges, or wrecks and, like gags, are attracted by either live bait, cut bait (squid, Spanish sardines, threadfin herring), or trolled plugs. Try prospecting these and other areas by trolling deep-running plugs such as the Mann's Neptune Stretch 30. Trolling is a tried-and-true way to cover more water and to find new spots to bottom fish.

Large spawning sheepshead can be found in late winter on many offshore rock piles. These fish are eager to eat, but sometimes are hard to catch. Smaller shrimp threaded onto heavy jig heads are a good choice of bait.

Cobia are found swimming near channel markers and over rock piles in deeper water, and king mackerel appear at random, feeding over bait pods that swarm over rocky bottom. It's always a good idea to free-line a live bait, such as a blue runner, rigged on a stinger rig for king mackerel while you're bottom fishing for grouper. Blue runners are hardy, frisky, and easily caught during warmer seasons on small jigs or Sabiki rigs. Cobia can be finicky eaters, and while a small live crab is excellent bait, heavy jig heads with long eel-like tails are attractive to them as well.

On any given day, pink mouth grunts and black sea bass will appear in areas inhabited by grouper and are very good table fare. They are the natural by-product of a bottom-fishing trip.

Getting Around

US 19/98 passes right through Crystal River, in sight of Kings Bay. CR 44 runs eastward toward Inverness and, eventually, Interstate Highway 75. Taking CR 44 (Fort Island Trail) westward will get you to the Fort Island boat ramp.

Ozello is located several miles west of US 19/98 on CR 494, locally known as the Ozello Trail. The road ends at the Pirates Cove boat ramp some ten miles from US 19/98.

Where to Stay

Crystal River

Best Western Crystal River Resort, 614 NW US 19, (352) 795-3171, 1-800-435-4409, www.crystalriverresort.com. Lodging, food, dockage, tackle shop, launching ramp for guests. The Best Western is owned by renowned angler Daryl Seaton and is conveniently located on King's Bay near the center of Crystal River.

Kings Bay Lodge, 506 NW 1st Ave., (352) 795-2850, www.kingsbay lodgefla.com. On Kings Bay, efficiency units, dockage for guests.

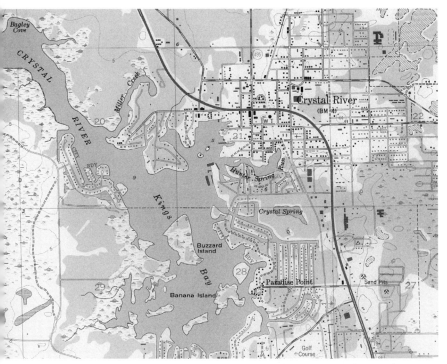

Kings Bay borders US Highway 19/98 and the town of Crystal River. Reprinted with permission from the full-color *Florida Atlas & Gazetteer*. Copyright DeLorme.

Kings Bay Lodge is an institution in Crystal River. Located on Kings Bay, it's independently operated, neat, and clean. It's free dockage for guests' boats is a big plus.

Days Inn, 2380 NW US 19, (352) 795-2111. Lodging, food, on the canal leading to Crystal River. A standard chain motel, the Days Inn is to the north of town. The canal to the main river involves at least a twenty-minute idle through a manatee zone.

Crystal Manatee Suites, 310 N Citrus Ave., (352) 795-2836. Extended stay suites. Not on the water.

The Plantation Inn, 9301 W Fort Island Trail, (352) 795-4211, www. plantationinn.com. Lodging, food, on Kings Bay. Golf, if you're interested.

The Port Hotel and Marina, 1610 SE Paradise Circle, (352) 795-3111, 1-800-443-0875, www.porthotelandmarina.com. Lodging, food, bar, dockage, launching ramp for guests, boat rentals, on Kings Bay.

Where to Eat

Peck's Old Port Cove, nine miles on CR 494 West, Ozello, (352) 795-2806. Lunch, dinner, seafood, bar, open every day. Enjoy the scenic trip to Peck's; then dig in to some great seafood.

Backwater Jack's Bar and Grill, six miles on CR 494 West, Ozello. Lunch, dinner, seafood, and bar.

Dan's Clam Shack, CR 44 East, Crystal River. Lunch, dinner, casual seafood. The fried shrimp at Dan's is worth the trip to the eastern side of town.

Caribbean Cravings on the Water, Best Western Crystal River Resort. Breakfast, lunch, dinner, authentic and casual Cuban food, tiki bar, dockage, on Kings Bay. Don't miss the Cuban sandwiches at this outside restaurant and bar.

Crackers Restaurant, US 19, Crystal River, adjacent to Best Western. Lunch, dinner, seafood, bar, tiki, dockage, on Kings Bay. Indoor and outdoor dining. Seafood is a specialty.

Charlie's Fish House, US 19, Crystal River. Lunch, dinner, seafood, bar, dockage, on Kings Bay.

Oyster's Restaurant, US 19, Crystal River. Breakfast, lunch, dinner, casual, seafood, home cooking. Excellent breakfasts!

Jones' Restaurant, US 19, Crystal River. Early breakfast, lunch, dinner, casual, home cooking.

Grannie's Restaurant, US 19 at CR 44 West, Crystal River. Early breakfast, lunch, dinner, casual, home cooking. A favorite breakfast and lunch spot for early-rising fishermen on the way to either of the Fort Island boat ramps.

Crystal Paradise Restaurant, W Citrus Avenue at 4th Street, Crystal River. Breakfast, lunch, home cooking.

M&E's Donuts and Subs, US 19 North, Crystal River. Donuts, subs, open from 4:30 a.m. until 1:30 p.m. M&E will pack sandwiches to go for fishing trips.

Crystal River Ale House at the Port Hotel and Marina, Crystal River. Lunch, dinner, bar, casual, dockage, on Kings Bay.

There are numerous restaurants other than those listed, including fast food, in the Crystal River area. Many local groceries (Publix, Winn-Dixie, and Sweet Bay) also have reliable delicatessens.

Marinas, Marine Supplies and Service, Bait-and-Tackle Shops, and Launching Ramps

Twin Rivers Marina, CR 44 at Salt River, Crystal River, (352) 795-3552. Wet slips, dry storage, overnight dockage, boat rentals, inboard and outboard repairs, live and frozen bait, tackle, gas and diesel, convenience store, showers. This marina is the closest one to the mouth of the Crystal River.

Pete's Pier Marina, on Kings Bay, Crystal River, (352) 795-3302. Wet slips, dry storage, overnight dockage, boat rentals, live and frozen bait, gas and diesel, adjacent to city launching ramp. This is a good place to launch if you plan to fish in and around Kings Bay. Free paved ramp, $5 car parking, $10 boat and trailer parking.

Crystal River Watersports, adjacent to Days Inn, Crystal River, (352) 795-7033. Overnight slips, launching ramp for guests, live and frozen bait, boat rentals, on canal leading to Crystal River. The canal here leads to the main river, just west of Kings Bay. It's about a twenty-minute trip at the mandatory idle speed.

Crystal River Marine, US 19/98, Crystal River, (352) 795-2597. Honda and Yamaha outboard service, boat and trailer storage.

Three Rivers Marine, US 19/98, Crystal River, (352) 563-5510. Honda outboard service.

Nature Coast Fly Shop, Best Western Crystal River Resort, US 19, Crystal River, (352) 795-3156. Extensive tackle, Orvis fly shop.

Ed's Bait & Tackle, 938 N US 19, Crystal River, (352) 795-4178. Live and frozen bait, extensive tackle, excellent repairs.

West Marine, US 19/98, Crystal River, (352) 563-0003 Complete marine supplies and gear, extensive fishing tackle selection.

Fort Island Boat Ramp, end of CR 44, Crystal River. Free paved ramp, limited parking, restrooms, small fishing pier. This ramp offers shallow-water access to the gulf.

Fort Island Trail Park Boat Ramp, CR 44, five miles west of US 19/98, Crystal River. Free paved double ramp, adequate parking, restrooms, small boat basin. Boats over 24-feet may have trouble launching in the narrow basin. The canal from this ramp leads to the slow-speed zone near the confluence of the Salt River. It's about a fifteen-minute ride from here to the gulf.

City boat ramp, at Pete's Pier off King's Bay Drive, Crystal River. Free paved ramp, $5 car parking, $10 boat and trailer parking.

City Boat Ramp, next to Charlie's Restaurant, US 19, Crystal River. Narrow free paved ramp, parking behind fire station across the highway. This ramp is right on King's Bay.

John Brown Boat Ramp, Ozello, six miles from US 19/98 on CR 494. Free ramp on the Salt River, shallow, adequate parking, no security. If you want to poke around the backwaters at Ozello or the Salt River, this is a great place to launch.

Pirate's Cove Boat Ramp, Ozello, ten miles from US 19/98 at the end of CR 494. Free primitive ramp with adequate parking, no security. Ditto the backwaters!

Marine Patrol Boat Ramp, US 19/98 at Cross Florida Barge Canal, north of Crystal River. Free paved ramp, small boat basin, immediate access to barge canal, four miles to gulf, adequate parking. The basin here is narrow, and longer boats might be hard to launch.

Local Fishing Guides

Capt. Dave Jefford, (352) 563-1689, fisherford@xtalwind.net. Inshore fishing, light-tackle, artificial-lure specialist. Be sure to ask Dave about his handmade One-Off topwater lures.

Capt Steve Fussell, (352) 753-2525, captfussell@earthlink.net, www.tarponstalker.com. Inshore, light-tackle, and fly fishing.

Capt. Rick Burns, (352) 726-9283, reelburns2001@yahoo.com, www.reelburns.com. Inshore light-tackle and fly fishing.

Capts. Dick and Janet Yant, (352) 746-9067. Inshore and offshore fishing.

Capt. Mark Zorn, (352) 400-1925, mzorn1@tampabay.rr.com, www.captainmarkzorn.com. Inshore fishing.

Capt. Roy Cunningham, (352) 302-7024, roybighog@tampabay.rr.com. Light-tackle inshore and backwater fishing from Ozello.

Capt. Jackie Bryant, (352) 302-4174. Inshore and offshore fishing.

Capt. Rich Hinde, (352) 564-8079. Offshore fishing.

Capt. Ken Lewis, (352) 634-6723. Offshore fishing.

Gulf Coast Charters, Capt. Roger Batchelor, (352) 860-1927. Inshore charters and bookings for multi-boat charters.

Apollo Deep Sea Fishing, 1340 NW 20th Ave., Crystal River, (352) 795-3757. Offshore fishing on a sixty-foot party boat.

Many guides from Homosassa and Yankeetown are familiar with the waters at Crystal River, and vice versa. Please consult the guide listings for Homosassa and Yankeetown, if necessary. Also, the Web site of the Florida Guides Association (www.florida-guides.com) has a complete listing of United States Coast Guard licensed-and-insured fishing guides.

4

Yankeetown and the Withlacoochee and Waccasassa Rivers

I sometimes refer to the Withlacoochee and the Waccasassa Rivers as the "Ws," which is a lot less complicated than the native names. Located in southern Levy County, they are two of the more beautiful natural rivers on the Gulf Coast of Florida. Neither is heavily developed near their entrances to the gulf, and each river leads to some good fishing, inshore and nearshore. Both are dark-water rivers, and the waters at their gulf entrances are often stained by dark-brown tannin.

This is an aerial view of the mouth of the Withlacoochee River made at extreme low tide.

The Waccasassa River winds a circuitous route toward Waccasassa Bay.

Of the two, the Withlacoochee is the larger river. It's actually one of Florida's longest, and its final two miles are virtually uninhabited, save the alligators, osprey, and summertime manatees.

The river, once continuous from its headwaters to its mouth, has been chopped up by development—specifically the Cross Florida Barge Canal, a project that was begun in the 1960s but never completed. Still, work did cease in time to save the river from being cut in half. That project, as well as the large power-plant complex to the south, changed the river's natural flow into the gulf, and many old-timers claim that fishing was "ruined forever." The truth, however, is that the area still maintains an outstanding fishery.

The Waccasassa River is completely undeveloped, with the exception of a county boat ramp and private fishing club near Gulf Hammock. Its channels are marked, but the government no longer maintains the markers. Care should be taken for rocks near the channel, particularly upstream of the last markers, which are just inside the river mouth. The closest amenities are those at Inglis and Yankeetown, about twenty miles to the south via US Highway 19/98. That being the case, many anglers fishing the gulf south of the Waccasassa

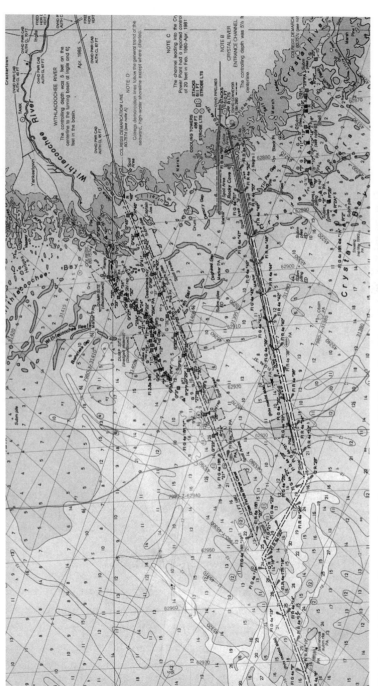

This chart detail shows the power-plant, barge-canal, and Withlacoochee River channels.

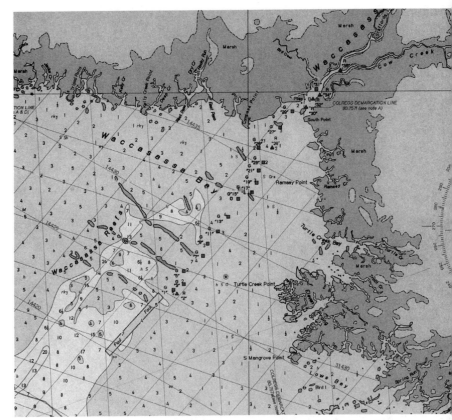

Waccasassa Bay, shown on this chart detail, is an excellent place to find redfish along the shoreline and trout on the interior flats.

River prefer to run there by boat from Yankeetown. Those fishing north of the Waccasassa often cross over from Cedar Key, to the west. Either way, it's worth the trip for the sights—and the fishing.

Inshore Fishing at Yankeetown and Waccasassa

While there is some inshore saltwater fishing in the Withlacoochee River, it's really a place best left to the freshwater anglers. Occasionally there are small redfish along the rocky banks and trout in deep holes in late fall and throughout the winter. The rare snook catch here brings reporters from local newspapers to the scene. A mile or

Creeks near the mouths of both the Withlacoochee and Waccasassa Rivers offer excellent protection from wind or cold weather.

so upstream from the gulf, to a turn called Pat's Elbow (just upriver from marker #46), is the summer home to some nice tarpon, which are usually caught by fishing cut mullet on the bottom or by trolling sub-surface lures such as Storm's Shallow Thunder 15. Still, the best bet remains to get out of the river into the gulf, and try your skills in the surrounding waters.

On cold days, local anglers launch at either the County Road (CR) 40 ramp or at one of the upriver ramps and head toward the Crystal River Energy Complex hot-water discharge. There are shortcuts to the discharge, but I don't recommend any for newcomers. It's best to head out the Withlacoochee channel to marker #18A before you turn toward marker #31 in the Barge Canal. Near marker #31, steer a course (about 145 degrees) through the spoil islands to waypoint N28 57.289 W82 46.990, and then run *slowly* toward the tall stacks. There is a large spoil island between the turn and the hot-water discharge. Pass very closely to its left and steer to N28 57.530 W82 44.571, Rocky Point, which is the western end of the jetty on the southern side of the discharge. Fish the entire channel with jigs, live shrimp, or trolled

MirrOlure 52M lures. It holds trout, reds, and even a few snook and cobia. The colder the weather and the lower the tide, the better the fishing here.

As the weather warms in early spring, so does the water on the nearby flats and bars. The water temperature rises more quickly southward toward the power plant, as the outflow can affect an area of many square miles, even to the end of the spoil banks at Long Point (N28 55.996 W82 49.326). An early spring influx of Spanish mackerel can usually be found in the Energy Complex channel near Long Point, and many locals consider the hot-water outflow a factor, even though it's several miles inshore. Shiny spoons or yellow-and red Floreos tipped with strips of mullet are favorite baits, but don't leave your steel leaders at home. Sea trout and redfish are also popular game along the northern side of the spoils all the way to shore. Sight-fishers, including those throwing flies, are often seen poling slowly all along this northern shore. The spoil banks along the sides of the Cross Florida Barge Canal are also great for reds, trout, flounder, and occasionally pompano. In late winter or fall the most southern and gulf-end bars seem to be the better fishing areas.

In spring, as the backwater temperature stabilizes with the gulf water and negates the influence of the hot-water discharge, there are many potential redfish spots behind Drum Island (N28 58.331 W82 44.577). The area tends to become less active as summer nears, but a few reds linger. This is very shallow territory, so navigate this bay carefully—don't get trapped by a falling tide. Finally, don't be fooled by thinking the hot-water discharge is good in late spring or during the summer. It's just too hot, even for the fish!

There's some great cold-weather inshore and nearshore fishing to the north of the Withlacoochee River, too. The rocky coastline, starting at the river, to Corrigans Reef east of Cedar Key, is treacherous. It's also perfect redfish habitat during the late fall and winter. Extreme tides trap fish in deeper holes behind Porpoise Point (N29 03.370 W82 48.421), Turtle Creek Point (N29 05.950 W82 49.531), and even well into Lows Bay. Many anglers move into these areas on high tides and stay for the entire tidal cycle, catching big reds on topwater lures

The creeks feeding Waccasassa Bay are shallow and rocky. Airboats are sometimes used to gain access to their upper reaches.

or on live shrimp. Others, with kayaks, canoes, shallow-water skiffs, and airboats, have the luxury of making their own schedules.

Once the spring winds ease, locals begin fishing the grass flats in Waccasassa Bay, which comprises all the water in this corner of coastline. Fed by the two rivers, numerous creeks, and bounded by the Cedar Keys on the west, the bay is a catch-all for many species of fish. Trout are abundant on the flats, as are cruising cobia and schools of Spanish mackerel. Rocky areas are found primarily on the eastern side of the bay in three to eight feet of water, while the deeper flats in the center of the bay are mostly covered in sea grass. The closer you find yourself to shore, in any direction, the rockier or rougher the bottom. Small rocky creeks northwest of the Waccasassa River's mouth hold fish in deeper holes, as does the river itself. A good place to begin drifting for trout with shrimp-sweetened jigs is the Trout Stake (N29 02.488 W82 50.405), located equidistant from the Withlacoochee Bird Cage (N28 58.879 W82 48.445) and the end of the

Waccasassa channel (N29 05.998 W82 51.716). Either of these river coordinates is a good place to turn directly toward the Trout Stake. Be sure to keep a big rod ready as you'll likely see cobia, tarpon, or even sharks cruising as you fish the flats, particularly if you drift northward over the Waccasassa Reefs near the channel.

Offshore Fishing at Yankeetown

Waccasassa has no real access to offshore water, and there are a couple of facts to consider if you plan to fish for offshore species out of Yankeetown. First, it's eighteen nautical miles from the Bird Cage to the Steel Tower (N28 58.515 W83 09.241) at the end of Seahorse Reef south of Cedar Key. From there, it's another twenty miles to the Barge (N29 00.512 W83 31.623), a popular fishing spot in fifty feet of water. That's a long haul. And second, the natural Withlacoochee channel joins up with the dredged Cross Florida Barge Canal channel and the Energy Complex barge channel, two newer access points to the gulf that weren't just dredged from sandy bottom but from solid lime rock. All other things equal, I think I'd fish closer to port and spend less money on fuel. These two channels are deep enough for the sea-going barges and tugboats moving coal and sand in and out of the area. The edges are craggy and steep and the rocks taken from their centers were distributed onto many areas, some as spoil islands and much as litter over the relatively flat bottom.

An excellent area to fish for offshore species, including grouper, cobia, and king mackerel, is near the junction of the three channels. The stretch from marker #28 on the Energy Complex channel (N28 55.620 W82 51.173) to Marker #18 on the Barge Canal (N28 56.500 W82 53.251) is an excellent place to troll Mann's Neptune Stretch 20s and 25s. The 30-size lure typically used offshore just runs too deep for this area and will hang up frequently. Troll right up against the edges of the channel, particularly on the southern side, at about four knots. Many a commercial grouper fisherman has earned a living fishing this stretch of bottom, so give it a try. Also, don't hesitate to check out the bottom structure outside the channel here. If you take care

A happy gathering of "grouper diggers" show off their day's catch.

The channel markers along the barge canal and Withlacoochee River channel often attract cobia and schools of Spanish mackerel.

and mind your depth sounder while trolling, you'll find some new bottom-fishing spots and probably catch a grouper or two at the same time. Don't neglect the areas of the Crystal River artificial reefs (approx. N28 54.900 W82 52.301) to the south. These older reefs can be productive for many species, and while they are fished heavily, they can be loaded with nice sheepshead in the late winter.

This channel junction area is also good for king mackerel and cobia in the warmer months. For kings, you might try trolling shallow-running lures—Yo-Zuri's Crystal Minnow would be a good choice—a bit higher in the water column while you're trolling near the bottom for grouper. Of course, slow-trolled live pinfish or blue runners do well, too. If you're the first on the scene, you'll likely find cobia cruising around many of the markers on the outer reaches of these channels. Brightly colored jigs, live white bait (caught near many of the markers), or small blue crabs are good choices for hooking up on a big cobia.

The long of this story is that the deep-water offshore spots really belong to Cedar Key, and the short is that there's plenty of good fishing for offshore species close to shore in the Yankeetown area.

Beware a northeasterly wind on a cold winter day; tides will sometimes be much lower than predicted.

Getting Around Yankeetown and Waccasassa

Yankeetown, about twelve miles north of Crystal River, is accessed by either CR 40, through Inglis, or by CR 40A from the northeast. Both roads lead from US 19/98. CR 40 runs eastward from Inglis to Dunnellon and then on to I-75.

Getting around Waccasassa is even easier. Head west on CR 32 from US 19/98 at Gulf Hammock, approximately twenty miles north of Inglis, and drive a mile or so to the end of the road.

By water, access to the Withlacoochee River is good, as the channel begins offshore near the Cross Florida Barge Canal and the Progress Energy channel. The Withlacoochee does have a rather long slow-speed zone in place during warm months, making the upstream run to the marinas and other amenities tedious. The Waccasassa River has no formal entrance, and its markers are no longer maintained.

Where to Stay

Inglis Motel, US 19/98, Inglis, (352) 447-2467. Rooms and efficiencies, adjacent to Port Inglis Restaurant.

Withlacoochee Motel, US 19/98, Inglis, (352) 447-2211. Lodging.

Pine Lodge B&B, CR 40, Inglis, (352) 447-7463. Upscale lodging, breakfast included.

Cattail Creek RV Park, 41 Cattail Lane, Yankeetown, (352) 447-3050. Full hookups, restrooms, showers.

B's Campground, Riverside Dr., Yankeetown, (352) 447-5888. RV hookups, dockage, boat ramp for guests, on Withlacoochee River.

Where to Eat

Port Inglis Restaurant, US 19/98, Inglis, (352) 447-2467. Early breakfast, lunch, dinner, bar, home cooking, adjacent to Inglis Motel.

Our Pub Restaurant and Lounge, CR 40, Inglis, (352) 447-2406. Lunch, dinner, bar.

Gobbler's Restaurant, US 19, (352) 447-6112. Early breakfast, lunch, dinner.

Inglis Shell Station, CR 40 and US 19/98, Inglis. Good deli, fried chicken, and sandwiches, open early.

Marinas, Marine Supplies and Service, Bait-and-Tackle Shops, and Launching Ramps

Yankeetown Marina, Hickory Ave., Yankeetown, (352) 447-2529. Gas and diesel, wet slips, dockage, $5 boat ramp, live and frozen bait, tackle, bulk ice. This is the only full-service marina on the Withlacoochee River.

Hook-Line & Sinker, CR 40, Inglis, (352) 447-5477. Live and frozen bait, ice, excellent tackle selection.

Yankeetown General Store, CR 40, Yankeetown, (352) 447-2532. Gas, deli, live and frozen bait, tackle, marine hardware.

Marine Patrol Boat Ramp, US 19/98 at Cross Florida Barge Canal, north of Crystal River. Free paved ramp, small boat basin, immediate access to barge canal, four miles to the gulf, adequate parking. The basin here is narrow and longer boats might be hard to launch.

CR 40 launching ramp, at the gulf end of CR 40. Free paved double ramp, adequate parking, no security. Be careful, as crosscurrents can make launching and loading boats difficult. There is *no* tie-up area or dock at this county ramp.

Vassey Creek primitive ramp (Cross the four-way stop at CR 40 and CR 40A and follow the dirt road to the end.) Excellent access to the Lows Bay backwaters for shallow-draft skiffs, canoes, and kayaks.

Levy County Boat Ramp, Waccasassa, west of US 19/98 on CR 32. Free paved single ramp, adequate parking, restrooms, access to upper Waccasassa River, approximately three miles to the gulf.

Yankeetown City Ramp. Riverside Drive next to Coast Guard Station, Yankeetown. Free paved single ramp, several miles upriver, roadside parking, small basin.

Local Fishing Guides

Capt. Rick LeFiles, (352) 447-0829, captain@ospreyguides.com, www.ospreyguides.com. Light-tackle and fly fishing.

Capt. Ky Lewis and Capt. Zack Lewis, (352) 447-3818, 1-800-844-5035. Offshore and inshore fishing.

Capt. Richard Steinhorst, (352) 447-5522. Inshore, light-tackle.

Capt. John Morris, (352) 447-2575. Inshore, light-tackle.

Capt. Jake Hearon, (352) 447-2625. Inshore, light-tackle.

Capt. Mark Taylor, (352) 821-3920. Inshore, light-tackle.

Capt. Rick Muldrow, (352) 629-3605. Inshore, light-tackle.

Capt. John Dickerson, (352) 536-0019. Inshore, light-tackle.

Capt. Bill O'Bry, (352) 220-9020. www.weketchum.com. Inshore, light-tackle.

Capt. Duane Walters, Waccasassa, (352) 318-3342. Inshore airboat fishing.

Many guides from Crystal River are familiar with the waters at Yankeetown and Waccasassa, and vice-versa. Please consult the guide listings for Crystal River, if necessary. Also, the Web site of the Florida Guides Association (www.florida-guides.com) has a complete listing of United States Coast Guard licensed-and-insured fishing guides.

5

Cedar Key and the Cedar Keys

Cedar Key is the town—the Cedar Keys are the place. This group of small islands, joined by causeways and small bridges, forms a peninsula about twenty-five miles from US Highway 19/98.

In this aerial photo of Cedar Key, North Key is seen near the horizon at the top.

Historically, Cedar Key was a shipping center for fish, timber, and wood products, including pencils made from local cedar trees. Jutting well into to the Gulf of Mexico, and with two main channels offering quick-and-deep access to offshore waters, Cedar Key is a good destination for deep-water anglers. Good shallow grass flats, as well as abundant oyster beds, are located both to the south and north of Cedar Key and provide very good habitat for many inshore species.

In an attempt to make itself chic and artsy, Cedar Key has become less of a fishing destination in recent years, with many angler-oriented amenities disappearing. Despite the crowds of trendy, non-fishing tourists, Cedar Key and its local and offshore waters are still teeming with anglers, including many who travel great distances to fish here.

Inshore and Nearshore Fishing at Cedar Key

The amazing thing about the inshore and nearshore fishery at Cedar Key is the range and variety of habitat. To the northeast and east into the northern reaches of Waccasassa Bay the bottom is generally muddy but strewn with rocky bars and hazards. To the southeast and south are islands and lush grass flats lined with deep cuts. To the west and northwest are the beginnings of some of the best creek fisheries on the Gulf Coast. The connecting channels and bays that separate the islands from the mainland are shallow but active areas to be considered by anglers. The geographic construction of the Cedar Key area gives it the big advantage of always having some productive fishing grounds in the lee of any wind.

Redfish and black drum are plentiful close to shore and around oyster bars, in creeks, and shallow waters. The deeper flats teem with baitfish, which attract sea trout, Spanish mackerel, and tarpon. And, while cobia are considered by many to be an offshore species, the fact that the Cedar Keys poke well into the gulf, nearer deep water than many other Big Bend ports, they are found along markers and flats well within the reach of smaller craft.

Anglers leaving from either of the city boat ramps or the ramp at the Number Four Channel and heading northeast will find the

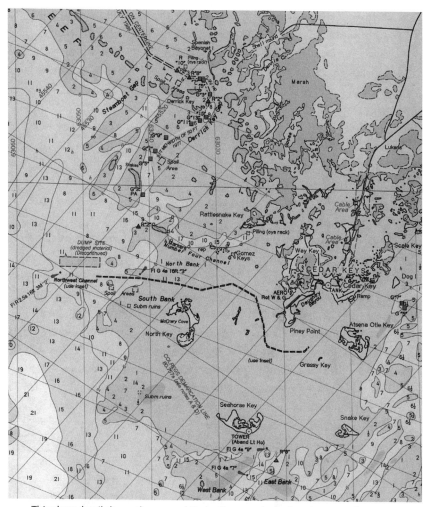

This chart detail shows the general Cedar Key area, including the rugged shoreline to the north.

shoreline and its adjacent rock and oyster bars a magnet for both redfish and trout. But, as with many great backwater-fishing areas, there are sometimes drawbacks. This water is largely uncharted and its hazards are not to be taken casually by visitors. Don't be fooled by boats running at full speed and piloted by locals, who know the exact locations of many rocks and bars by heart. It's pretty safe to run at cruising speed from the harbor until you get to marker #7 of the South Bar Channel (N29 08.013, W83 00.780), but after that, take it easy—countless outboard-motor lower units have been lost in the upper reaches of Waccasassa Bay. Run slowly from marker #7 toward the tip of Corrigans Reef (N29 09.170 W82 58.167). From there, head north toward the shoreline and look for bars, sloughs, and jumping baitfish. This is perfect water to fish on days when the winds are either westerly or northerly, as there's plenty of protection afforded by the structure of the shoreline.

In spring, fall, and on warm winter days, you'll find schools of mullet jumping along the shoreline, in sloughs between bars, and near creek mouths, particularly on rising tides. This is a good sign that reds and trout are hanging around, too. In fact, you may even see tailing red or black drum grubbing up a meal of crabs or snails. Use a pushpole, a trolling motor, or a slow drift to quietly get within range of the baitfish and fish the outside edges of the school with noisy top-water lures or poppers. Predators such as reds and trout home in on noise that might be considered *gill rattle* and strike readily. If you're fly fishing, consider some big noisy poppers on a floating 8-weight line. In either case, short erratic retrieves can be quite effective.

While many anglers regularly fish for sea trout and redfish in deeper water with jigs or slow-sinking plugs, this just isn't the place to do it. You'll spend lots more time re-rigging and less time fishing. Besides, I think top-water plugs catch bigger fish and the action keeps you on your toes. If you see black drum tailing, try a piece of cut bait or dead shrimp in front of them—and hang on. Fishing this side of Cedar Key in the hot summer months is similar, but sometimes the water is just too hot, moving all but the hardiest red and black drum out onto the deeper flats. Early-morning and late-afternoon trips can be fun, too, but plan accordingly, as the dark part of the ride can be difficult and dangerous. Cold winter days in the upper reaches of the bay can be fun, but extreme low tides make it difficult for many anglers to approach the area. If you can plan a late-afternoon trip on a rising tide, count on the morning's sunshine to warm the bars and make for some exceptional trout and redfish action.

The deeper flats to the southeast of Cedar Key are great places

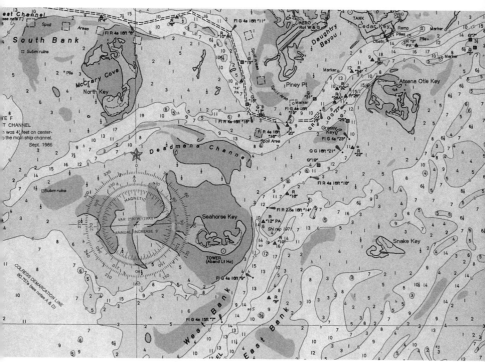

This chart shows the areas near the town of Cedar Key.

to drift and fish during the warmer months. From marker #7 of the South Bar Channel all the way to the entrance of the unofficial channel at the Waccasassa River (N29 05.998 W82 51.716) and south for several miles, you'll find lush grass flats. Sea trout cruise the edges of the deeper cuts and white-sand patches, and schools of Spanish mackerel chase schools of white bait. Don't be surprised to see cobia and tarpon cruising in search of almost anything they can get their mouths around. Locals favor natural baits for trout and often use live shrimp or pinfish rigged about two feet under popping corks. Anglers fishing artificials rely on the same rigs but with jig heads and soft plastics, typically in bright flashy colors. When drifting and trout fishing, remember to keep a heavy rod in the rod holder with a live pinfish under a cork drifted behind the boat—cobia, tarpon, and even sharks are always a fun surprise.

To the south of Cedar Key, in particular the areas close to Snake

Key and then farther south and southwest from there are excellent year-round fisheries. Vast grass flats with deep cuts hold baitfish in the warmer months and the shallows provide warmth for all fish on cold days. These flats also attract fish rounding the corner at Cedar Key in their seasonal migrations. Pelagic species, Spanish mackerel in particular, are almost always found here on rising tides during spring and autumn. And, if you're heading out to these flats, don't neglect the edges of Snake Key itself; its southwestern shoreline and eastern bars have surrendered many a redfish and trout.

Assuming that the Main Ship Channel from Cedar Key to the gulf is the dividing line between east and west, the southwestern quadrant includes North Key, Seahorse Key, and some pretty nice grass flats. Several specific areas deserve mention. First, between Seahorse Key and North Key there are flats on both sides of Deadmans Channel and the deep channel itself. Entering the area from marker #16 of the Northwest Channel (N29 07.246 W83 03.567) and heading almost due west, you'll be in Deadmans Channel. A deep slough, it runs nearly to the deep waters of the gulf and attracts many inshore spe-

During winter, the extreme shallows near Snake Key provide good conditions for fly-fishermen who want to sight-fish for redfish.

cies, particularly on a falling tide when bait wash off the adjacent flats. The flats themselves teem with bait in the warmer months, and in winter, you'll find both reds and trout seeking the sun's warmth up on top of the flats. This is a great shallow-water spot to toss either flies or top-water lures.

These flats are also accessible on moderate tides from the eastern end of Seahorse Key. A second spot to consider is the slough running eastward from waypoint N29 05.275 W83 05.254, southwest of Seahorse Key. This channel doesn't connect to the Main Ship Channel, but running slowly between the spoil banks and the island will get you there. Similar to Deadmans Channel, this is another deep cut through shallow, fertile flats.

Finally, the islands of Seahorse Key and North Key offer interesting shorelines and structure. McCrary Cove, on the western side of North Key has some interesting oyster bars along its northern edge (and a great picnic beach to the south). Just outside the cove and to the northwest you'll find nice grass flats. The South Bank spoil area along the Northwest Channel is also a great spot to sight-fish for redfish, cobia, and tarpon in warmer months. The eastern side of North Key is littered with a few small coves and oysters, and the southern side, adjacent to Deadmans Channel, can be an active spot in cool months, especially if you're patient enough to fish live bait on the channel's edge.

Seahorse Key is home to a retired lighthouse and a marine research facility. There are restricted areas into which access by boats is forbidden in certain seasons along the southern and inner shorelines. If you have the ability to make long casts, don't hesitate to work the bars and flats alongside this island during any season. Being that it's the most southern island toward the open gulf makes it a natural throughway for all species of game fish.

I'd like to also mention the southernmost end of Seahorse Reef, as it's sometimes accessible by smaller boats. Other times, it can be downright dangerous, so have a plan B ready on a day when you set off toward the end of Seahorse Reef. The reef runs about ten miles from Seahorse Key and is marked at its end by the Steel Tower (N28 58.515 W83 09.241). The reef is generally deep and sometimes navigable, but it gets shallow on its crest near the end at a spot called the Hook (N28 59.930 W83 08.181), which is a grassy hump known for great sea-trout and Spanish-mackerel fishing. Here, if you anchor on top of the reef, chumming and free-lining live shrimp has always been good for trout. When the Spanish mackerel are running and the birds start diving, it's easy to get your limit of Spanish while trolling Floreos or Clarkspoons, tipped with fish belly strips and rigged with wire leaders. The Steel Tower is also a great close-in spot to fish for big spawning sheepshead in the late winter and early spring. These

Seahorse Reef, to the south of Cedar Key, is a famous hot spot for anglers targeting Spanish mackerel.

During the cold months, sheepshead are found spawning over many of the nearshore reefs at Cedar Key.

fish are certainly found all around offshore rock piles, but the fact that they show up here gives inshore anglers an even chance to catch a couple of these tasty bait-stealers.

North and west of the Northwest Channel, the coastline is ragged, pocked with deep waters close to shore and accessible creeks opening into the gulf. The water here is sometimes affected by the massive outflow of the Suwannee River and can be less clear than that south of Cedar Key. This area marks the southern end of Florida's Big Bend creek system, famed for excellent catches of redfish, sea trout, and black drum.

Inshore anglers leaving Cedar Key's main boat ramps at the City Boat Basin by way of the Northwest Channel usually pass Gomez Keys (N29 08.955 W83 04.367) and the tip of North Key before heading northward up the Derrick Key Channel. Many fishermen stop to fish Gomez Key, North Key, and Piney Point (N29 07.607 W83 03.078), which are near the channel and have some nice natural shorelines. This marked channel is an old inshore route from Cedar Key to the Suwannee River's East Pass. Shoaling has reduced the depth in the upper half of the route significantly in recent years, making it viable for shallow water boats only. The southern half, northward to a deep wash called the Tarpon Hole (N29 11.334 W83 04.761), is an easy way to get inshore near Spanish Bayonet Island, the Raleigh Islands, and Deer Island, which provide barriers for several creek mouths and protection from the elements, particularly on colder days. The Tarpon Hole is a great spot to anchor up and fish for tarpon, sharks, and cobia that ambush baits washing around the tip of the Cedar Keys. Deep jigging with lures such as the D.O.A. TerrorEyz, or BaitBuster is a popular method, but many anglers take their chances and bottom fish with cut mullet or drift live pinfish under corks. These methods will provide lots of action, but you may find more small sharks or rays than you have energy to fight, especially in the summer.

Don't overlook the shoreline between Deer Island (N29 14.602 W83 04.805) and the mouth of Big Trout Creek (N29 15.935 W83 05.156). And, if you have the ability to maneuver in very shallow water, the Preacher Hole (N29 14.000 W83 04.001) is another top spot for trout and reds, but it's tricky getting there. While more fish hole up in these deeper creeks and holes during cooler months, some are present year-round, sometimes moving outside the creeks and onto the flats. Live shrimp, cut mullet, or pinfish rigged under a popping cork is a local favorite for all species. Look for jumping mullet along the shorelines, and you'll likely find game fish there. Look up into the creeks for big wagging fish tails, signs of huge black drum—sometimes hard to hook but always fun to catch. Incidentally, the launching ramp at Shell Mound is in these backwaters and makes an excellent departure point for anglers in canoes, kayaks, and super-shallow boats.

Offshore Fishing at Cedar Key

What Cedar Key lacks in terms of fishing-related conveniences (adequate boat and trailer parking, a deep-water marina, and dockside fuel) it makes up in access to some great Big Bend–style offshore fishing. With deep water fairly close to shore and rocky natural bottom a natural geologic extension of the islands, the trip to productive fishing in depths of fifty or more feet can be less than thirty miles from the boat-ramp area. The mainstay of Cedar Key offshore fishing is grouper, but there's no shortage of kingfish, cobia, amberjacks, sheepshead, and smaller bottom fish. Rock piles and live bottom hold baitfish, and baitfish attract these predators for your fishing pleasure.

Live bottom, in contrast to vast sandy prairies, is essentially sea grass growing over limestone bottom that is peppered with clumps of sponges and other sea growth. This type of bottom is plentiful off Cedar Key and will hold remarkable numbers of offshore fish, even in less than thirty feet. Much like inshore flats, this bottom can be mixed with areas of barren sand. Three good areas easily reached from Cedar Key are the Kingfish Hole, the Ten-Three Hole, and the Grouper Grounds. These are not specific spots but general fishing areas. The Kingfish Hole (N29 02.696 W83 10.474) is in more than twenty feet of water to the northwest of the Steel Tower (N28 58.515 W83 09.241) on Seahorse Reef. Trolling deep-diving lures or live baits such as blue runners rigged on stinger rigs in the spring and fall will produce good catches of king mackerel and sometimes a large grouper. The Ten-Three Hole (N29 03.460 W83 18.191), so-named because it's ten miles at 300 degrees from the entrance to the Northwest Channel, is another convenient offshore area. Like the Kingfish Hole, this area is mostly hard live bottom, and anglers are often surprised to find big grouper hiding behind relatively small rock outcrops.

Heading southwest from the Main Ship Channel entrance, the area called the Grouper Grounds (N28 49.590 W83 11.581) is worth a try, and it tends to be a bit rockier than the water farther north. Here, piles of rocks are scattered among huge sand prairies and provide the only cover to schools of baitfish. Serious offshore fishermen will tell you that these areas are often inhabited by the largest grouper, and you can also count on marauding king mackerel, cobia, and amber-jacks.

The area to the southwest of the Grouper Grounds toward way-point N28 47.103 W83 20.732 is a good place to troll deep-running plugs in hopes of pinpointing a nice rock pile. Note a big strike by hitting the "Man Overboard" button on your GPS or by tossing a marker on the spot. Then, using your bottom finder, try fishing the same rock pile with live or cut bait. This is one method by which great offshore numbers are best found, and there are some nice ones, many still unknown, in this general area. Bottom structure and relief are always important to offshore fishermen, and there's sometimes nothing better than a wreck or artificial reef. Luckily, there are several in the gulf within easy reach of Cedar Key. The Barge (N29 00.512 W83 31.623) is a good wreck in about fifty feet of water about twenty miles due west of Seahorse Reef. At times, this wreck will attract bait and grouper, but the amberjacks, barracudas, and resident goliath grouper can be pesky, as each will steal bait that is sinking to the bottom or game fish being reeled in.

Good artificial reefs to the west of Cedar Key are GOFC #1 (N29 07.594 W83 13.327) and GOFC #3 (N29 06.841 W83 25.603). These reefs were originally placed by the Gainesville Offshore Fishing Club and are popular areas. GOFC #3 is located farther offshore than GOFC #1, but it is on the edge of the 30-foot contour. In addition to holding grouper and kingfish, both of these reefs are good habitat for spawning sheepshead in the winter and early spring. Another artificial reef worth considering, almost thirty miles from Cedar Key, is the White City Bridge (N29 10.000 W83 39.081). Great construction rubble means great hiding spots for lots of predators, and this is one of the best.

Getting Around Cedar Key

Cedar Key isn't hard to get around, either by boat or by car. The main highway from US 19/98 is County Road (CR) 24, which passes through Otter Creek on its way from Gainesville and Interstate 75.

An alternative route from the north is CR 345 from Chiefland, which intersects State 24 at Rosewood, northeast of Cedar Key. Once you're in town, the road dead ends at the city boat basin and downtown. While there are some accommodations and eateries along State Road (SR) 24, most are found within easy reach of the city boat ramps and dock area.

Many visiting anglers find the layout of Cedar Key confusing and sometimes disheartening. All three big channels lead to the downtown area and a small boat basin. The South Bar Channel runs to the southeast and is not very deep, essentially dumping out onto the flats. The Main Ship Channel leads from town southward alongside Seahorse Key toward the Steel Tower, and the Northwest Channel cuts close by North Key and is a logical route for boats heading northward along the coast. Smaller channels, including the Number Three and Number Four Channels, are used mostly by locals and by shallow-draft boats. The Number Four Channel, for instance, actually snakes from the gulf through the maze of islands to the north of Cedar Key and into the upper reaches of the backwaters on the eastern side. These treacherous smaller channels are not for the faint-of-heart, even on higher water.

Where to Stay

Faraway Inn, 3rd & G Streets, 1-888-543-5330, www.farawayinn.com. Cottages and motel, pets welcome, small private beach, efficiencies available, on the gulf. This small, friendly place is clean, convenient, and lots of fun.

Old Fenimore Mill, 1-800-767-8354, www.fenimoremill.com. Rental condos. Located bayside, but still close to the boat basin and launching ramp. There's also plenty of parking for trailers.

Dockside Motel, 491 Dock St., 1-800-541-5432, www.dockside-cedar key.com. Lodging, near boat basin, ramp, and city dock.

Seahorse Landing, 1-877-514-5096, www.seahorselanding.com. Rental gulf-front condos, pool.

Beach Front Motel 1-866-543-5113. Lodging, pool, efficiencies.

The Island Place, 550 1st St., 1-800-780-6522, www.islandplace-ck. com, info@islandplace-ck.com. Rental condos.

Gulfside Motel, 552 1st St., 1-888-543-5308, www.thegulfsidemotel. com, gulfse@bellsouth.net. Lodging, boat dock, pets okay, efficiencies available.

Cedar Cove Beach and Yacht Club, 192 2nd St., 1-800-366-5312, www. cedarcove-florida.com. Lodging.

Park Place in Cedar Key, 211 2nd St., 1-800-868-7963, www.parkplace incedarkey.com, parkplace@inetw.net. Lodging, efficiencies, pets okay, across from city beach.

Nature's Landing Condos and Vacation Rentals, 7041 Depot St., 1-877-832-9161, www.natureslandingcondominiums.com. Rental bayside condos.

Rainbow Country RV Campground, SR 24, (352) 543-6268. Five and a half miles east of Cedar Key.

Where to Eat

Cook's Café, 434 2nd St. Breakfast, lunch.

The Island Room at Cedar Cove, (352) 543-6520, Casual, upscale menu, weekday dinner only, brunch on Sundays.

Annie's Café, SR 24, Breakfast, lunch.

Blue Desert Café, SR 24, (352) 543-9111. Dinner, closed Mondays.

Frog's Landing, on the Dock, (352) 543-9243. Lunch, dinner.

Seabreeze, on the Dock, 310 Dock St. Lunch, dinner.

Fishbonz Sandwich Shop & Bait & Tackle, 509 3rd St, Breakfast, lunch, closed Mondays. Excellent sandwiches served alongside bait and tackle.

Anne's Other Place, 360 Dock St. Breakfast, lunch, dinner.

Tony's Seafood Restaurant, 597 2nd St. Dinner, upscale seafood.

Robinson Seafood, 6991 SW SR 24, (352) 543-5051. Lunch, dinner, closed Mondays and Tuesdays. Worth the 7½-mile trip eastward for excellent fresh seafood. Carl and Eve Robinson also operate a fresh seafood market on the premises, so you know the fish is fresh.

Island Jiffy Mart, SR 24. Convenience store, deli, gas, ice.

The Market at Cedar Key, SR 24 at 3rd Street. Full-service grocery store with deli, beer, wine.

Marinas, Marine Supplies and Service, Bait-and-Tackle Shops, and Launching Ramps

Cedar Key Marina, SR 24 at Number Three Channel, (352) 543-6148. Fuel, dry storage, bait, minor service, marine supplies, some tackle. Difficult to reach by water as the Number Three Channel is very shallow.

Doug and Wendy Rains Seafood and Bait, SR 24, (352) 222-9383. Next to Jiffy Store, live, frozen, and artificial bait. Doug and Wendy work hard and are always glad to see new customers.

Fishbonz Tackle, 509 3rd St. Tackle, bait, ice, convenience store.

Marina Hardware Store, at boat basin. Live and frozen bait, tackle, ice, marine supplies. Closed Sundays, and only open until noon on Saturdays.

Kayak Cedar Keys, (352) 543-9447, www.kayakcedarkeys.com. Fishing kayak rentals.

Island Hopper Rentals, city marina on Dock Street, (352) 543-5904, www.cedarkeyislandhopper.com. Boat rentals.

Municipal Boat Ramps. Gulfside, nice paved ramps, one ramp is inside the boat basin and the other outside, $10-per-day parking fee, $130 yearly pass available, some overnight slips. Bridge clearance is very low allowing only smaller boats to use the inside ramp.

County Boat Ramp, SR 24 at Number Four Channel. Free, paved single ramp, adequate parking, restrooms. This ramp allows good access to the shallow backwaters north of Cedar Key. Much of this area, however, will be out of water on wintertime low tides.

Shell Mound Ramp, CR 326 at Shell Mound. Free paved public ramp near shallow coastal backwaters, camping, showers. Plan your shallow-water expedition from this ramp around the tides.

Local Fishing Guides

Capt. Phil Muldrow, (352) 543-9930. Offshore bottom fishing for grouper.

Capt. Bill Blair, (352) 316-6389, www.fishinfireman.com. Offshore bottom fishing for grouper.

Capt. Tracy Collins, (352) 843-4067, www.cedarkeybarhopper.com. Inshore, light-tackle, and offshore fishing.

Capt. Carl Robinson, (352) 543-5051, Inshore and offshore fishing.

Capt. Danny Allen, (352) 215-3686, www.gulfcoastflatsfishing.com, captdanny@gulfcoastflatsfishing.com. Inshore, light-tackle fishing.

Capt. Dennis Voyles, (352) 486-3763, www.voylesguideservice.com, davoyles@aol.com. Inshore fishing for trout, redfish, and tarpon.

Capt. Lloyd Collins, (352) 543-9102, www.captlloyd.com. Inshore fishing for trout and redfish.

Capt. Steve Kilpatrick, tarpononfly1@aol.com. Light-tackle and fly fishing, tarpon fishing.

Many guides from Waccasassa, Yankeetown, and Suwannee are familiar with the waters at Cedar Key. Please consult the listings for those areas, if necessary. Also the Web site of the Florida Guides Association (www.florida-guides.com) has a complete listing of United States Coast Guard licensed-and-insured fishing guides.

6

Suwannee

The town of Suwannee sits on the northern bank of the Suwannee River about twenty-four miles from US Highway 19/98 at what locals call Suwannee Old Town.

While it lies at the mouth of a huge river, the community of Suwannee has remained small and inhabited mostly by weekenders who come to there to fish. The town is located on a peninsula formed

This photo shows the settlement at Suwannee, with Salt Creek in the foreground.

by Salt Creek to the north and the main river to the south. Offshore access is through one newer major channel that runs toward the west. Two natural, not dredged, channels are navigable only by shallow-draft boats. Popular inshore-fishing areas are oyster-lined creeks and the shallow bars that lie just outside their entrances to the Gulf of Mexico and nearby grass flats.

Suwannee has remained small and quiet due to its distance from the "beaten path." However, that isolation is the key to finding less-crowded and abundant fishing grounds year-round.

Inshore and Nearshore Fishing at Suwannee

Don't expect to find the gin-clear waters of Cedar Key's southern flats or Steinhatchee's Deadmans Bay at Suwannee. If you do, you'll likely be there at a time of severe drought. Even though the Suwannee River is fed by many springs along its long course from southern Georgia, it is a dark-water river by the time it reaches the gulf, meaning that rainfall and runoff can sometimes cause muddy or stained water many miles offshore.

Suwannee's greatest inshore assets are its creeks and adjacent close-to-shore oyster bars. Some of these areas are accessible by bay-style boats, affording good opportunities for almost everyone, but most require shallow-draft boats or even canoes or kayaks.

Redfish, black drum, and trout are the game of choice for inshore anglers here year-round. Spring and fall bring schools of Spanish mackerel close to shore, and sheepshead are abundant on the nearshore reefs during late winter and early spring. Winter is the time to fish deep holes in creeks or the main river itself for spotted sea trout.

To the south of Suwannee are the shoreline and creeks shared with anglers from the Cedar Keys. The areas in and around Deer Island and the mouths of Little Trout, Big Trout, and Giger Creeks are spots to begin a Suwannee inshore trip. There is a line of bars to the outside of this shoreline that keeps wind-driven wave action to a minimum and the flats maintain a reasonable four-foot depth during moderate tides. In fact, the entire area between the shoreline and the bars,

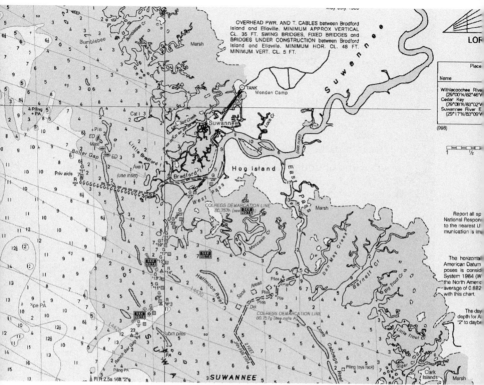

The Suwannee River mouth is shown on this chart detail.

which run from just south of the river's East Pass to just west of Deer Island, is good for drifting live baits for trout during warmer months. While the water levels here are workable during most tides, be very careful during extreme winter low tides. The best access to this area is from the Suwannee River's East Pass, slowly skirting the shoreline past the mouth of Barnett Creek and steering roughly southeast toward the north end of Deer Island (N29 14.602 W83 04.805).

At Deer Island, fish the island's northern shore, and if possible, get into the areas behind the island. In winter months, plan a trip timed around a rising tide and you'll find some nice reds here waiting to ambush mullet seeking the warmth of the late afternoon sun. As the water warms past seventy degrees, the reds will move outside the creek mouths and the trout will seek cooler water near the outer bars.

The Suwannee River and numerous creeks feed the gulf, from Cedar Key to Horseshoe Beach. Reprinted with permission from the full-color *Florida Atlas & Gazetteer*. Copyright DeLorme.

Always keep your eyes peeled for big black drum rooting around the oyster bars if you get up into one of these creek mouths. The closer the water temperature is to bath water, the more these big drum show their wagging tails above the surface. Jigs tipped with pieces of live shrimp or crab, and pitched to the bottom in front of tailing black drum are a good bet for a hookup.

Barnett Creek is the first creek to the south of East Pass and probably the busiest of the Suwannee area creeks during the winter. Dan May Creek, just north and inside the mouth of East Pass, is a close second. These are big creeks, rivaling some of the Big Bend rivers in size. They are peppered with oyster bars and some relatively deep holes, particularly at the mouths of their tributaries. During times of extremely cold weather, nice fat trout invade Barnett and Dan May Creeks, as do scores of boats and eager fishermen. While many locals still fish live shrimp under popping corks in the creeks, I believe that a slow-trolled or slow-retrieved MirrOlure does equally well for wintertime creek fishing. The TT series of MirrOlures works very well, as they sink deep and resemble tiny trout, one of the favored foods of big trout. Troll at about three knots until you have a strike, then start casting near the spot where the hit occurred.

East Pass is almost as wide and deep as some parts of the main river channel. It runs south from a point upriver (N29 18.965 W83 07.202), from the town of Suwannee, and winds almost due south, where it flows alongside Hog Island and finally floods onto the flats. There is an old marked channel, but silting has taken its toll, making it useable only on higher water. While you're likely to catch largemouth bass at the junction with the main river, you'll find wintertime trout near the mouth, and tarpon and redfish along the southern banks in summer. Trolled plugs or cut mullet are good choices if you try for tarpon. Reds respond well to jigs fished deep and tipped with shrimp. Trout succumb to deeply trolled MirrOlures in the winter, but you'll find these deep-water fish want the lure to move a bit more slowly than in the nearby creeks.

Popular wintertime fishing spots in the main river are the deep holes along the northern shore, west of the Miller's Marina canal. Using your depth finder, you can spot trout stacked up and waiting for a live shrimp or deep-diving MirrOlure to pass. Many anglers troll this stretch, and it can become hectic at times. The colder the day, in particular the last day of a very cold spell, the better the fishing here.

Hog Island is the name given to the piece of very swampy land that's bounded by the main channel of the Suwannee River and East Pass. Along its gulf shore are several creeks, including Moccasin Creek. Anglers willing to brave the numerous oyster bars crossing its mouth (N29 17.095 W83 08.129) will find great year-round fishing here. And, if you're willing to chance the tides and potential snags, a trip to the swampy headwaters is worth the trip just for the scenery.

The main river channel, like the southern channel from East Pass, has in recent years become silted-in by the river's discharge from upstream, making another least-favored exit to the gulf. However, don't

This photo shows the entry to Moccasin Creek, just south of the main river channel at Suwannee.

The creeks near Suwannee are scenic and lined with rocky oyster bars.

neglect the areas behind Halfmoon Reef (N29 16.723 W83 08.741), the Ranch Bar (N29 15.312 W83 10.082), and the south side of the McGriff Channel, or northwest channel, for trout and redfish. Hot summertime water may run the trout towards deeper, cooler flats, but reds cruise these areas all year. Topwater lures, thrown on early or late falling tides, are very productive.

The McGriff Channel is now the deepest entry to the gulf from the Suwannee River. However, September 2001 soundings showed only three feet of water at low water. The area that seems to have become shallow is between markers 6 and 7, and should be noted by all boaters.

The line of bars through which the McGriff Channel is cut is another good spot to fish for reds and trout. On the incoming tide, bait from the deep offshore flats washes through cuts in the bars where predators lay in ambush. The slightly deeper, shoreward sides of the bars get fairly active with bait fish in the mid-summer months and are good areas to drift using live bait or jigs. Schools of Spanish mackerel sometimes venture into these waters, and the occasional tarpon is jumped here by startled light-tackle fishermen.

To the northeast, against the marshy shoreline, is Cat Island (N29 19.722 W83 10.625), just outside the Salt Creek Channel. There's an interesting and sometimes productive cut between Cat Island and the shoreline, but it's usually heavily trafficked by boats heading northward. Salt Creek has cool-weather potential, but it's shallow, and bigger boats have limited access. As in many of the creeks along the Big Bend's rugged shoreline, you'll likely see many more airboats and jet-driven johnboats here than traditional outboard-powered boats.

North of Cat Island are Bumblebee, Sanders, and Johnson Creeks. Sometimes heavily fished by locals, these three creeks provide great structure for redfish year-round and sea trout in winter. Oysters line and barricade the mouths of these creeks, which feature deep holes along the turns and stretch several miles back into the California Swamp. While the mix of tidal flow from the adjacent flats and backwater runoff allows these creeks to hold fish well back toward their headwaters, the first quarter-mile or so of each is probably best fished by the average angler. Kayakers, canoeists, and airboaters have a decided advantage in their far reaches.

Offshore Fishing at Suwannee

Suwannee is one of those places that epitomize offshore fishing along the Big Bend. Locals joke about the depth increasing only a foot for every mile. That's not far from the truth. The influence of the Suwannee River has pushed the ten- and twenty-foot shelf out a bit further than at other places along the Big Bend. Luckily, as the shoreline receded in past millennia, ancient creek beds left their mark, as evidenced by many uneven depth contours, a few trenches, and even small reefs. Hedemon Reef (N29 17.074 W83 15.544) and Red Bank Reef (N29 19.165 W83 15.438) are excellent examples of close-to-shore reefs reachable by smaller boats. They are only about three miles from the end of the McGriff Channel (N29 18.576 W83 12.018) and are both five-foot grassy humps sitting between the ten- and twenty-foot contours.

Running out the McGriff Channel and heading offshore from Suwannee, you're likely to encounter boats fishing from Cedar Key, Horseshoe Beach, and even Steinhatchee. It takes a bit longer to reach fifty feet here, but you'll find grouper, kingfish, cobia, amberjack, and wintertime sheepshead on the scattered rock piles and even over deeper live bottom, which contrasts to vast sandy prairies with its sea grass growing over Swiss cheese limestone bottom and clumps of sponges and other sea growth. This type of bottom is plentiful off Suwannee and will hold remarkable numbers of offshore fish, even in less than thirty feet. Much like inshore flats, this bottom can be mixed with areas of barren sandy bottom.

The area of live bottom known locally as Spotty Bottom (approx. N29 16.202 W83 19.567) is close to shore and, despite its shallow depths, is a great spot for spring and fall kingfish and Spanish mackerel.

Anglers trolling large diving plugs occasionally hook up with keeper red and gag grouper over this mixed bottom as well. Note a big strike by hitting the "Man Overboard" button on your GPS or by tossing a marker on the spot. Then, using your bottom finder, try fishing the same rock pile with live or cut bait. This is one method by which great offshore numbers are best found, and there are some nice ones, many still unknown, in this general area.

Bottom structure and relief are always important to offshore fishermen, and there's sometimes nothing better than a wreck or artificial reef. Luckily, there are several in the gulf within easy reach of Suwannee. One artificial reef worth considering, about twenty-five miles from Suwannee, is the White City Bridge (N29 10.000 W83 39.081). Mostly rubble, it's a good spot to try on a calm day.

Two other artificial-reef areas to the south are GOFC #1 (N29 07.594 W83 13.327) and GOFC #3 (N29 06.841 W83 25.603). These reefs were originally placed by the Gainesville Offshore Fishing Club and are popular fishing areas. GOFC #3 is located farther offshore than GOFC #1 but is on the edge of the thirty-foot contour. In addi-

Suwannee is an excellent jumping-off spot for grouper fishermen.

tion to grouper and kingfish, both of these reefs are good habitat for spawning sheepshead in the winter and early spring.

Getting Around Suwannee

Highway 349 is the main artery into Suwannee from US 19/98 at Old Town. In fact, it's just about the only artery. Suwannee Town is largely residential, with no nightly accommodations and only a few restaurants. There are promises of a motel, and weekend or weekly condo rentals are available. While the two marinas do stock some convenience items and can pump gas into your car, many visitors stop in Old Town or Cross City for provisions. There is one small but reasonably stocked grocery store in Suwannee.

As I mentioned, of the three original channels into Suwannee from the gulf, only the McGriff Channel is reasonable to navigate, and larger boats should wait for high water. Once inside the river, the channel is marked and deep. Access to the two marinas is by way of canals on the north bank.

Where to Stay

Bill's Fish Camp, Suwannee, (352) 542-7086. Weekly lodging.

Suwannee Gables Motel, 27659 US 19, Old Town, (352) 542-7752. Lodging.

Cadillac Motel, 7490 N US 19, Fanning Springs, (352) 463-2188. Lodging.

Park Inn, US 19, Chiefland, (352) 463-2069. Lodging.

Carriage Inn, 16872 SE US 19, Cross City, (352) 498-3910. Lodging, adjacent restaurant.

Condominium Rentals, Billy Miller, (352) 542-7349.

House Rentals, Sonja Reed, (352) 542-0704.

Where to Eat

Salt Creek Restaurant, County Road (CR) 349, Suwannee, (352) 542-7072. Lunch, dinner only on Mondays and Tuesdays.

Sarah's Suwannee Café, CR 349, Suwannee, (352) 542-0500. Breakfast and lunch daily, 6 a.m. to 2 p.m.; dinner Friday and Saturday, 5 to 9 p.m.

Crown's Waterfront Market, Canal Street, Suwannee, (352) 542-9600. Groceries, but limited produce and meat, beer, ice.

Carriage Inn Restaurant, US 19, Cross City, (352) 498-0888. Breakfast, lunch, dinner, dinner buffets. The seafood buffet on Friday and Saturday nights is popular.

Lighthouse Restaurant, US 19, Fanning Springs, (352) 463-2644. Lunch, dinner, seafood.

Homestead Restaurant, 17313 NW US 19, Fanning Springs, (352) 463-0040. Buffet and menu, breakfast, lunch, dinner, open everyday, takeout. The Friday and Saturday seafood buffet at the Homestead is worth the trip to Fanning Springs.

Huckleberry's BBQ, 7440 US 19, Fanning Springs, (352) 463-0355. Breakfast, lunch, dinner, takeout.

Hitchcock's Foodway, CR 349, Old Town. Small, full-service supermarket.

Marinas, Marine Supplies and Service, Bait-and-Tackle Shops, and Launching Ramps

Miller's Marina and Houseboat Rental, Suwannee, (352) 542-7349, 1-800-458-2628. Gas and diesel, dockage, dry storage, sanitary pumpout, campground, frozen and live bait, snacks, tackle, ice, launching ramp. Miller's is the closest marina to the mouth of the Suwannee River.

Suwannee Marina, Canal St., Suwannee, (352) 542-9159. Gas, dockage, dry storage, frozen and live bait, snacks, tackle, ice, launching ramp, closed Tuesdays. This marina is easy to reach. It's just inside the river mouth; look for signs.

Suwannee Shores Marina, US 19, Old Town, (352) 542-7482. Full outboard service, new boat and motor sales, extensive marine supplies, closed Mondays. While not actually in the town of Suwannee, Suwannee Shores Marina is your best bet for local marine repairs.

Local Fishing Guides

Capt. Craig Holcomb, (352) 542-9159, -1901. Inshore and nearshore.

Capt. Ron Hall, (352) 542-0358. Inshore.

Capt. Butch Thorpe, (352) 542-9375. Inshore.

Capt. Les Flaherty, (352) 542-0327. Inshore and offshore.

Capt. Jon Farmer, (352) 542-7145. Inshore and offshore.

Capt. Howard Hamilton, (352) 542-3278. Inshore and offshore.

Capt. Reggie Bielling, (386) 365-5057. Inshore and offshore.

Capt. Joe Basin, (352) 542-2266. Inshore.

Many guides from Cedar Key and Horseshoe Beach are familiar with the waters at Suwannee. Please consult the listings for those areas, if necessary. Also the Web site of the Florida Guides Association (www. florida-guides.com) has a complete listing of United States Coast Guard licensed-and-insured fishing guides.

7

Horseshoe Beach

Horseshoe Beach has no beach unless you count the twenty-foot strip of white sand next to the county boat ramp. You *will* find horseshoe crabs there.

A small commercial fishing village, Horseshoe Beach is located on a small spit of gulf coastline between Suwannee and Steinhatchee. By road, it's about twenty-five miles from Cross City, a major town on US Highway 19/98. A well-maintained channel leads to the Gulf of Mexico and its deeper water. Horseshoe Beach marks the northern end of the Suwannee River's effect on water clarity. Unless muddied by winds or torrential rains, inshore and nearshore waters here remain clear for most of the year.

Facilities at Horseshoe Beach are limited, and many visiting anglers rely on the amenities at Cross City. If you're willing to put up with the lack of some conveniences, you'll find this a great secluded fishing destination. On the way into town, there's a sign proclaiming Horseshoe Beach as "Florida's Last Frontier." That's the truth!

Inshore and Nearshore Fishing at Horseshoe Beach

The point of land that makes up the town of Horseshoe Beach seems to act as a catch basin for all sorts of bait and inshore species that move from the south heading north, where equal number of game fish await.

To the south, there's a visible effect of the Suwannee River's dis-

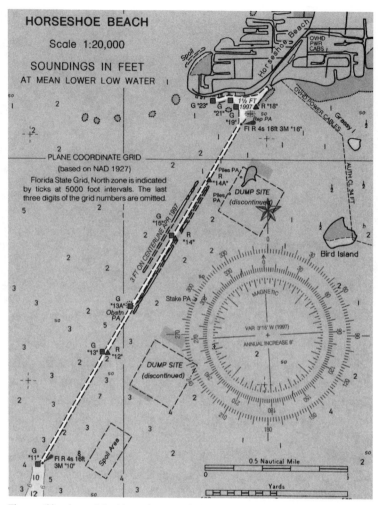

The spoil banks and the Horseshoe Beach channel are good places to look for trout that are hiding from cold winter weather.

charge. Stained water is the norm, and downright muddy water occurs sometimes as far north as the Horseshoe Beach channel, during times of heavy rain. To the north, the water remains surprisingly clear the closer one gets to shore and to the Pepperfish Keys.

The shoreline of Horseshoe Cove, between Horseshoe Beach and Shired Island, is rugged, formed by creeks and barrier bars. It does

The islands to the south of Horseshoe Beach are excellent redfish habitat.

make a westward turn, forming a *hook* that seems to trap game fish, particularly trout, redfish, flounder, and occasional black drum. The closer anglers can get to the mouths of Shired, Fishbone, Amason, and Butler Creeks, the better they'll find the fishing. And don't hesitate to head south of Shired Island, particularly if you launch there. The only reason I've included Shired Island in this chapter is that it's accessed by road from County Road (CR) 351, leading to Horseshoe Beach from Cross City. The creeks toward Suwannee are similar and equally fishy.

The shell and oyster bars along the creekfronts in Horseshoe Cove are excellent for wade-fishing. Some anglers use kayaks and canoes, launched at Shired Island; others come in light skiffs from Horseshoe Beach. Slow-moving rising tides seem to be best spring through fall. Quicker, spring tides seem to push baitfish over the bars too fast, but action can pick up at the peak of the tide. Anglers should always be aware of the tide in this backwater, moving out as the tide falls. This is not a fun spot to be stranded for the night. The set of bars called Seven Brothers (N29 23.897 W83 14.509) is a good place to

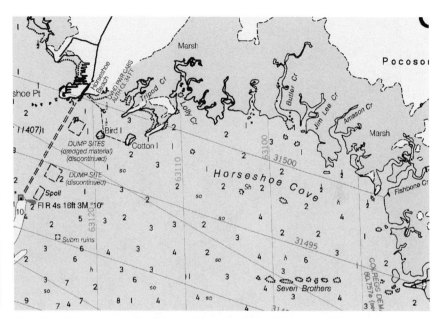

Horseshoe Cove is a natural "catch point" for trout and redfish north of the Suwannee River.

start a trip to Horseshoe Cove. They're offshore a fair distance. Special care should be taken to not run through or interfere with any of the clam-lease areas in the outer cove, but otherwise, reaching Seven Brothers is easy. Should the tide drop, give Seven Sisters (N29 22.863 W83 14.731) a try. They're about a mile to the southwest and are good bars to fish on a falling tide, either from the boat or wading. Popular baits are D.O.A. shrimp (¼oz, darker colors) or D.O.A. TerrorEyz jigs (¼oz, root beer glitter), as they can be worked slowly over the craggy shelly bottom. Typically, reds eat the TerrorEyz and trout eat the shrimp. Topwater plugs work well, too, and you'll likely catch a Spanish mackerel, bluefish, or even jump a tarpon. A good rule here and around any other bar structure is to fish into the current, making your lure appear to be washing along with the tide. Action along the outer bars slows in cold weather, and the bigger trout and reds move inside the creeks. Butler and Fishbone Creeks are local favorites in the winter.

While there are grassy flats off the southern side of Horseshoe

Wade-fishing with light tackle on shell bars between Horseshoe Beach and Suwannee is a popular and easy way to catch lots of nice fish.

Beach, they are best fished when the water is fairly clear. A good general area is about three miles southeast of marker #5 near waypoint N29 21.304 W83 16.923, where you'll find deep cuts through some grassy bottom.

The flats to the north of the Horseshoe channel seem to attract more anglers. There are three old bird racks in the general vicinity of N29 26.313 W83 22.839 that mark the edge of some nice flats off Boggy Creek. A drift to the northeast in the summer months, fishing shrimp or artificials under corks, will usually produce a limit of trout. As you get closer to shore and near the mouth of Boggy Creek (N29 28.221 W83 19.289), you'll start seeing redfish and schools of mullet.

Look for large sea trout cruising the shoreline north of Horseshoe Beach during the cool months. Big slow-moving plugs will get them to bite.

Changing to topwater plugs will likely get a red aboard, particularly in the late spring or early fall. And, just as in most Gulf Coast creeks, cold weather and cold water move trout, reds, and even flounder into the creeks' deep holes.

The Pepperfish Keys are rocky islands about six miles northwest of Horseshoe Beach and seem to be the *de facto* boundary between anglers from Horseshoe Beach and Steinhatchee. I think both groups make mistakes by not crossing the boundary.

To the north of the islands is a deep cut, probably the ancient creek bed of Cow Creek, and to the south is some of the best rocky bot-

The Pepperfish Keys are rocky islands to the north of Horseshoe Beach. The shallow rocky flats along the southern side of Pepperfish are good for spring and summer trout.

tom and shoreline along this stretch of coast. Fishing the Pepperfish Channel (approx. N29 30.429 W83 24.229) to the north, or Stuart Point (N29 29.230 W83 20.640) to the south, should not be missed.

Offshore Fishing at Horseshoe Beach

Offshore anglers visiting the Big Bend often overlook Horseshoe Beach, as the public ramp can't handle bigger boats and trailers. However, the local marina has a sling that will handle boats up to 12,000 pounds. The sixty-foot contour comes pretty close to shore here, and many grouper, kingfish, and snapper spots remain undiscovered.

Some of the best offshore fishing at Horseshoe Beach is reached by running on a 270-degree compass heading from the end of the channel until you reach depths of fifty feet. This general area is shared by anglers from Suwannee and Steinhatchee, but the crowds thin out beyond sixty or seventy feet. Many locals recommend trolling deep-diving lures just above the bottom at four to five knots, as soon as fifty feet is reached. This method of prospecting is highly effective, and many times will catch more and bigger gag grouper than bottom fishing. Other prospectors prefer to slowly drift over large areas, fishing live bait, cut bait, or jigs near the bottom. Drift-fishing can also be a good technique for catching red grouper, which seem to enjoy live bottom with less relief than the rocky ledges and piles inhabited by gags.

Lamb Spring (N29 26.628 W83 50.627) and The Crack (N29 23.819 W83 42.722) are good natural offshore spots. They're not big but can hold grouper, cobia, amberjack, and even a few barracuda. They are about seven miles apart, and slow trolling between them can be productive. In forty to fifty feet of water, these spots can hold fish in the colder months, too.

Two artificial reefs worth noting are the White City Bridge (N29 10.000 W83 39.081), about twenty-three miles to the southwest, and the Buckeye Reef (N29 39.000 W83 54.310), about thirty-five miles to the northwest.

Getting Around Horseshoe Beach

If you travel too far down CR 351 from Cross City toward Horseshoe Beach, you'll simply run into the gulf. About halfway on the twenty-four-mile trip you'll see the intersection of CR 357 on the left. That's the road to Shired Island, where there's a boat ramp and county park.

In town, everything is located pretty much along the highway. The marina is across the canal that borders the highway to the south, but the turn is well marked. The public launching ramp is down a residential road to the right, and signs show the way.

From the gulf, the Horseshoe Beach Channel leads in from what's left of a natural channel in about eight feet of water. The entrance to the channel at marker #2 (N29 23.264 W83 20.403) is safe to approach from offshore. Care should be taken to stay inside the channel inshore of marker #5 (N29 23.872 W83 19.456), especially on the northern side. Anglers using small boats and wishing to fish the southern shoreline of Horseshoe Cove can begin a slow and cautious easterly run from marker #10 (N29 23.872 W83 19.456). There is an old channel running from Horseshoe Point to the western flats, but it's best to follow someone on your first trip. The canal to the marina has recently been dredged, as has the turning basin, offering safe access at most tides.

Amenities are precious at Horseshoe Beach, and many visitors prefer to provision in nearby Cross City.

Where to Stay

Compass Realty, Jimmy Butler Jr., (352) 498-2400, 1-877-498-2402. Condominium and house rentals.

Tina's Dockside Inn, (352) 498-5768. Cabins, kitchenettes, sleeping rooms.

Carriage Inn, 16872 SE US 19, Cross City, (352) 498-3910. Lodging, ample trailer parking, adjacent to restaurant. The folks at the Carriage Inn welcome fishermen willing to make the drive to or from Horseshoe Beach.

El Dorado Motel, 16148 SE US 19, Cross City, (352) 498-3307. Lodging.

Where to Eat

Horseshoe Beach Café, CR 351, (352) 498-7061. Breakfast, lunch, dinner.

Lily Creek General Store & Café, CR 351, (352) 498-7515. Convenience store, tackle, deli items, take-out foods.

Carriage Inn Restaurant, US 19, Cross City, (352) 498-0888. Breakfast, lunch, dinner. The seafood buffet on Friday and Saturday nights is popular.

Cypress Inn Restaurant, US 19, Cross City, (352) 498-7211. Breakfast, lunch, dinner.

Midtown Café, 660 NW US 19, Cross City, (352) 498-5050. Breakfast, lunch, dinner.

Smokey's Steakhouse and BBQ, 16368 US 19, Cross City. Lunch, dinner, closed Sundays.

Marinas, Marine Supplies and Service, Bait-and-Tackle Shops, and Launching Ramps

Horseshoe Beach Marina, CR 351, (352) 498-5687. Gas and diesel, ice, large-capacity boat lifts, wet and dry storage, convenience-store items, frozen bait, tackle. Low tides, particularly in winter, can make access to the canal difficult for larger boats.

Kight's Shrimp, CR 351, (352) 498-7767. Live bait, shrimp.

Panama Paul's General Store and Discount Marine Supplies, CR 351, (352) 498-3148. Convenience store, marine supplies, bait and tackle.

El Sea's Fish Camp, (352) 498-5021. RV park.

County Boat Ramp. Paved single ramp, adequate parking, restrooms, limited security, camping allowed. The channel leading to the gulf can be a problem, even for smaller craft, on low water.

Shired Island Boat Ramp, CR 357. Paved single ramp, adequate parking, no facilities, limited security, camping nearby. This ramp offers very shallow access to the gulf and Shired Creek. If you launch here, try wading some of the oyster bars to the north.

Local Fishing Guides

Capt. Gary Patterson, (352) 498-2017, captpat@atlantic.net. Inshore and offshore.

Capt. John Squires, (352) 498-7479, www.captainjohnsquires.com. Inshore.

Capt. Cecil Kight, (352) 498-2809, -0018. Inshore.

Capt. Jerry Chewning, (352) 214-9553. Inshore.

Many guides from Steinhatchee and Suwannee are familiar with the waters at Horseshoe Beach. Please consult the listings for those areas, if necessary. Also the Web site of the Florida Guides Association (www.florida-guides.com) has a complete listing of United States Coast Guard licensed-and-insured fishing guides.

8

Steinhatchee

First things first—Steinhatchee is pronounced *STEEN-hatchee*, not *STINE-hatchee*. If you use the *Stine* pronunciation, locals will immediately know you're an outsider. No matter though, as many folks at Steinhatchee are outsiders anyway.

Located just up the coastline from Horseshoe Beach, Steinhatchee is closer to both US Highway 19/98 and South Georgia than are Cedar Key, Suwannee, and Horseshoe Beach. And, while many of Florida's other coastal towns attract visitors from adjacent states, Steinhatchee has become a strong magnet for out-of-towners wanting to fish. For good reason, too, as Steinhatchee provides easy access to relatively unspoiled rocky shoreline and deep offshore waters.

Steinhatchee has also become the focal point for recreational scalloping on the Big Bend. While other ports from Homosassa to Mexico Beach attract scallopers, Steinhatchee has turned the entire scallop season (July 1 to September 10) into a lively crowded festival. Visiting anglers should plan their visits to Steinhatchee accordingly and well in advance.

The town of Steinhatchee occupies the northern side of the Steinhatchee River in Taylor County. On the southern side, in Dixie County, the small town of Jena is less settled but growing quickly. Real-estate development has reduced the number of marinas, but the remaining three are all excellent, with full services. The upside of the real-estate boom here is that the quality of lodging and food services has greatly improved since the mid-1990s.

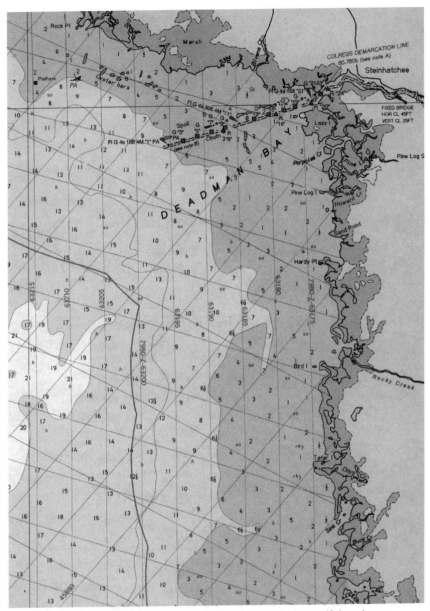

The flats and craggy shoreline south of Steinhatchee are legendary redfish and trout fisheries.

The marinas and the boat ramp at Steinhatchee are near the river mouth.

Inshore and Nearshore Fishing at Steinhatchee

Inshore and nearshore fishing here is legendary. From just a few feet to as many as five miles offshore you'll find grass flats in depths from one to eight feet. The coastline from the Pepperfish Keys (N29 30.275 W83 24.352), about nine miles to the south, to Big Grass Island (N29 44.069 W83 34.214), eight miles to the northwest, is easily reached by anglers leaving the Steinhatchee River. Care should be taken not to run too close to shore on lesser tides as some of Steinhatchee's famous rocks extend several miles into the Gulf of Mexico. I recommend that inshore fishermen consider marker #9 (N29 39.641 W83 26.295) as a safe turning point to either the northwest or to the south. If you plan to fish within a mile of shore, I recommend you idle or use a trolling motor within that limit, especially if you are a newcomer to the area. Don't be fooled by locals running on plane—they know every inch of the bottom.

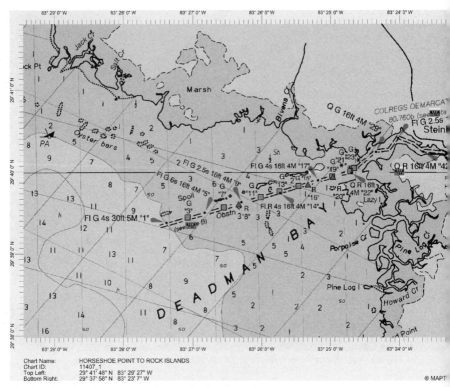

Chart Name: HORSESHOE POINT TO ROCK ISLANDS
Chart ID: 11407_1
Top Left: 29° 41' 48" N 83° 29' 27" W
Bottom Right: 29° 37' 58" N 83° 23' 7" W
                                                         ® MAPT

The Steinhatchee River empties into rocky Deadman Bay.

Dixie and Taylor Counties are home to coastal creeks (Cow, Buck, Sink, Rocky, Howard, Pine Log, Porpoise, Bevins, Jack, Dallus and Clay Creeks—listed from south to north) that feature rocky shallow entries, making each a potential holding area for baitfish and game species. The rocky shoreline is almost always exposed during low tides, particularly in the winter months. Extreme care should be taken by boaters even on higher tides, as the published depths at these creek mouths can still be less than one foot at mean low water. Grass beds, mostly turtle and manatee grass, sometimes reach well up into the creeks. There are primitive launching ramps where Cow Creek crosses County Road (CR) 361 and inside Rocky Creek (both to the south) and Dallus Creek (to the north). These are useful for launching small motorboats, kayaks, and canoes.

Cobia are fun to catch—and all sizes make great table fare.

Sea trout are the staple at Steinhatchee for inshore fishermen, with redfish taking a close second. Trout are found in all sizes and at all depths throughout the spring, summer, and fall. They move into the creeks and the river during the cold winter months, generally fattened and ready to spawn. Reds are found close to shore all year, with fall and spring the best seasons, particularly for fly fishermen, who prefer to see their prey. In the springtime and throughout the summer, invading schools of Spanish mackerel and bluefish will steal their share of light leaders and lures from trout and redfish anglers. Flounder are plentiful along the edges of rocky bars and are easily targeted. Cobia, usually considered an offshore species, are sometimes found cruising the flats and channel markers in the warmer months. And an occasional tarpon, moving northward from warm southern gulf waters in late spring or summer, will be seen, but the species is rarely targeted here.

If it's bitter cold, the best bet for Steinhatchee sea trout is in the river. The Suicide Hole (where trout go to commit suicide in the win-

Frigid winter days push sea trout into the Steinhatchee River. This spot is just downstream from the Sea Hag Marina.

ter) is located mid-channel just a few yards south of the Sea Hag Marina. Also, the deep drop-offs along the channel edges near markers #21 and #23 attract trout and dozens of boats on cold winter days. Be careful not to anchor here, as this area is outside the river's idle-speed zone and boat traffic can be fast and furious. Live shrimp on ⅜-ounce jig heads are local favorites, as are deep-sinking TT-style MirrOlures.

Another wintertime option, often ending up with many over-slot fish, is to fish the oyster and rock bars along creek mouths on a late-afternoon rising tide. Winter low tides are extreme, and sunny days warm the bottom. Trout, and a few reds, prowl these areas as the tide covers the bars in the late afternoon. While live shrimp work well for these fish, slow-suspending lures such as Corky Mullet, MirrOlure Catch 2000s and MirrOminnows, or Brown Lures' jig bodies seem to be most productive. These fish also give fly fishermen a good target on cold days and attack patterns such as Bendbacks and Clouser Minnows. Trout season is closed in February, and of course, that's when the big fish show up. Catching them is fun, but be sure to carefully release these spawners. Rock Point (N29 41.239 W83 29.206) to the north of the river is a good place to fish on winter afternoons, as are the rocky bars near Rocky Creek (N29 36.221 W83 24.874) and Bull Cove (N29 31.738 W83 23.959), both to the south.

Trout are easy to catch at Steinhatchee, making for a fun family outing.

It's difficult to recommend a single or even a dozen areas to fish the flats for sea trout near Steinhatchee. Unless there have been recent storms and big rains, the water here is generally very clear and the sea grasses healthy. There are literally miles and miles of great fishing.

Two areas come to mind that are close to the river's mouth. The Trout Flat (Approx. N29 38.271 W83 26.273) is the general area in Deadman Bay to the south of marker #9 in four to five feet of water. The areas inside and outside the Trout Bars (N29 40.621 W83 28.598) to the northwest are also lush deeper flats. If you don't mind a bit

Lush grass flats surround this large sandbar, north of Steinhatchee and west of Dallus Creek.

Big Grass Island is a popular picnic spot and is located between Steinhatchee and Keaton Beach.

Local guides use specialized boats and gear to approach wary redfish in the Steinhatchee backwaters.

more of a run, try the expanse of grass between Dallus Creek and Big Grass Island (Approx. N29 42.691 W83 34.300) to the north or the edges of the sandbar off Pepperfish Keys to the south (N29 32.439 W83 27.139). Drifting spots such as these and fishing with either live or artificial baits is the standard drill at Steinhatchee.

Offshore Fishing at Steinhatchee

A substantial part of any day of offshore fishing at Steinhatchee (or at most Big Bend ports) involves a long boat ride. Grouper, the primary offshore species targeted here, are almost always found in water deeper than thirty feet. That depth doesn't appear quickly on your depth sounder, as the shallow plain of coastline extends many miles into the gulf. And, while the nearshore areas of Taylor and Dixie Counties are rocky, there's an awful lot of plain-sand bottom before you get to thirty feet. Other offshore species, including spawning sheepshead in the winter, king mackerel in spring and fall, and cobia in summer, are more likely found closer to shore thus alleviating the need for long runs, particularly on windy days. Smaller, less-glamorous species such as black sea bass and "Florida snapper" (white grunts) are fun to catch and excellent to eat. There's always some sort of offshore action at Steinhatchee.

Some of the best offshore fishing here is reached by running on a 240-degree compass heading from marker #1 until a depth of fifty feet is reached. Depending on whether or not there's floating grass on the surface, many locals recommend that anglers begin trolling deep-diving lures, such as Mann's Stretch 30s, just above the bottom at four to five knots, when they reach fifty feet. This method of prospecting is highly effective, and many times will catch more and bigger gag grouper than bottom-fishing. Other prospectors prefer to slowly drift over large areas, fishing live bait, cut bait, or jigs near the bottom. Drift-fishing can also be a good technique for catching red grouper, which seem to enjoy live bottom with less relief than the rocky ledges and piles inhabited by gags.

If you're interested in bottom fishing, locate a piece of rough bottom and anchor over it. Larger rock outcroppings such as Lamb Spring (N29 26.628 W83 50.627) and The Crack (N29 23.819 W83 42.722) will also hold big schools of baitfish in the warmer months. Those bait pods in turn attract king mackerel, cobia, and an occasional barracuda. A live pinfish or white bait, free-lined on a stinger rig, will sometimes result in the catch of a lifetime. Don't neglect slow-trolled (at one to two knots) live bait; this is a favorite technique of king-mackerel experts. If you're trolling plugs for grouper in the spring or fall, put a smaller, shallower-running plug or feather in your prop wash for king mackerel.

In cooler months, many larger grouper will hide close to rock piles, as will spawning sheepshead. Anglers wishing to stay close to shore in colder months (or affected by mandatory closures of grouper) do well for big sheepshead around structure, including the Steinhatchee Reef (N29 39.900 W83 37.591), the remnants of Big Bend marker #18 (N29 40.100 W83 35.400) or the Taylor County Reefs (N29 45.890 W83 43.640).

While there are good grouper spots in shallow water, it's the fifty-
to sixty-foot contour that regularly produces big fish here, both to
the southwest and out toward the Air Force V Tower (N29 24.961
W84 20.695) in seventy-plus-feet of water. Many anglers out of Steinhatchee fish the same spots that are within reach of other ports in the
eastern panhandle, including the Alphabet Towers south of Carrabelle as well the upper reaches of the Florida Middle Grounds. The V
Tower is one of those. Offshore fishing from Steinhatchee takes place
over a large area with many scattered rocky piles and vast prairies of
spongy live bottom. No single location is capable of sustaining great
numbers of fish, but in total, the area is highly populated with deep-
water dwellers year-round.

Getting Around Steinhatchee

There are two major highway access routes to the Steinhatchee area,
including Jena, which is on the southern side of the river. Both lead
from US 19/98.

Traveling south on US 19/98 from Perry, turn west on State Road
(SR) 51, which intersects the bigger highway at Tennille, about twenty
miles south of Perry. It's about ten miles to Steinhatchee.

Traveling northbound, drive about thirteen miles from Cross City
to the intersection of CR 358. Take CR 358 six miles to Jena. If your
destination is Steinhatchee proper, turn right at 10th Street and cross
the Steinhatchee River Bridge.

Riverside Drive runs alongside the river, essentially an extension
of SR 51. CR 361 runs northward from town toward Dallus Creek and
southward from Jena to Rocky Creek and Cow Creek.

Accessing the Steinhatchee River by water involves staying well
offshore until you're able to make an almost due east turn toward
marker #1 (N29 39.383 W83 27.376). The old Big Bend markers have
been removed, but some older NOAA charts may show their locations. These were good offshore reference points. Knowing the former locations of Big Bend #16 (N29 28.400 W83 28.400) and #18 (N29
40.100 W83 35.400) can be useful if approaching Steinhatchee from

There are few places to hide from bad weather along this stretch of coastline. Be aware of the weather at all times.

the deep gulf. Once in the river channel, follow the marked channel upstream. Most amenities here are located along the riverbanks.

Where to Stay

Smuggler's Cove at the Sea Hag, Riverside Drive, (352) 498-3008, www. seahag.com. Lodging, adjacent to marina, kitchenettes, RV cabins. Professionally managed lodging at the closest marina to the gulf.

Pace's Cottages, Riverside Drive, (352) 498-3008, www.seahag.com/ paces.htm. Lodging, across from marina. Managed by the Sea Hag Marina crew.

River Haven Marina & Motel, Riverside Drive, (352) 498-0709, www. riverhavenmarinaandmotel.com. Lodging, across from marina.

Gulfstream Motel and Marina, CR 358, Jena, (352) 498-8088, www. gulfstreammotelmarina.com. Lodging, adjacent to marina, kitchenettes, RV cabins.

Pelican Pointe Inn, Riverside Drive, (352) 498-7427, www.pelican pointeinn.com. Lodging, dockage, adjacent to Fiddler's Restaurant.

Steinhatchee Landing Resort, Highway 51, (352) 498-3513, www. steinhatcheelanding.com. Rental homes and condos. The Landing, located upriver, is quaint and quite a bit more upscale than the average marina or fish-camp motel.

Steinhatchee River Inn, Riverside Drive, (352) 498-4049, www.stein hatcheeriverinn.com. Lodging, across from River Haven Marina, kitchenettes, wireless Internet. Same ownership but less stately than Steinhatchee Landing Resort.

Nature's Coast RV Resort, CR 358, Jena, (352) 498-7344. Full-service RV Park, swimming pool.

Steinhatchee Rivergate, Front Porch Realty, (352) 498-5151, www.fla-living.com. Upscale rental homes and condos.

Sunset Place Condominiums, 1st Street, (352) 498-0860, www.the sunsetplace.com. Condo rentals.

Where to Eat

Roy's Restaurant, SR 51, (352) 498-5000. Breakfast buffet, lunch, dinner, seafood, open seven days a week. An excellent salad bar is included with entrees, but be careful not to fill up on the excellent Greek-style potato salad and spoil your dinner.

Fiddler's Restaurant, Riverside Drive, (352) 498-7427. Lunch served Friday, Saturday, Sunday. Dinner nightly. Sunday lunch buffet, seafood.

Lynn-Rich Restaurant, SR 51, (352) 498-0605. Breakfast, lunch. Great pancakes, but the service can be slow and leisurely.

Mel's Crab Shack, CR 358, Jena, (352) 498-8088. Bar and grill at Gulfstream Marina.

Hungry Howie's, Riverside Drive, (352) 498-7100. Pizza, sandwiches, riverside with dockage, local delivery.

Casey's Cove, CR 358, Jena, Convenience store with deli, breakfast, lunch, and dinner.

Mason's Market, 1st Street, (352) 498-3028. Full-service supermarket with hot and cold deli. Mason's chicken finger snacks are lunchtime favorites at Steinhatchee.

Marinas, Marine Supplies and Service, Bait-and-Tackle Shops, and Launching Ramps

Sea Hag Marina, Riverside Drive, (352) 498-3008, www.seahag.com. Gas and diesel, lodging, transient dockage, wet and dry storage, convenience store, live and frozen bait, tackle, full marine service and repairs, marine supplies, tiki bar, full-service dive shop, boat rentals. Professional, courteous and well stocked—need I say more?

River Haven Marina & Motel, Riverside Drive, (352) 498-0709, www. riverhavenmarinaandmotel.com. Gas and diesel, lodging, boat rentals, trailer-boat launching with 30,000-pound lift, transient dockage, sanitary pump station, wet slips, convenience store, marine supplies, live and frozen bait, tackle, kayak rentals and sales, tiki bar.

Gulfstream Motel and Marina, CR 358, Jena, (352) 498-8088, www. gulfstreammotelmarina.com. Gas and diesel, lodging, boat rentals, transient dockage, wet slips, boat ramp for guests, convenience store, live and frozen bait, tackle, bar and grill.

Tackle Outlet, CR 358, Jena, (352) 498-5424. Live and frozen bait, tackle.

Steinhatchee Ace Hardware, 1st Avenue, (352) 498-7269. Tackle, marine supplies.

Public launching ramp, end of CR 358, Jena. Free, paved single ramp with floating dock, limited parking. This ramp is the only public ramp on the river. Expect crowds on weekends and during scallop season. Roadside parking is available but limited.

Rocky Creek ramp, CR 361, five miles south of Jena to SW 459th Avenue, then one mile west. Primitive ramp near creek mouth, shallow access to gulf, limited parking, no security. Motor slowly out of here—Rocky Creek is called Rocky Creek for a good reason.

Cow Creek access, CR 361, ten miles south of Jena. Canoe and kayak access to Cow Creek at road crossing, shallow canoe and kayak access to gulf, parking on roadside, no security. Watch the tides here.

Dallus Creek Landing, CR 361, five miles north of Steinhatchee, then three miles by dirt road. Primitive ramp near creek mouth, very shallow access to gulf, limited parking, no security.

Sand Ridge/Pine Log Ramp, three miles from CR 361 in the Jena Wildlife Management Area off the southern end of Rocky Creek Cutoff Road. A primitive ramp with access to Howard and Porpoise Creeks, very shallow access to gulf, limited parking, no security. This ramp is excellent for canoes or kayaks on windy days. There are good fishable oyster bars and deep holes within yards of the ramp.

Local Fishing Guides

Capt. Steve Rassel, (352) 376-4336, www.lastcastrass.com, srassel@ yahoo.com. Inshore, nearshore, scalloping.

Capt. Randall Hewitt, (386) 208-3823, www.naturecoastfishing.com, captrandall@hotmail.com. Inshore, nearshore, scalloping.

Capt. Tommy Thompson, (352) 284-1763, www.flanaturecoast.com/capttommy, captain@twotree.net. Inshore and backcountry, light-tackle, fly fishing.

Taylor County Fly Fishing Guides, www.taylorcountyflyfishing.com.

Capt. Walt Carlson, (352) 498-3176, wcarlson@svic.net. Inshore and airboat, offshore, scalloping.

Capt. Brian Smith, (352) 498-3703, www.bigbendcharters.com, fishing@bigbendcharters.com. offshore, nearshore, scalloping.

Capt. Wiley Horton, (352) 284-0990, www.tunersportfishing.com, w_horton@bellsouth.net. Offshore sport fishing.

Capt. Steve Hart, (352) 498-0299, www.legallimitscharters.com. Offshore.

Capt. Pat Brooke, (386) 961-1094,, www.captainpat.com. Inshore, nearshore, scalloping.

Capt. Steve Kroll, (352) 222-4085, www.pepperfishkey.com. Inshore, nearshore.

Capt. Terry Joyner, (352) 498-2349, www.joynerguideservices.com, captainjoyner@aol.com. Inshore and nearshore.

Capt. James Chesser, (352) 498-2705, www.boogercharters.com. Offshore.

Capt. Jim Zurbrick, (352) 498-2371, www.jollyrogersii.com, jim@jollyrogersii.com. Overnight offshore fishing and dive trips.

Many guides from Horseshoe Beach and Keaton Beach are familiar with the waters at Steinhatchee. Please consult the listings for those areas, if necessary. Also the Web site of the Florida Guides Association (www.florida-guides.com) has a complete listing of United States Coast Guard licensed-and-insured fishing guides.

9

Keaton Beach to the Fenholloway River

Unlike Horseshoe Beach, Keaton Beach does have a beach. It's not very big, and you're likely to be swimming alongside wade-fishermen who are tossing lures at lunker sea trout, but it is a beach.

Located seventeen miles up a scenic road from Steinhatchee, Keaton Beach is considered part of the Apalachee Bay coastline. The community straddles a long canal that leads from the main channel back to the public boat ramp and exits the flats close to shore, allowing easy access to the Gulf of Mexico for offshore fishermen. Inshore and nearshore fishing are popular on the excellent grass flats that extend well into the bay.

The gulf shoreline northward from Keaton Beach to the mouth of the Fenholloway River (N29 58.572 W83 47.296) and southward to Big Grass Island (N29 44.069 W83 34.214) is rocky and treacherous, making shallow approaches by boat difficult, but fishing excellent. The area is also relatively uncrowded (by anglers).

Like Steinhatchee, Keaton Beach and its nearshore waters attract a lot of scallopers from July 1 to September 10 each year. Facilities for anglers and visitors are good here but limited. Excellent amenities, however, can be found a half-hour drive away at Perry, on US Highway 19/98.

Inshore and Nearshore Fishing at Keaton Beach

The close shoreline near Keaton Beach can be deserted at times, and on a weekday, it's not unusual to see only one or two other boats fish-

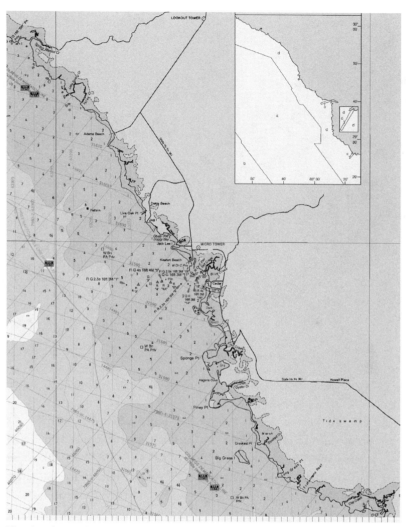

The shoreline to the north and south of Keaton Beach is rocky and rough. Move a mile offshore, however, and you'll find some of the most pristine grass flats in Florida.

ing the rocky points and creek mouths. The deeper flats can be a bit more crowded but still nothing like Steinhatchee or Crystal River. The fact that there's little angler pressure makes Keaton Beach a popular spot for anglers wishing to tackle trophy sea trout and schools of roaming redfish.

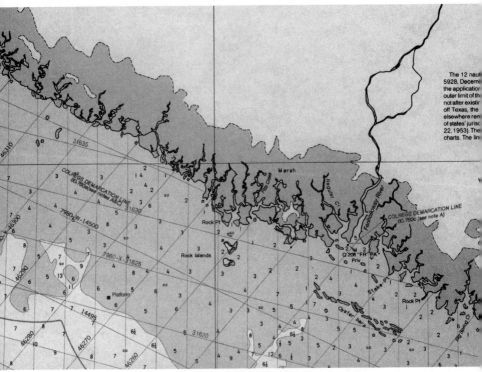

The shoreline north of Keaton Beach is ragged and rarely crowded.

From Keaton Beach marker #4 (N29 48.931 W83 36.625), it's pretty safe to run due south onto the grass flats off Sponge Point (N29 46.964 W83 35.348) and Piney Point (N29 45.588 W83 35.130). These flats are particularly productive, as they lie offshore of Hagens Cove and stretch to a tongue of deeper water just a few miles offshore. If you're within a mile of the shoreline, you'll find the water shallow and should exercise care, but the outer flats are deep enough to run at cruising speed.

In warmer months, these deeper flats, mainly structured with seagrass beds and pock-marked with white-sand holes, can hold trout and the entire gamut of inshore species, including cobia, tarpon, sharks, and flounder. And don't be surprised to find schools of Spanish mackerel or bluefish attacking schools of small baitfish. Drifting live shrimp or imitations (D.O.A. or Gulp!) beneath corks

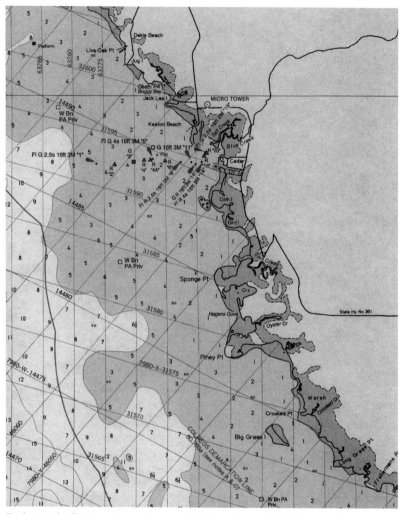

To the south of Keaton Beach, be sure to fish near Sponge Point, Hagens Cove, and Big Grass Island.

is a popular method of fishing the deeper water. Some fishermen use jig heads to weight their baits toward the sea grass tops, but others prefer fishing their baits with only a circle hook and no weight or sinker. The D.O.A. shrimp is a soft-plastic lure that is available in ½- or ¼-ounce configurations. Its lifelike appearance and action make it a good choice for bigger fish, as little ones sometimes peck

Sight-fishing for redfish is popular in the shallow clear waters near Keaton Beach.

away expensive live shrimp or smelly artificials. Several guides at Keaton Beach rely heavily on live pinfish, which are plentiful, for trophy trout. They are easily trapped or caught on small hooks anywhere on the flats in warmer weather but require an aerated live well to keep them frisky. Bird Rack #3 (N29 43.438 W83 34.373) is located southeast of Big Grass Island, and Bird Rack #2 (N29 47.076 W83 37.129) is just west of Sponge Point. These structures, originally built to gather bird guano for fertilizer, were abandoned years ago but remain good GPS waypoints by which to navigate this stretch of coastline. Bird racks were typically constructed on the edge of deeper, more navigable, water.

It's about twelve miles from the Keaton Beach Channel to the Rock Islands (N29 58.625 W83 49.712) off the mouth of the Fenholloway River. Taking a northwesterly course from the #4 marker, anglers in bay boats or flats skiffs will have no trouble staying in comfortable water depths until the bars northwest of Big Spring Creek are approached. Anyway, at this point, it's best to take it slowly and start fishing.

On the flats, staying in three to five feet of water anywhere along or outside of your course from Keaton Beach is worthwhile, as the grass flats are cut with fingers of deeper water and fed by scores of shoreline creeks that wash baitfish into the gulf. There are a couple of prehistoric creek beds lying off the coast that offer good fishing. One is the Spring Warrior Hole (N29 54.132 W83 41.482) which lies perpendicular to the coastline about seven miles up the coast to the

The Rock Islands, near the mouth of the Fenholloway River, offer good structure for trout and redfish.

northwest. Another is the Fenholloway Cut (N29 57.285 W83 48.138), which runs from offshore to the bars just off the mouth of the Fenholloway River. These deep channels are natural passages for fish moving to and from the shoreline. On both rising and falling tides, bait and predators are attracted to their depths and safety.

It's sometimes worth fishing an entire tidal cycle in channels and cuts such as these. Floating live bait (pinfish or shrimp) beneath corks as well as bottom fishing with cut bait can be successful. I'd recommend both and would also advise fishing jigs along the grassy edges while waiting for the stationery rods to bend. Expect cobia, tarpon, sharks, and a king mackerel to bite your live or cut bait, and expect trout, reds, Spanish mackerel, and bluefish to attack your jigs from the safety of the grass.

As the seawater cools down in the fall, many meat fishermen fish the deep flats and continue to catch keeper trout until the very coldest days. Even then, there will be an occasional fish, but catching them is hard work. From Big Grass Island to the Fenholloway, you'll find that cooler water means the trout and reds are close to shore, many times in water so shallow that they're easily spotted by anglers with high perches, such as poling platforms. Cooler water usually means clearer water, too, except near the Fenholloway, which is a black-water river, stained by tannin and industrial effluent. Rainfall and freshwater discharge from the many creeks can also decrease water clarity and limit sight-fishing opportunities, but I don't think clarity really affects the general quality of the fishing.

Chilly water along the Taylor County coast brings out the plug-casters. If possible, fish as close to shore as you can get, and be as quiet as you can—no loud talking or yelling. And don't feel like you need to get there early as you would do in the summertime. An afternoon rising tide on a sunny bitter-cold day will push big fish toward the tops of bars and rock piles and into shallow creeks. Big Spring Creek (N29 56.811 W83 45.037) and Spring Warrior Creek (N29 55.286 W83 41.297), both to the north, have excellent barrier bars and are good creeks to try when it's cold outside. The dark bottom and rocks just off Dark Island (N29 48.093 W83 35.679), south

Big sea trout invade the rocky shoreline at Keaton Beach during the cool months.

of Keaton Beach, attract hordes of trout and reds, providing you can reach them in the shallows. And, if you want to fish on foot, get out your insulated waders, jump in the car, and try Hagens Cove, located south between Piney Point and Sponge Point. This area is not as rocky as other areas, but it is protected by the enclosing points and fed by a small creek. The Adams Beach and Yates Creek areas to the north can also be reached by car. The creeks' muddy bottoms warm quickly in the winter sunshine and are excellent points to begin a canoe or kayak trip.

Due to the abundance of rocks scattered over the shallow flats at Keaton Beach, you'll see little high-speed boat traffic close to shore.

Offshore Fishing at Keaton Beach

If you launch your offshore boat at the Keaton Beach public boat ramp and head due west about fifty-five miles, you'll run aground at Carrabelle long before you hit fifty feet of water. And that's based on the supposition that you can get your deep-draft rig out of the residential canal to the main channel to begin with. Apalachee Bay and the northeastern Gulf of Mexico just aren't very deep.

Despite those drawbacks, there's a fair amount of offshore fishing from Keaton Beach. Heading a bit south of west will get you to fifty feet and some nice live bottom within thirty-five miles, and the K Tower (N29 39.966 W84 22.153) at about forty miles. One of the Alphabet Towers that are south of Carrabelle, the K is a good spot to find amberjack, king mackerel, and snapper in the warmer months. This tower is within easy reach of some nice live bottom to the northeast. Many anglers heading home to Keaton Beach pull deep-running lures such as the Stretch 30s and 40s with thin braided line and attract lots of nice keeper gag and red grouper. Fishing live bottom here is much like flats fishing for inshore anglers, just deeper. While there are occasional rock piles, ledges, and cracks, they are small and scattered. Understanding the display on your depth finder can make a big difference fishing this relatively flat bottom. The ability to *see* baitfish pods, the upside-down Christmas-tree structure of a school of red snapper, or the air bladder of a big grouper will give you a decided advantage over anglers who don't take the time to read their instruction book's chapter on "Adjusting the Gain." Seeing the fish before they hit is always a thrill.

Offshore anglers shouldn't neglect the areas generally considered the property of anglers from Steinhatchee. The Buckeye Reef (N29 39.000 W83 54.310) is in about forty-five feet of water and eighteen miles southwest of Keaton Beach, but it can be crowded not only with anglers, but also with amberjacks, grouper, Florida snapper, red snapper, king mackerel, and cobia. The same is true for Lamb Spring (N29 26.628 W83 50.627), which is twenty-five miles out and almost due west of Horseshoe Beach. Should you try either of these spots, fish them as you would any reef or rock pile—troll first, then bottom fish if you get strikes.

While the depths to the northwest of Keaton Beach are shallow, there are still lots of live sponges and other sea growth that hold bait. Look in depths ranging from ten to thirty feet for pods of bait with king mackerel attacking them in the summer and fall, and troll the outsides of the pods with shallow-running plugs, Clarkspoons, or live blue runners. And if you find a small rock outcrop or ledge while trolling, mark it for a late-winter sheepshead trip. The big spawning sheepshead, some more than ten pounds, enjoy their mating rituals in these moderate depths. An example of a good shallow-water spot is the Taylor County Reef (N29 45.890 W83 43.640, which is a known sheepshead hangout in about twenty feet of water and about seven miles southwest of Keaton Beach. Wintertime anglers usually anchor here and fish with live shrimp on heavy jig heads for these striped bait-stealers.

Getting Around Keaton Beach

Located about seventeen miles north of Steinhatchee on County
Road (CR) 361, Keaton Beach enjoys its isolation. The main road runs
alongside the canal leading from the boat ramp and is fronted by
canal-side and gulf-side homes, a marina, and a restaurant and hot-
dog stand. There is one convenience store, but the marina seems to
be the center of activity in this fishing-oriented village. The upscale
residential communities of Dark Island and Cedar Island are a mile
or two down CR 361 toward Steinhatchee. There are other residential
communities, some with rental properties, at Dekle Beach and near
Adams Beach, both near the highway (CR 361) on the way to Perry,
which is farther north.

From the water, Keaton Beach is approached best directly from
the west by way of a two-mile channel. Marker #1 (N29 48.726 W83

The settlement at Keaton Beach is dissected by a canal leading from the public
boat ramp to the Gulf of Mexico.

37.752) is shown to be in an average depth of six feet. There is no turning basin, as the channel makes a severe turn at the end of a breakwater and stops. This is the beginning of the residential canal that leads to the public boat ramp and marina, but care should be taken on moderately low tides. New dredging is contemplated and rumored.

Where to Stay

Keaton Beach Marina and Motel, (850) 578-2897, www.keatonbeach marina.com. Motel rooms, efficiencies, RV sites with hookups.

Captain's Quarters Lodge, Keaton Beach, (850) 578-2850. Lodging.

Eagles Nest Waterfront Vacation Retreats, Dekle Beach, (850) 584-7666.

Beach Realty, (850) 578-2039. Rental homes and condos.

Big Bend Properties, (850) 578-2898. Rental homes and condos.

Hampton Inn Perry, Byron Butler Parkway, (850) 223-3000. Lodging.

Best Budget Inn, Byron Butler Parkway, Perry, (850) 584-6231. Lodging.

Chaparral Inn, Byron Butler Parkway, Perry, (850) 584-2441. Lodging.

Gandy Motor Lodge, Byron Butler Parkway, Perry, (850) 584-4947. Lodging.

Royal Inn, Byron Butler Parkway, Perry, (850) 584-7565. Lodging.

Where to Eat

Keaton Beach Hot Dog Stand and Restaurant, (850) 578-2675. Lunch, dinner. Where else can you eat and then go wade-fishing?

Keaton Beach Gas & Grill, (850) 584-4467. Breakfast, lunch, dinner.

Mama's Italian Restaurant, Byron Butler Parkway, Perry (850) 223-

1109. Lunch weekdays, lunch and dinner weekends. Mama's serves excellent home-style Italian food.

Deal's Famous Oyster Bar, US 98 West, Perry, (850) 584-4966. Seafood, lunch, dinner.

Chaparral Steakhouse, Byron Butler Parkway, Perry, (850) 584-8700. Lunch, dinner.

Goodman's BBQ, Byron Butler Parkway, Perry, (850) 584-3751. Lunch, dinner.

Pouncey's Restaurant, Byron Butler Parkway, Perry, (850) 584-9942. Breakfast, lunch, dinner. Fried mullet and swamp cabbage, anyone?

Pepperhead's, US 19/98 at State Road 30, Perry. Convenience store, deli, take-away food. Great fried chicken and barbecue.

Marinas, Marine Supplies and Service, Bait-and-Tackle Shops, and Launching Ramps

Keaton Beach Marina and Motel, (850) 578-2897, www.keatonbeach marina.com. Gas, ice, live and frozen bait, wet slips, dry storage, trailer boat storage, tackle, boat launching with lifts, convenience store.

Wilson's Bait and Tackle, Byron Butler Parkway, Perry, (850) 584-6157. Frozen bait, tackle, convenience store items.

Big Bend Marine, 3482 US 19/98 South, Perry, (850) 584-5977. New and used boats and motors, parts, service, marine supplies.

Keaton Beach Public Ramp, CR 361. Two paved ramps, $5 parking fee, adequate parking, restrooms, access to gulf via residential canal.

Dark Island Boat Ramp, off CR 361. Paved single ramp, free, limited parking, restrooms, access to gulf via *very* shallow channel.

Hagens Cove Boat Ramp, Hagens Cove Park, off CR 361. Very shallow airboat ramp, picnic area, adequate parking, limited security.

This ramp is suitable for canoes and kayaks, too. Hagens Cove is also a popular spot for wade-fishing and scalloping.

Spring Warrior Creek Boat Ramp, Spring Warrior Road, Very shallow ramp. This ramp offers good access to the rocky coastline north of Keaton Beach. Small boats only.

Local Fishing Guides

Capt. Pat McGriff, (850) 584-9145, onemorecast@gtcom.net. Inshore trout specialist.

Capt. Dwayne Valentine (850) 843-2441, redzonecharters@yahoo.com. Inshore.

Capt. Rick Moseley, (850) 578-2627, fishrick@gtcom.net, www.scales ntales.com. Inshore.

Capt. Edward Thomas, (386) 209-1233, captainedward@tgifcharters. com, www.tgifcharters.com. Inshore.

Many guides from Steinhatchee and Econfina are familiar with the waters at Keaton Beach. Please consult the listings for those areas, if necessary. Also the Web site of the Florida Guides Association (www. florida-guides.com) has a complete listing of United States Coast Guard licensed-and-insured fishing guides.

10

The St. Marks, Econfina, and Aucilla Rivers

The port of St. Marks is at the confluence of the St. Marks and Wakulla Rivers. An early Spanish settlement, the current community caters to anglers who come here to fish the shallow shoreline or to take advantage of the relatively shallow offshore fishing grounds to the south. The St. Marks River channel is well maintained and marked, thanks to the needs of commercial vessels. Marine facilities at St. Marks are excellent, and while there are a few good restaurants and some lodging, local options are limited.

My decision to include the Econfina and Aucilla Rivers with St. Marks is arbitrary. They could easily be paired with Keaton Beach as they are an easy distance by boat and similar in terms of shoreline structure. But many anglers who ply the St. Marks make the short trip to the Econfina and Aucilla, which are dark, rocky, and relatively short. While neither is navigable by deep-draft boats, both rivers have launching ramps upstream that offer inshore and nearshore anglers with trailer boats quick access to the Gulf of Mexico. Amenities on the Econfina are excellent and convenient, while those on the Aucilla are very limited and well upriver at US Highway 98.

Inshore and Nearshore Fishing at St. Marks

The top of Apalachee Bay can be a lonely place, particularly if you're an inshore fisherman. And that can be a good thing.

If you run a straight course from marker #1 (N30 01.528 W84

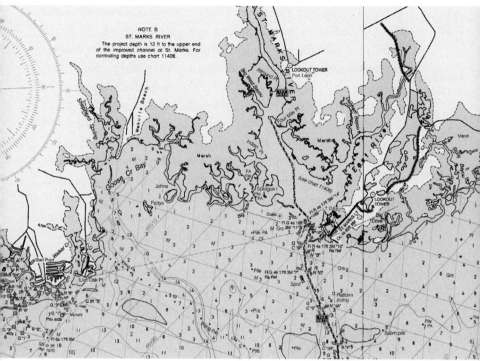

Shown on this chart detail, the St. Marks River is large and navigable.

10.563) at the southern end of the St. Marks River channel to the Econfina River mouth (N30 01.894 W83 56.169), you'll travel about twelve miles. If you take the long way and investigate every small creek mouth and estuary along the shoreline, you'll probably travel about 100 miles—but you'll almost always have a great fishing trip. This bay is where many fish species moving northward along Florida's western gulf coast stop and feed before heading westward along the panhandle. And, while some fish move on, others hang out year-round along the rocky shoreline or in the fertile nearshore shallows.

There's no need to run all the way out the St. Marks channel if you're interested in fishing close to shore. In fact, don't run too far or you'll miss some good spots at the shell bars just inside the river's mouth or up its many tributaries, including the East River. The area to the west of marker #26 (N30 05.846 W84 11.667) is three to five feet deep and crossed by a number of bars running northeast to south-west. Depending on how much fresh water is flowing—the St. Marks River is fed partially by the huge springs at Wakulla—these bars at-tract trout, redfish, flounder, and even an occasional tarpon. Drift-ing live or artificial (D.O.A. or Gulp!) shrimp under popping corks along the up-tide side of any of these bars is a popular technique. These bars have good wade-fishing potential. If the tide's right and you're comfortable anchoring your boat and walking, you'll have a stealthy advantage over other anglers, even those with trolling motors on their boats. A wading belt such as the WadeAid (www.wadeaid.com) is advantageous as you can carry an extra rod, a fish gripper, and spare tackle all around your middle. Don't neglect the topwater plugs that you've been saving for that perfect fishery either. Bright-colored MirrOlure Top Dogs and Popa Dogs are excellent artificials, and have hooks strong enough to handle the biggest red or tarpon. If you're willing to lose a few jigs to the rough bottom, you might try them near the points of bars for reds and flounder. D.O.A.'s TerrorEyz jigs—root-beer color for the dark water; chartreuse on the clear out-side flats—work very well on rocky or rough bottom as they hit the bottom with the hook oriented upward. Slow-sinking plugs such the MirrOlure Catch 2000 and Corky Mullet work well, too, but you'll likely lose more of these expensive lures than you'd like to the bottom monsters.

Warm water and warm weather attract heat-tolerant species such as redfish and flounder to the river's bars, but trout seem to hold on the outside flats from late spring until early fall. Tarpon, trav-eling from the south on their annual spring migration, are often distracted by the huge schools of mullet and other baits in the St. Marks estuary. Once there, they often stay for the summer. In the late fall, the trout move into the river and are found feeding along-side the bars and in their backwash. However, as the weather chills, particularly after long bitter cold spells, they can be found far up-river in deep holes and in the channels of both the St. Marks and the Wakulla Rivers. The barge anchorage and power-plant discharge in the St. Marks River above Shields Marina can be good deepwater trout hangouts.

Barrier bars and dredge lumps are plentiful downriver from St. Marks and offer excellent fishing in quick-moving water.

Bars, some natural, and others created by dredging, border the main channel outside the St. Marks River. The edges of these bars, particularly those near the channel, are worth investigating for springtime cobia and summertime tarpon and redfish. Try fishing long-tail jigs for tarpon and cobia, and gold spoons for the redfish. Sight-fishing can be good here, too, and fly fishermen throw bright toad patterns for tarpon and cobia. This is a similar fishery to the one found farther west near Alligator Point but with much less competition.

There are two options for inshore fishermen wishing to travel east from St. Marks. One is to stay very close to shore and run slowly or fish toward Cobb Rocks (N30 04.782 W84 02.539) about midway to the Econfina River. The other choice is to run a bit deeper (safer and faster) and make a slow, northerly turn to approach the shoreline from the south. The early-morning action for trout and reds is excellent to the south of Palmetto Island (N30 05.118 W84

Don't miss an opportunity to fish the grassy edges in the many creeks feeding the St. Marks River and the Gulf of Mexico.

07.005) and to the north of Gray Mare Rocks (N30 04.752 W84 05.392) in the spring, summer, and early fall. Small topwater lures, like the MirrOlure Top Dog, Jr., are lots of fun over rocky bottom or along the shoreline. As the sun comes up, move southward to the deeper flats in five to seven feet of water. Here, live shrimp, pinfish, or shrimp imitations under corks are the local favorite for trout. Also, keep your eyes peeled for schools of Spanish mackerel chasing baits on these flats in all but the coldest times, and either troll or cast small Clarkspoons or Flowering Floreo jigs for lots of action. In winter, avoid the deep flats, and fish the shoreline on cold, sunny days only after the sun has had time to warm the close-in bars. Jumping mullet are the sign that trophy trout are moving toward whatever warm water they can find. Show me the mullet, and I'll show you the trout.

The inshore fishing west of the St. Marks River mouth is similar to that near Cobb Rocks but has the advantage of several old channels leading from the deep flats almost to Wakulla Beach. These sloughs act as a natural funnel for bait- and game fish on falling tides and are worth your time. The upper reaches of Goose Creek Bay (at Wakulla

Beach) are strewn with oyster bars that provide good year-round habitat for redfish and excellent trout fishing in the colder months. And, if your boat has shallow-water capability, don't neglect fishing the north–south shoreline on the eastern side of Live Oak Point (N30 03.701 W84 16.392).

Inshore and Nearshore Fishing at Aucilla and Econfina

The Aucilla and Econfina areas need separate mention from the St. Marks. These are *bona fide* inshore fisheries with no formal access to the gulf. While it is possible to run from St. Marks, it's best to launch at Econfina, make the short run to the gulf, and fish close to the mouths of these rivers. There's not much in the way of a boat ramp

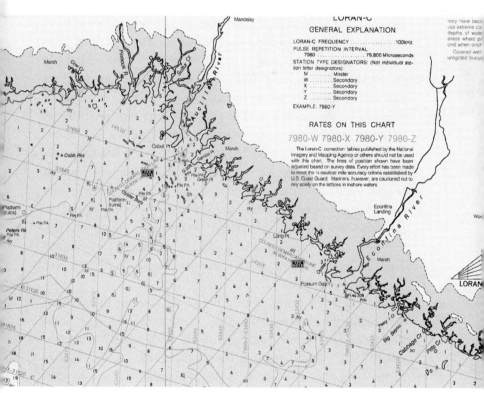

To the east of St. Marks, rocks pepper the coastline, but lush grass flats are just offshore.

near the mouth of the Aucilla and even JR, from J.R.'s Aucilla Store, sends folks to launch up the road at Econfina. The Econfina is treacherous, but not nearly so much as the Aucilla. In the case of either river, a leisurely boat ride at low tide can give you lots of information as to the location of deep holes and shallow rocks, otherwise— boaters beware!

Like most of the Big Bend shoreline, this is trout country. It seems that folks traveling from other places in Florida and Georgia, who make up the bulk of visiting anglers here, would rather take home a limit of trout (currently five) than a limit of reds (one). And besides, trout are easier to catch on the deep flats without endangering your outboard's lower unit on the rocky shoreline bars. But if you're willing to take it slow or have a trolling motor or pushpole, there's lots of action just outside the Aucilla and Econfina. Canoes and kayaks are the perfect craft for fishing this coastline. Just get as close to shore as you can, toss slow-sinking jigs (Brown Lures), suspending plugs (Corky Mullet or MirrOlure Catch 2000s), or small topwater lures. In the warmer months, you'll likely find reds closer to shore, as they're tolerant of high water temperatures, but big trout will also cruise the shoreline just as the sun rises or sets. As it gets cooler, all sizes of trout and reds become more predictable, entering creek mouths and hanging out near bars frequented by mullet. On the coldest of winter days, fish inside these rivers with shrimp under popping corks or MirrOlure TT baitfish imitations. Cast the cork rigs toward points and to known rocky holes. Troll the MirrOlures very slowly, note the spots you hook up, then go back and cast the lures to that spot. Wintertime trout are known to bunch up in deeper temperate water and many can be found well upstream in these black-water rivers, even into fresh water.

Both the Aucilla and Econfina have close-to-shore sloughs running from deeper water toward the existing river mouths. These sloughs are not necessarily deep nor particularly navigable, but they offer some game fish, including trout, cobia, mackerel, and bluefish, shelter from the even shallower water of the flats. The inshore point of the Aucilla Channel (N30 04.167 W83 59.926) is a good spot to begin fishing as the tide rises. The outside of the Aucilla Flats (N30

Big sea trout are wary and sometimes hard to catch. Plugs seem to attract the gators.

02.490 W84 01.091) is fishy as a falling tide pulls bait away from the shoreline and through the cuts. Using the same tactics, fish the inside of the Econfina Channel (N30 01.378 W83 56.509) as the water rises and the outside (N29 59.793 W83 57.506) as it falls. Dropping a chum bag over the side or chunking cut pieces of junk fish is a good way to increase your chances in deep sloughs such as these.

Offshore Fishing at St. Marks

Even though the St. Marks area is tucked away at the top of Apalachee Bay, it still has much offshore fishing potential. It's about ten miles from the river's mouth due south to marker #24 (N29 51.486 W84

09.976), and then you're on your way to deep water, provided you run southwest and not southeast. Southeast is shallow, and some of the best offshore spots are south of Carrabelle in sixty to eighty feet of water. This area of ledges and deep trenches is good for grouper, snapper, king mackerel, and amberjack. It's also the beginning of the very deep water of the northern gulf and an occasional tuna, wahoo, or dolphin (mahi-mahi) can wander in from the west and appear near the Air Force towers.

Using the K Tower (N29 39.966 W84 22.153), the V Tower (N29 24.961 W84 20.695), and the O Tower (N29 32.127 W84 37.081) as the three points of a triangle, you'll enclose some nice bottom. There's about fifteen miles on each leg of the triangle, so that's lots of ground to be covered. Trolling big deep-diving plugs such as Mann's Stretch 30s with 30-pound super-braid line (PowerPro) at five knots will get them down to at least fifty-five feet, within the striking range of both red and gag grouper. While this area does have some rocks, the bottom here is mostly live, with sponges, grasses, and a few ledges and undercuts. That being the case, it's not unusual to see fish on your depth finder and to have them strike a few seconds later. This bottom just doesn't have the "hidey-holes" of the southern Big Bend. Red snapper are known to stack up above small ledges to feed, showing like an inverted Christmas tree on the fish finder. Grouper appear as spots above the grass tops. If you're accomplished at anchoring accurately in deep water, bottom-fishing with live bait (white bait or pinfish) at the site of a strike is always good. However, accurate anchoring is a practiced art and may be a waste of time if you're new to these depths. Trolling burns fuel but covers lots of ground quickly.

Another course to consider if you're trolling is the edge of the thirty-foot contour due east of marker #26 (N29 48.107 W84 20.522), which is south of Alligator Point. Working this edge you'll likely find king mackerel in spring and fall, and smaller but keeper grouper throughout the year. There's no need to troll the bigger plugs in these shallow depths—the smaller Stretch 25s do just fine.

Many St. Marks fishermen frequent the closer offshore waters just south and west of the #1 marker. Shallow-water trolling with shallow-running lures (Stretch 15s) or spoons (#1 Clarkspoons) can be fun in spring and fall when the kings are crashing bait schools. And, jigging the deep flats can also be productive, as trout and Spanish mackerel invade this area in the summer months.

Getting Around St. Marks, Aucilla, and Econfina

St. Marks is about forty miles west of Perry, where US 19/98 splits, and US 98 becomes the main coastal highway, heading west toward the Emerald Coast. St. Marks is also about twenty-five miles south of Tallahassee and I-10. The village is located about five miles south of US 98 on County Road (CR) 363 (Port Leon Drive), which dead-ends at the river. You'll have no trouble finding the marinas, restaurants, or launching ramp here, as it's a small place. And the natives are friendly.

The Wakulla River is fed by several large springs while the St. Marks River is smaller with a dark-water outflow. There are several industrial sites, including oil terminals and a small power plant, on the St. Marks River just upstream of Shields Marina.

Due to some commercial vessel traffic, the St. Marks River channel is well maintained and leads southward into the gulf and about fifteen feet of water.

There's no getting around Aucilla, as it's really just the spot where the Aucilla River crosses US 98 at J.R.'s Aucilla Store. If you launch at the ramp by the highway here, expect to travel about six miles down this rocky river before you reach the gulf.

The settlement at Econfina is about five miles down CR 14, which intersects US 98 twenty-five miles west of Perry. The road passes the store, motel, and campground before ending at the boat ramp. The Econfina river is rocky and shallow, but much more navigable than the Aucilla. Expect a tedious two-mile run to reach the gulf if you launch at the US 98 ramp on the Aucilla River.

Where to Stay

Shell Island Fish Camp, Shell Island Road, St. Marks, (850) 925-6226. Motel rooms, cabins, adjacent to marina. Shell Island Fish Camp is not fancy but is one of the last of the classic fish camps along the Gulf Coast.

Sweet Magnolia B&B, Port Leon Drive, St. Marks, (850) 925-7670. Upscale lodging.

The Inn at Wildwood, US 98, Crawfordville/Medart, (850) 926-4455, www.theinnatwildwood.com. Lodging, adjacent restaurant.

Wakulla Springs Lodge, Wakulla Springs, (850) 224-5950, www.florida stateparks.org/wakullasprings. Lodging, meals. If you plan to fish several local areas, consider staying here. Wakulla Springs is one of the largest and most beautiful springs in Florida.

Econfina River Resort, CR 14, Econfina, (850) 584-2135. Motel and rental condos, RV park, store, adjacent to public ramp.

Where to Eat

Riverside Café, end of Port Leon Drive, St. Marks, (850) 925-5668. Breakfast, lunch, dinner, seafood, bar, dockage, open seven days a week.

Two-Nichols Seafood Restaurant, Port Leon Drive, St. Marks, (850) 925-4850. Breakfast, lunch, dinner, open seven days a week.

Ouzt's Too Oyster Bar and Canoe Rental, US 98, Newport, (850) 984-5370. Lunch, dinner, not far from St. Marks.

The Bistro at Wildwood, US 98, Crawfordville/Medart, (850) 926-4455, www.theinnatwildwood.com. Breakfast, lunch, and dinner, open seven days a week. This restaurant is adjacent to the Inn at Wildwood.

Marinas, Marine Supplies and Service, Bait-and-Tackle Shops, and Launching Ramps

Shields Marina, St. Marks, (850) 925-6158, www.shieldsmarina.com. Gas and diesel, dockage with shore power, marine sanitary dump station, dry storage, showers, boat sales and service, ice, live and frozen bait, tackle, convenience store, excellent launching ramp.

Shell Island Fish Camp, Shell Island Road, St. Marks, (850) 925-6226. Gas, dry storage, dockage, marine service, frozen bait, tackle, convenience store, launching ramp, adjacent motel rooms and cabins.

Jerry's Bait & Tackle, Woodville Highway, Crawfordville, (850) 421-3248, www.jerrysbait.com. The folks at Jerry's keep tabs on the local fishing scene and are always willing to give advice on the current bite.

J.R.'s Aucilla Store, US 98 at Aucilla River, (850) 584-4595. Bait, tackle, fresh-water launching ramp across highway, convenience items. J.R.'s is pretty far upriver from the gulf. There is a boat ramp downstream, but it's primitive and many locals use the ramp at Econfina for gulf access.

Rocky's, US 98, west of Perry, (850) 584-6600. Bait, tackle, fuel, convenience store, deli, campground.

St. Marks Public Ramp, confluence of the St. Marks and Wakulla Rivers. Free ramp and adequate parking, restrooms, easy access from town.

St. Marks Lighthouse Point Ramp, at the end of CR 59, eleven miles from US 98 at Newport. Public ramp with excellent access to the river mouth.

Econfina River Public Ramp CR 14, Econfina. Free paved ramp, near lodging, and convenience and bait store.

Local Fishing Guides

Capt. Rusty Jenkins, St. Marks, (850) 997-0164, www.fishfulthinking. com, ishoe4utoo@aol.com. Inshore and nearshore, light-tackle and fly fishing.

Capt. Jody Campbell, St. Marks and Shell Point, (850) 926-1173, www. bigbendguides.com, gail@talweb.com. Inshore and nearshore, light-tackle and fly fishing.

Capt. Pat Kennedy, St. Marks, (850) 514-0812, redfish233@earthlink. net. Inshore.

Capt. R. A. Grimes, St. Marks, (850) 251-9519. Offshore.

Capt. James Burke, Econfina, (850) 508-1411, captjburke@aol.com. Inshore.

Capt. Tom Erle, Econfina, (850) 997-4521. captaintomerle@yahoo. com. Inshore and offshore.

Capt. Gary Mears, Econfina, (850) 584-4532. Inshore, airboat.

Capt. Randy Peart, Econfina, (850) 320-4214. Inshore and fly fishing.

Many guides from Shell Point, Panacea, and Keaton Beach are familiar with the waters from St. Marks to Econfina. Please consult the listings for those areas, if necessary. Also the Web site of the Florida Guides Association (www.florida-guides.com) has a complete listing of United States Coast Guard licensed-and-insured fishing guides.

11

Shell Point to Lanark Village,
and Ochlockonee Bay

This is a complex stretch of Florida's coastline. It represents not only the beginning of the panhandle but also the transition from shallow rocky coastline to white-sand beaches. It's just this complexity that makes fishing here exceptional—and varied.

From Shell Point westward, through Oyster Bay, past Panacea, and to Mashes Island, you'll find backwaters similar to the coastline at St. Marks. And, west from the mouth of Ochlockonee Bay, the sands get whiter and the water clearer and deeper.

Traveling by car, you'll notice that the main highway (US Highway 98) runs fairly close to the Gulf of Mexico. There's no need for long trips down secondary roads to reach launching ramps or marinas. But, travelers beware, US 98 to the west can disappear into the gulf after big storms, and detours are not necessarily convenient. Paying attention to news of current gulf storms and a quick call ahead to any marina or tackle shop should answer any questions about access to your favorite gulf fishing spot.

Shell Point has until recently been a quiet residential community built on a series of canals. Plans are underway for a condominium and marina that will change the face of the area, and that will no doubt make it busier. Despite the growth, Shell Point is a comfortable jumping-off spot for anglers who wish to fish the upper reaches of Oyster and Goose Creek Bays.

Panacea, located on US 98, is a classic Florida fishing village that

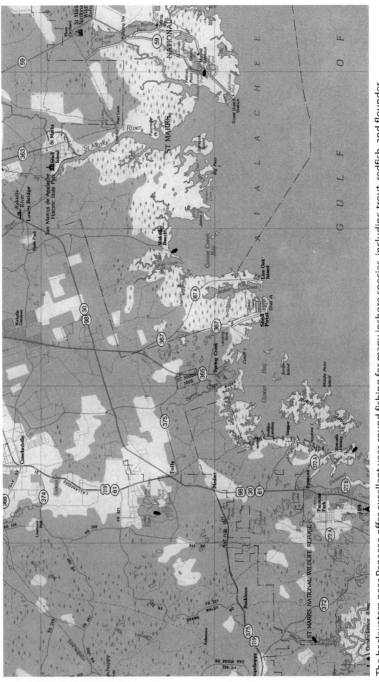

The backwaters near Panacea offer excellent year-round fishing for many inshore species, including trout, redfish, and flounder. Reprinted with permission from the full-color *Florida Atlas & Gazetteer*. Copyright DeLorme.

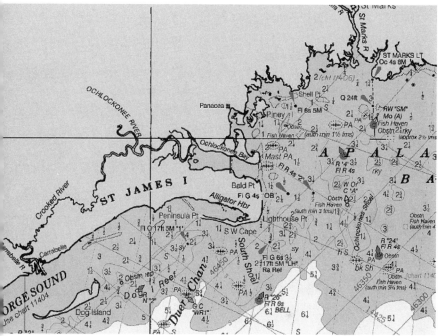

St. James Island and Alligator Point are popular hangouts for fish—and for weekenders!

still counts on commercial fishing as a major part of its economy. It is very fisherman-friendly, with good amenities and resources.

Although fed by several rivers, Ochlockonee Bay is mostly salt-water. Resembling a big lake, its backwaters offer excellent fishing for redfish, trout, and flounder, while its mouth is deep enough to attract larger species, including king mackerel, cobia, and tarpon.

Crossing the Ochlockonee Bay Bridge from Panacea, you'll come ashore on St. James Island. The Ochlockonee River and a tributary, the Crooked River, which runs into St. George Sound at Carrabelle, form this pseudo-island. Rental and vacation homes dot the area, but large-scale beachside developments have begun to pop up willy-nilly. It's here that the beaches begin and angler-oriented amenities, including boat ramps, are fewer. Many fishermen visiting Saint Teresa and Alligator Point stock up on supplies in nearby Panacea, or in Craw-fordville, on the inbound trip.

Panacea's marina is well supplied, has good dockage, and good food.

Alligator Point is best described as the peninsula of St. James Island that bounds Ochlockonee Bay to the south. Alligator Harbor, a good inshore fishery, is enclosed by Southwest Cape, which almost touches land at Saint Teresa.

Lanark Village is about halfway between Turkey Point, which is the site of the Florida State University Marine Laboratory, and Carrabelle. I'm including Lanark in this section because it's the closest public launching ramp to the west of Alligator Point, and it's not really that close—fourteen miles from Lighthouse Point, the southeastern tip of Alligator Point.

Inshore and Nearshore Fishing, Shell Point to Lanark Village

You'll notice that the deep-water contours on your fishing charts creep noticeably closer to shore as you move west of St. Marks. That doesn't necessarily mean that there's no good inshore fishing out "west." To the contrary, the backwaters north of the mouth of Ochlockonee Bay are really good—and they're not necessarily crowded.

Don't expect to launch from Shell Point or Panacea and blast off to some great shallow-water spots without first scouting the area. Sure, you can head out of the marked channels and drift about, taking potluck, but exploring the fishery can really make a difference. Take into consideration your boat's draft, and push its limits by slowly running—with a trolling motor, if you have one—or poling into the far reaches of Oyster Bay on a falling tide. Pay attention to deep holes and shell bars, and note their locations. You'll get to fish some, but the value of this trip is in what you learn. Travel as far as you can, let the tide rise and then fish the spots you've discovered. You'll be surprised how much information you can garner on a low-tide scouting trip.

In warmer months, plan your trip into these backwaters early in the day and throw big topwater plugs such as MirrOlure Top Dogs or Popa Dogs for big sea trout. These big fish travel solo, chasing mullet

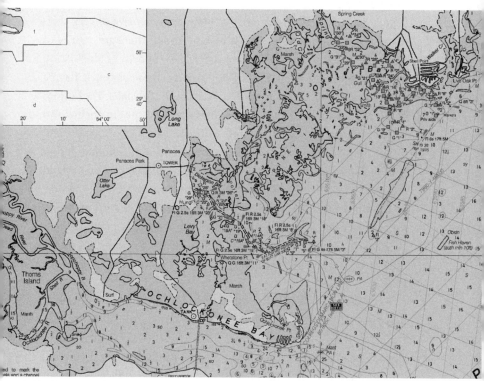

Ochlockonee Bay feeds into the gulf between Panacea and Lanark Village.

schools. Smaller trout opt for deeper water when it's warm. Redfish are also plentiful here, and local favorites are gold spoons, D.O.A. TerrorEyz jigs, or spinner-type baits. When it's cold and sunny, wait until afternoon and fish slow-sinking plugs such as Corky Mullet, D.O.A. Bait Busters, or MirrOlure Catch 2000s very slowly over bars that have warmed all morning. If it's cold and *not sunny*—stay home or try fishing a deep hole or spring. The big powerful spring at Spring Creek, northwest of Shell Point, has been a longtime favorite on cold days, but its flow has diminished in recent years. If it pumps again, expect big trout (and crowds of anglers) there on very cold days, warming in its 72-degree water. Wintertime fish get lockjaw when they can't keep warm. Spring Creek is accessible by boat from Shell Point.

The entire expanse of Oyster Bay, particularly the area behind Piney Island, is an excellent inshore fishery. However, if you're timid, have a new inshore boat, or are just plain apprehensive of very shallow water, try some of the deeper inshore spots. There are a series of deep cuts through the shallows to the east and north of Shell Point, off Live Oak Point (N30 03.701 W84 16.392). These channels form a natural funnel for fish moving off the flats as the tide falls. The bottom of the funnel at N30 02.199 W84 13.699 is a good spot to anchor and fish live pinfish or cut bait when it's warm outside. Cobia, tarpon, and lots of sharks follow bait as it washes toward the gulf. Another option is to fish the top of the funnel, beginning southwest of Pattys Island at N30 04.623 W84 15.687, and drift southward with the falling tide. Fish the channel's edges with free-lined live or D.O.A. shrimp during the warm months, and try slow-sinking plugs when it's cold. There are also similar cuts through moderately deep water south of the #4 marker on the Panacea channel and into the mouth of Ochlockonee Bay.

Accessible more easily from the Mashes Sand ramp, the entire area between Bald Point (N29 57.056 W84 20.171) and the Ochlockonee Bridge is good for general drift-fishing with live or artificial baits, rigged deep under popping corks. The bridge itself is also known to hold numerous schools of bait in warm weather. Fish the edge of bait

pods for predators such as tarpon, jacks, and ladyfish, and try tossing jigs or live baits into the cool shade of the bridge for big redfish.
There are also channels along the northern and southern shorelines
of Ochlockonee Bay that provide not only refuge to fish from the
flats but also a steady stream of fresh water—and baitfish—from the
feeder rivers. Fish the deep spots in cold weather and the edges of
adjacent flats when it's warm. The northernmost channel is marked
and leads to the mouth of the Sopchoppy River; the southern cut,
leading to the Ochlockonee River, is slightly deeper. As is the case in
many estuaries in Florida, the flow of fresh river water doesn't seem
to scare away redfish, sea trout, flounder, or tarpon.

The stretch of beach from Lighthouse Point (N29 53.841 W84
20.641) westward along Southwest Cape to the #2 marker of the
Alligator Harbor (N29 55.286 W84 27.135) is prime close-to-shore
habitat for fish species washing around the point. In the spring, cobia
cruise the beach and are game for sight-fishermen. Free-lined live
pinfish or long rubber eels are excellent baits for these fish and for
the tarpon that follow them in early summer. Tarpon pluggers favor 52M MirrOlures, and fly fishermen have had good luck in recent
years with brightly colored toad-style flies. While many anglers chase
cobia and tarpon along this stretch of beach, others simply anchor
up and let the fish pass within comfortable casting range. Don't let
the lack of a boat hinder your fishing along Southwest Cape. Wade
fishermen with beach access do well in the summer by fishing in the
surf for pompano. Half-ounce Flowering Floreos or live sand fleas on
small hooks bounced slowly off the bottom just past the surf line get
plenty of action for wading anglers. And, in the fall, tossing the same
Floreo jig or a #00 Clarkspoon, but with more action, will get plenty
of strikes from fat Spanish mackerel or bluefish.

Alligator Harbor is about four miles long and a mile wide. On
each tide cycle, the water moves past Peninsula Point (N29 54.751
W84 26.146) and over the Bay Mouth Bar. With that tidal movement,
bait and predators move in or out of the harbor. The eastern end of
the harbor is shallow and marshy, making it good redfish habitat.
At the western end, with more tidal movement, you'll more likely

find sea trout along the shoreline from Wilson Beach (N29 55.724 W84 26.795) to Turkey Point (N29 54.565 W84 29.579). If docks remain along this shore from the last hurricanes, fish around their pilings and under boats on lifts on cold days with free-lined D.O.A. or live shrimp. Pilings hold daily heat, and boat lifts typically have deep washes underneath caused by propellers. Take care to fish near private docks in a respectful manner. Don't hit boats with lures, and if the owner asks you to leave, be polite and do so.

There is a dredged and marked two-mile channel into the FSU Marine Lab at Turkey Point. Marker #2 (N29 52.505 W84 30.307), at the channel's mouth, is safely located outside the Turkey Point Shoal. There are spoil banks or dredge lumps to the west of the channel and shell bars along the shoreline between the lab and the physical prominence of Turkey Point. These structures afford refuge to game fish throughout the year, and fishing the deep edges of this narrow channel and the bars on fall and spring days has potential for trout and redfish. On hot days, particularly those with falling afternoon tides, try jigging the deep channel with the soft bait of your choice, or take a chance with cut mullet on a circle hook. You never know just what's lurking down on the cool bottom waiting for food to wash off the surrounding flats.

In wintertime, fish the same deep channel for trout and reds that attempt to stay out of the cold. A dark TerrorEyz or a live shrimp on a jig head worked slowly along the bottom should get results.

There are about five miles of shallow grass flats between Turkey Point and Lanark Village, which sits directly ashore from the high point of Lanark Reef (approx. N29 52.312 W84 35.319). A good fishery for trout and redfish, this stretch of shoreline, including the shallow top of the reef, can be crowded with scallopers from July 1 to September 10. Early-rising fishermen can usually manage to get a few hours of topwater action before the partiers arrive, usually mid-morning. A slow walk-the-dog action on a floating MirrOlure is fun near the shoreline. In fact, you'll often see anglers wading from the shore here, while others leave their boats at anchor and wade the shallow top of Lanark Reef itself. Before and after the annual scallop season, it's a

Wade fishermen are happy anywhere they can find a beach to walk.

pretty good bet to drift these inshore flats with soft plastic or live bait under popping corks for whatever bites. Sea trout, bluefish, flounder, and Spanish mackerel are all likely to strike. The flats offshore of the reef are obviously deeper, attracting not only keeper sea trout during most of the warm months but also larger species such as cobia and king mackerel making their spring and fall migrations. Many local trout fishermen chum with small amounts of frozen commercial chum blocks or just chunks of leftover bait while drifting. They also drift for kings with a live pinfish or blue runner on a cork behind their boat and they have a pitch rod handy and rigged, ready to toss live bait to a cruising cobia on the deeper flats.

Depending on the seaworthiness of your inshore boat, you might consider fishing the nearby shoals and close-in reefs. From a geologic perspective, they all seem to be extinct shallow peninsulas or barrier islands.

The Ochlockonee Shoal is about eight miles due east of Lighthouse Point, and it rises to three feet from a surrounding water depth of over twenty feet. The reef top is a popular local spot for Spanish mackerel in the spring and fall, and sea trout are often caught along its deep edges in summer, often at depths of fifteen feet. The shallow top of the shoal is located at approximately N29 54.002 W84 12.223.

The South Shoal is a five-mile-long underwater extension of Lighthouse Point. It's end, and high spot, is a three-foot hump at approximately N29 48.733 W84 21.014. Tarpon, cobia, and king mackerel cruising the edge of the thirty-foot contour often feed along the shallow bar top and edges. Trolling colorful Flowering Floreos or small (#00) Clarkspoons during the warm months is a good bet for Spanish mackerel or bluefish, while fishermen willing to anchor and chum will almost certainly attract sea trout to a live shrimp or pinfish.

If Dog Island were extended twice its current length to the northeast, it would include the Dog Island Reef. The northeastern end is marked by a green flashing marker (N29 52.248 W84 26.702) that represents the eastern approach to Carrabelle from the gulf. The crest of this reef, like that of Ochlockonee Shoal and South Shoal, is very shallow and grassy. And, like the others, it attracts trout, Spanish mackerel, cobia, tarpon, and occasional bull redfish.

Offshore Fishing, Shell Point to Lanark Village

Accept the Air Force K Tower (N29 39.966 W84 22.153) as the example. K and its surrounding fifty- to sixty-foot depths, is about seventeen miles from Lanark Village and about twenty-four miles from Shell Point. True offshore fishing does get easier to the west of the Big Bend.

Don't get me wrong. The run from Shell Point to fifty-plus feet is still tolerable compared to a similar trip from places such as Steinhatchee and Crystal River, farther down the Big Bend. And the upper reaches of Apalachee Bay offer some good mid-depth fishing, too.

The entrance to the Shell Point channel is at marker #1 (N30 02.352 W84 17.680) and is indicated by flashing a white light. It's at the northern end of a shoal that acts as a barrier across the entrance of Oyster Bay. The entry to the Panacea channel is marker #2 (N30 00.395 W84 18.710), located at the southern end of the same shoal.

At either entrance, give way to any recent erosions or extensions of the shoal, and proceed toward marker #2 (N29 56.038 W84 15.743) between Bald Point and the Ochlockonee Shoal. From this marker, which has a red flashing light, you've got pretty good seaway to the south, the thirty-foot contour, and the open gulf.

Several reputable charter captains claim that live bottom doesn't extend much past the Air Force K Tower. I take issue with the word *much*. Live, or encrusted, bottom just doesn't stop and big sandy prairies begin at one point. There certainly is a change in bottom structure, but it's a gradual transition, beginning south of St. Marks and extending almost to the C Tower (N29 24.706 W84 51.339), which is south of St. George Island and Apalachicola.

That geology lesson over, assume you'll need to fish both live bottom and artificial reefs in the deep gulf south of Shell Point, Panacea, Ochlockonee Bay, and Lanark Village.

Live bottom generally means grouper hanging out around sponges and grassy bumps. Fishing for them over this bottom usually means trolling large lipped plugs, such as the Mann's Stretch series. A Stretch 30 will easily dive to fifty feet or more if trolled far enough behind a boat at five knots, provided it's attached to an ultra-thin super-braid line such as 30-pound-test PowerPro. Even in seventy feet, grouper will come up to strike a trolled plug twenty feet above. Trolling for grouper in the eastern gulf doesn't necessarily mean you won't get a chance to bottom fish. Trolling along the rough edges of a natural contour, you'll likely find a few bigger natural rocky outcroppings and even a ledge or two. Mark them with the "Man Overboard" button on your GPS and return to fish for more grouper—or even better, American red snapper. Bottom fishing for grouper isn't hard, as grouper eat most anything from frozen squid to live pinfish or white bait. Snapper, on the other hand, are picky eaters and are prone to eat at night. On the depth finder, a school of snapper looks like an upside-down Christmas tree; if you see the shape, come back for a night trip and bring plenty of live white bait. Small pinfish will do, but alewives and cigar minnows are their favorites. Try trolling the edge of the sixty-foot contour to the south of the K Tower toward the east.

The point of deep water northeast of the O Tower (N29 32.127 W84 37.081) at approximately N29 37.469 W84 31.208 is a good general area for trolling, more easily reached from Lanark Village than from Panacea or Shell Point.

The artificial reefs in this part of the gulf are scattered, relatively old, and heavily fished. They are worth fishing if you have a crew of kids or folks just wanting to catch some Florida snapper (white grunts) or black sea bass. These reefs and the Air Force towers do attract many species of baitfish during the spring, summer, and fall. In turn, anglers slow-trolling live baits, such as blue runners and cigar minnows, will find king mackerel and even a wahoo. Those anchoring and chumming over reefs will attract amberjacks, some snapper, and the occasional cobia, to which live pinfish and white bait are irresistible.

Getting Around Shell Point to Lanark Village

If you're traveling west from Perry toward Carrabelle and Apalachicola on US 98 and for some reason want to avoid this area, take US 319 from Medart to Sopchoppy and then down to Turkey Point. You'll avoid some traffic and have the opportunity buy a jar of genuine tupelo honey at Sopchoppy, but you'll miss some great fishing if you don't stop along the St. James Island peninsula for at least a day or two. With the exception of Shell Point and the southeast cape of St. James Island, most of the area's amenities, including marinas, launching ramps, motels, and restaurants, are located on or near US 98. Shell Point is about five miles south of US 98, by way of Spring Creek Highway (County Road 365) and Shell Point Road (CR 367). The areas along the southeast cape, generally known as Alligator Point, are accessed from US 98 by CR 370, south of the Ochlockonee Bridge.

From the gulf, there are good deep approaches to Shell Point, Panacea, and Ochlockonee Bay. However, shoaling is always an issue and is dependent upon recent storms. Likewise, the entry to Alligator Harbor can have a mind of its own.

Major hurricanes destroyed many of the homes on Alligator Point, but rebuilding is moving forward—and rentals are available.

Where to Stay

The Landing Motel, Coastal Highway (US 98), Panacea, (850) 984-4996. Lodging, adjacent restaurant.

Best Western Garden Inn & Suites, Coastal Hwy, Crawfordville/Medart, (850) 926-3737. Lodging.

The Inn at Wildwood, US 98, Crawfordville/Medart, (850) 926-4455, www.theinnatwildwood.com. Lodging, adjacent restaurant.

Coastal Shores Properties, (850) 984-5800, www.coastalshores.com. Vacation and beach rentals.

Ochlockonee Bay Realty, (850) 984-0001, www.obrealty.com, obr@obrealty.com. Vacation and beach rentals.

Holiday Park & Campground, Coastal Highway, Panacea, (850) 984-5757. Full-service RV park and campground, fishing pier on Ochlockonee Bay.

Where to Eat

Posey's Steam Room & Oyster Bar, Coastal Highway, Panacea, (850) 984-5243. Seafood, lunch, dinner, closed Mondays. It's worth the trip to Panacea just to eat here. You might even find fried mullet gizzards on the menu.

Spring Creek Restaurant, end of CR 365 at Spring Creek, (850) 926-3751. Fresh local seafood, dinners Tuesdays–Fridays, lunch and dinner weekends, closed Mondays.

The Landing Restaurant, Coastal Highway, Panacea, (850) 984-4996. Breakfast, lunch, dinner, adjacent to motel, lunch and Sunday buffets.

Coastal Restaurant, Coastal Highway, Panacea, (850) 984-4986. Breakfast, lunch, dinner, open seven days a week, lunch and Sunday buffets.

Hook Wreck Henry's Dockside Café, Rock Landing Road at Panacea Harbor Marina, Panacea, (850) 984-5544. Seafood, lunch, dinner, closed Mondays.

Hamaknocker's Oasis BBQ and Sports Bar, US 98 west of Panacea, (850) 984-8130. Lunch, dinner, steak night Fridays and Saturdays, closed Sundays.

Angelo and Son's Seafood Restaurant, Panacea, at the eastern end of the Ochlockonee Bridge, (850) 984-5168. Lunch, dinner, scenic views. After being blown away by recent hurricanes, Angelo and Son's has been totally rebuilt.

Frank's Good Food, US 98, Medart, (850) 545-4909. Barbecue and seafood, lunch, dinner, closed Mondays. Frank's is basically a large catering trailer that spends some of its time here and the rest of the time at the RV park at Carrabelle Beach, based on the owner's whim.

The Bistro at Wildwood, US 98, Crawfordville/Medart, (850) 926-4455, www.theinnatwildwood.com. Breakfast, lunch, dinner, open seven days a week. This restaurant is adjacent to the Inn at Wildwood.

Marinas, Marine Supplies and Service, Bait-and-Tackle Shops, and Launching Ramps

Panacea Harbor Marina, Rock Landing Road, Panacea, (850) 984-5844. Full-service marina adjacent to free public boat ramp, gas and diesel, wet and dry storage, dockage, live and frozen bait, adjacent restaurant, tackle, showers.

Crum's Mini Mall, 1321 Hwy. 98, Panacea, (352) 984-5501. An amazing place full of tackle, marine supplies, clothing, hardware, and just about anything the recreational angler needs. Bulk ice and live and frozen bait round out the selection.

Jerry's Bait & Tackle, 664 Woodville Hwy., Crawfordville, (850) 421-3248, www.jerrysbait.com. Jerry's is the local hangout for fishermen. Expect up-to-the-minute fishing reports from the friendly folks here.

Lanark Village Market and Marina, Lanark Village, (850) 697-4600. $10 paved launching ramp, $100 annual permit, secure parking, gas, ice, live and frozen bait, tackle, convenience store. You'll see everyone from professional tarpon guides to local crabbers here. Parking can be a problem at the height of scallop season.

Advantage Marine, US 98, Medart, (850) 926-6020. Bait, tackle, boat sales and service, parts, open seven days a week.

Mike's Marine Supply, US 98, Panacea, (850) 984-5637. Boat sales and service, parts, tackle.

AMS Marine Supply, US 98, Medart, 1-800-726-3104, www.rmsmarine.com. Tackle, marine supplies, traps, trailer parts, frozen bait. AMS, formerly RMS, is a good source for local fishing reports and hard-to-find marine and electronics parts. This is where many commercial fishermen buy their gear.

Bayside Marina, up Ochlockonee Bay on Surf Road (CR 372), (850) 984-5548, www.baysidemarina.com. Gas and diesel, wet slips, transient slips, frozen bait.

Spears' Fish Camp and RV Park Ramp, at the end of CR 365 at Spring Creek. $5 paved ramp, few services. This is a great spot to launch a small boat for quick access to the Spring Creek bite on cold winter days.

Panacea City Ramp, Rock Landing Road, next to Panacea Harbor Marina. Free paved ramp, adequate parking.

Mashes Sand Ramp, CR 372 at Ochlockonee Point. Three paved public ramps, adequate parking, restrooms. This ramp offers excellent access to the mouth of Ochlockonee Bay.

Ochlockonee Landing Ramp, at the western foot of the Ochlockonee Bridge on the bay. Shallow sand ramp, adequate parking. This ramp is popular for anglers launching kayaks and canoes.

Leonard's Landing, US 98 on Alligator Harbor. Shallow sand ramp. This roadside ramp gives boaters with small craft good access to the upper reaches of Alligator Harbor.

Local Fishing Guides

Capt. Jody Campbell, Shell Point, Panacea and St. Marks, (850) 926-1173, www.bigbendguides.com, gail@talweb.com. Inshore and near-shore, light-tackle and fly fishing.

Capt. Adam Hudson, Lanark Village and Carrabelle. (850) 566-5599. Light-tackle and fly fishing.

Capt. David Zeigler, Lanark Village. (850) 228-6091, www.z-horse. com. Light-tackle, inshore, and nearshore.

Capt. Vic Davis, Panacea. (850) 925-6660, www.bigbendfishing.net/ barefoot. Inshore fishing, scalloping.

Capt. Bill Coman, Alligator Point. (850) 349-2414. Offshore.

Capt. Edgar Metcalf, Panacea. 850) 984-5645. Offshore.

Capt. Don Porter, Capt. Dallas Porter, Panacea. (850) 984-4803. Inshore and offshore.

Many guides from Carrabelle and St. Marks are familiar with the waters from Shell Point to Lanark Village. Please consult the listings for those areas, if necessary. Also, the Web site of the Florida Guides Association (www.florida-guides.com) has a complete listing of United States Coast Guard licensed-and-insured fishing guides.

12

Apalachicola, Carrabelle, and Their Barrier Islands

Some maps and charts show Apalachicola and Carrabelle only as two small dots, representing towns on Florida's Gulf Coast just east of Cape San Blas and ashore of St. George and Dog Islands. It's hard to convey the importance of either with a simple illustration. Long a center for commercial and recreational fishing, the Gulf Coast of Franklin County has survived hard economic times, natural disasters, and now struggles to keep up with the demands of tourism and development. The impact of recent growth has certainly affected fishing in the area but not to the extent seen in the southern part of the state. Yes, launching ramps are crowded, motel reservations are sometimes hard to get at short-notice, and there's sometimes a thirty-minute wait for a table at the better seafood restaurants. But, considering the quality of the fishing here and the character of the towns with all of their amenities, it's still worth the aggravation.

Carrabelle sits at the mouth of the Carrabelle River on the southwestern tip of St. James Island. The river is short, formed upstream at the confluence of the New River and the Crooked River, which along with the Ochlockonee River makes St. James Island a geographic entity even though most visitors don't even realize it's distinct from the mainland of Florida. Carrabelle has the first deep-water harbor with facilities for large boat repair west of Tarpon Springs, and it also boasts the first in a series of United States Coast Guard stations west of Yankeetown.

Apalachicola is the larger of the two towns. It lies at the mouth of the Apalachicola River, which runs from the confluence of the Chattahoochee and Flint Rivers at Lake Seminole on the Florida-Georgia border. The river also serves as the entrance to the westward section of the Gulf Intracoastal Waterway (ICW), which begins in St. George Sound. There is a 150-mile open-water gap between this section of the ICW and the end of the southern section at Tarpon Springs, and

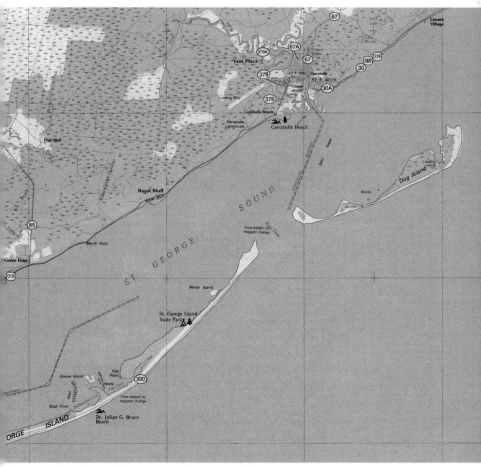

The sound behind St. George Island and Dog Island is big enough to attract pelagic species such as Spanish mackerel and king mackerel. Tarpon are also seen along the beachfronts in summer. Reprinted with permission from the full-color *Florida Atlas & Gazetteer*. Copyright DeLorme.

The Carrabelle River is wide at spots near town, making it a good anchorage for cruising anglers.

many boaters transiting the Big Bend are glad to get some protection from the elements in the sheltered waterway. Several other smaller rivers, including the St. Marks River and the East River, empty into the upper reaches of the bay here, but above the US Highway 98 bridge.

St. George Island, St. Vincent Island, and Dog Island are barrier islands forming the southern boundaries of St. George Sound, St. Vincent Sound, and Apalachicola Bay. St. George is largely a residential and beach community, connected to the mainland at Eastpoint by a modern bridge. The eastern end of St. George Island is a state park, and the western end is a private, gated residential development. The Bob Sikes Cut, a deep-water gulf-to-bay channel, separates what is now called Little St. George Island from the main island. St. Vincent Sound and St. Vincent Island make up the western area toward Cape San Blas. Dog Island, off Carrabelle, is residential

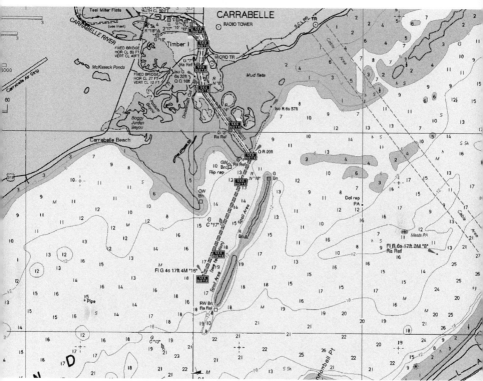

The Carrabelle River flows into the eastern end of St. George Sound. Be careful of strong sea breezes here on warm spring and summer days.

and private, and accessed only by small boats and ferries. While the sound and bay do provide protection for boaters and anglers, don't be fooled. The protected waters here are more than thirty miles long and at least five miles wide. That's lots of water, and a big westerly breeze can whip things up in a matter of minutes. What the islands do protect is an excellent fishery, including the famous Apalachicola oyster beds.

Amenities at Apalach are excellent, and include marinas, lodging, and eateries. Carrabelle offers good choices for marine services and food, but lodging has been limited until recently. The village at St. George is becoming upscale, due to the influx of renters and beachgoers but still retains the character of an inshore fishing destination. Eastpoint is still Eastpoint—and still the real Florida.

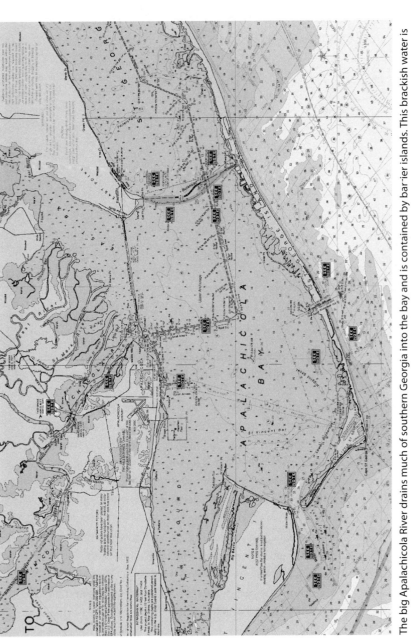

The big Apalachicola River drains much of southern Georgia into the bay and is contained by barrier islands. This brackish water is responsible for some of the world's best oysters—and the fish that are attracted to their beds.

East Pass, between Dog Island and St. George Island, can be treacherous, particularly when the outgoing tide bucks a sea breeze.

Long a popular destination for visiting anglers, "Apalach" has many levels of lodging.

What more could an angler want?

Inshore and Near Shore Fishing at Carrabelle

Many anglers think that unless they travel a great distance, they're not going to catch any fish. Carrabelle is the classic example of the opposite. Commercial fishing towns weren't built in spots where boatmen had to row or sail great distances to get their work done. The steady outflow of the Carrabelle River has created some pretty interesting close-in fishing spots, mostly to the east and into the sound right behind Dog Island. The mainland shore to the west, past Carrabelle Beach, is deeper and less structured.

Outbound from Carrabelle, you'll find a series of small spoil islands to the east, starting just past marker #6 (N29 50.445 W84 39.850). If your boat will handle the shallows, try fishing this area in the fall or winter for redfish and trout. This is a spot to fish a late-afternoon

A sizeable offshore charter fleet operates out of Carrabelle.

high tide on a bitter cold sunny day. Try slow-sinking plugs such as D.O.A.'s Bait Buster or Corky Mullet. Retrieve your lure slowly over the dark bottom and bars that have warmed all morning during the extreme low tide of winter. As the tide rises, baitfish (mostly mullet) will move closer, followed by big trout and reds. If you can't get through the islands, go out to marker #4 (N29 49.782 W84 39.348) and fish the deep edge of the flat that runs to the northeast toward the range marker at N29 50.255 W84 39.093.

This is also a good spot to try in the dog days of summer. In general, sea trout will tend to hang out around cool, deep holes and along channel edges in hot weather, but a few solo gator trout will attack noisy topwater lures (MirrOlure Top Dogs and Popa Dogs) in the shallows. Redfish and flounder, more tolerant of the heat, are not afraid to get shallow in the late spring, summer, and early fall. The same rules hold for the dead of winter, as trout go deep, seeking warmth. They get lethargic, though, and don't want to work for their food. Slowly jigged live shrimp, D.O.A. TerrorEyz jigs, or soft-plastic grubs on jig heads work well in the river channel, and even upriver, well past the bridge.

Lanark Reef is a five-mile-long shallow bar that extends from just east of Carrabelle about a half mile off the coastline. The western end is surrounded by a deep slough that provides cool shelter for game fish in the late spring and throughout the summer. Inshore and to the northeast, the slough empties on to an expanse of grass flats that reach the other end of the bar and on toward Turkey Point. These flats provide excellent drift fishing for trout, redfish, and flounder when the water's warm. Popular lures are topwater plugs at sunrise or sunset and live or artificial D.O.A shrimp rigged under popping corks in the interim. These shallow-water grass flats extend from shore to the top of Lanark Reef and are also popular for bay scallopers from July 1 to September 10 each year. Outside the reef, the water depth increases quickly, and anglers often find schools of Spanish mackerel. Outside the reef, toward the eastern tip of Dog Island (N29 49.588 W84 34.376), trolling with Flowering Floreo jigs or #00 Clarkspoons is effective if there are schools of white baitfish visible. Fly-fishers can also have lots of fun if the Spanish mackerel are chewing.

To the west of the river's mouth, outside the point of shallows at marker #4, is a secondary channel, or slough, that runs shoreward through the mud flats, past some old bars, and actually into the marshy areas behind Timber Island. The slough begins at about N29 49.448 W84 39.951 in eight feet of water. This is redfish country, but access can be difficult. Reds and a few flounder are found here in every season. Local anglers favor popping corks and live shrimp, but topwater lures will also attract the attention of a hungry red in warm months. Gold spoons (spin or fly versions) and slow-moving live or artificial shrimp do well up into the marsh as the water cools.

Depending on the direction of the wind, the run to Dog Island can be rough but productive, particularly in the summer. The deep flats behind the island offer refuge to huge schools of baitfish and shelter from the Gulf of Mexico. Sea trout forage the fifteen-foot-deep grass bottom in search of shrimp or pinfish. A light-colored D.O.A. shrimp, dragged slowly over the grass tops, is a good choice here, as pinfish will make a quick meal of any shrimp or shrimp imitation. Spanish mackerel chase bait schools along the western tip of the island (N29 47.168 W84 40.554) in the spring, summer, and early fall. Trolling Clarkspoons or Floreos is effective, as is fishing free-lined white bait along the edge of bait pods. Short steel leaders can help decrease cut-offs, but I prefer to take my chances (and get more hits) by using 40-pound fluorocarbon material. And if you're interested in chasing sharks, tarpon, or cobia with light tackle or fly rods, consider fishing due west of marker #5 (N29 45.594 W84 39.649) in East Pass toward the eastern tip of St. George Island (approx N29 45.735 W84 41.682). The beach side, or outside, of Dog Island offers excellent warm-water pompano fishing. Anglers with beach access wade the shoreline, but on calm days, boats are able to approach the beach and surf. Locals count on short-skirted jigs (trimmed Floreos) tipped with shrimp or Fishbites to attract pompano in the surf. In the fall, the targets for beach anglers are redfish. These fish come closer to shore from the depths of the gulf and cruise the beach, eating almost any live or artificial bait that's carefully placed in front of their nose. Accurate long casts, particularly with fly rods, are the secret to hooking these fish that feed primarily by smell, rather than by sight.

Inshore and Nearshore Fishing at Apalachicola

Fishermen can access Apalachicola Bay, St. Vincent Sound, and the western waters of St. George Sound from Apalachicola, East Point, or the bay side of St. George Island. The size and draft of your boat will determine which ramp is best for you. Larger boats should consider using the more substantial ramps at Apalachicola or up in East Bay at Sportsman's Lodge near Eastpoint.

The western area of St. George Sound acts like the big end of a funnel. Water carrying bait and game fish washes northward between Alligator Point and Dog Island and through East Pass. This tidal action, and the fact that the other outlets to the gulf from the sound (Bob Sikes Cut, West Pass, and Indian Pass) are all minor ones, makes the water here more likely to move quickly and to be clear and clean. In general, the sound holds abundant numbers of sea trout, redfish, and flounder. Summertime anglers will find trout in the cooler depths in the middle of the sound and redfish roaming the mainland shoreline. Anglers should pay attention to eddies created by moving water. Slack water during times of fast tidal movement will hold predators that aren't willing to expend too much energy chasing prey. A good example is the small point of land about halfway between Carrabelle and Eastpoint at N29 46.917 W84 45.341. This combination of marshy shoreline, shallow bars, and the protruding point makes for some good angling close to shore. Another example is the area around Goose Island (N29 42.326 W84 48.405) near the boat ramp at Bruce Beach in the St. George Island State Park. A quick look at a chart will give you a picture of the complexity of the area, and its bars and coves. There's no wonder trout, reds, flounder, and even tarpon are found near here. There are good opportunities for nearshore enthusiasts to fish for larger species toward the St. George bridge and mid-sound, particularly along the ICW. Trolling deep-running plugs such as the Stretch 25+ here will sometimes yield small grouper or big king mackerel in the late summer or fall. Troll the big plugs near the bottom and pull a few small Clarkspoons or Floreos for Spanish mackerel at the same time. The five-mile section of channel between ICW marker #22 (N29 43.323 W84 48.625) and the main span of the bridge is a good place to begin. Sharks also roam the entire bay in summer and are fun to catch using cut bait. Chumming or chunking will attract lots of sharks to the boat, and if you're brave, you'll want to give them a try with your big fly rod.

The bridge has been re-designed and rebuilt in recent years. In that process, a 3,000-foot section of the old bridge was left for fishermen at both the northern (Eastpoint) and southern (St. George Island) ends. These walk-on piers, with their structure above an almost solid oyster bottom, provide a year-round fishery for trout, reds, sheepshead, black drum, and Spanish mackerel. Fishing for trout and reds seems to be best from the northern pier, while the southern pier holds sharks and pelagic species, such as Spanish mackerel and king mackerel. Both ends of the old bridge offer good fishing for flounder

The old bridge abutments running alongside the new bridge to St. George Island still hold many species of game fish.

and black drum. There is good car parking available at either pier, and pier-fishing is always an option when the weather's not perfect for boating.

The area comprising Apalachicola Bay and East Bay (above the US 98 bridge) is a very distinctive estuary. Fed by gulf waters *and* by the outflow of the Apalachicola River system, its salinity levels are such that vast beds of living oysters cover the bottom. These bars support not only the local economy but also an excellent inshore fishery. While oystermen tong the bars, redfish, sea trout, and flounder lurk in hopes of finding crabs, shrimp, or small baitfish. Rising tides will always push predators to areas that were inaccessible on the last low tide, and wintertime high tides in the afternoon push everything toward the warmth of the dark bars. If you're fishing in three-foot depths, try popping corks with live or artificial D.O.A. shrimp or slow-sinking lures such as the Corky Mullet or MirrOlure Catch 2000. If it's shallower, go to a topwater plug (MirrOlure Top Dog or Popa Dog) or weedless gold spoon such as the Mann's Tidewater Spoon.

All the East Bay shoreline, from the mouth of Cash Creek (N29 48.021 W84 51.624) to downtown Apalach is a perfect year-round fishery for redfish and flounder and a great cool-weather habitat for big sea trout. This, however, is not an area for the faint at heart. It's tricky to navigate, shallow, and the bottom isn't smooth and sandy. Take the draft of your boat into consideration and spend some time poking around on a rising tide. Get as close as you can, then come out comfortably as the tide falls. Of course, fish as you go, but take some time to explore the area for fishing on other days.

The minor rivers here (Little St. Marks, St. Marks, and East) are fairly deep, but I stress the importance of a scouting trip, as changes can occur quickly due to gulf storms and upstream rainfall. Don't count on charts that are several years old for up-to-the-minute accuracy. The Apalachicola River breaks off to the north about five miles northwest of town and the ICW continues through the old Jackson River to Lake Wimico and then westward. Redfish and sea trout are often found as far upstream as Lake Wimico and certainly in the deeper rivers in winter and spring. They'll also be mingling with freshwater largemouth bass. Gold spoons cast toward riverbanks or shrimp (live or artificial) drifted into deep holes are excellent choices in the deep rivers and the far reaches of creeks.

Apalachicola Bay, outside the bridge, is big water. It's rarely deeper than twelve or fifteen feet but can get choppy as afternoon sea breezes pick up or as weather fronts arrive from the northwest. Care should be taken if you plan to cross the bay in a smaller craft. The northern shore from the municipal boat ramp (under the western end of the US 98 bridge) toward Green Point (N29 42.414 W85 02.021) is worth considering for reds, trout, and flounder if the wind's from the north. There's a secondary channel between Green Point and town, with adjacent spoil islands that are worth fishing, usually in cooler weather. The channel can be entered from the bay at N29 41.531 W85 00.753, in about six feet of water.

If you are able to launch at the shallow ramp at Bulkhead Point, near the end of the bridge on St. George Island, all the better when it comes to fishing the island's bay side. Crossing Apalachicola Bay can be a wet and wild adventure, but it's sometimes worth the trip when you arrive on the northern shore of the island. From spring through fall, you'll find schools of Spanish mackerel, bluefish, and huge ladyfish attacking white bait on the trip. Remember that these predators eat almost anything that moves quickly, whether cast or trolled. Mackerel are excellent to eat, blues are pretty good if fresh, and ladyfish are just plain fun. Running from the municipal ramp in Apalachicola, take the main channel to its eastward turn past marker #1 (N29 39.982 W84 58.171) and continue south toward the bay side of Bob Sikes Cut (N29 37.782 W84 58.065). There's at least ten feet of water here—until you're within a half-mile of shore.

The Cut is a favorite local fishing spot. It was dredged to favor the southbound passage of boat traffic and lessen the long run through East Pass. Huge amounts of water pass through the channel, and depending on the flow, bait and game fish follow. Slow tides usually mean fish gather closer to the rocky shore and quicker ones mean predators gather either inshore or offshore. This is *the* spot for big redfish in the fall, and it can be crowded with boats on weekends. Shore-bound anglers who are residing in the gated community also have access, but having a boat allows fishermen to adjust their position in relation to the tidal flow. In the cold months, big spawning sheepshead are found along the rocks, and anglers fishing live fiddler crabs or shrimp on heavy jig heads usually catch more than they should. In summer and early fall, expect to troll inside the Cut for Spanish mackerel and even hook the occasional cobia, tarpon, or king mackerel as they venture into the protected waters of the bay.

The north shorelines of St. George Island and Little St. George Island generally hold some sort of bait year-round. Mullet are the predominant species, and finding them close to shore usually means game fish are waiting. The oyster bars and shallows on both sides of Cedar Point (N29 38.939 W84 55.321) between the Cut and the St. George bridge are favored spots among locals for redfish, trout, and flounder. The same could said for the entire shoreline from the Cut to West Pass. If you see schooling or jumping mullet, rig a topwater plug or a gold spoon and approach the area slowly and quietly. Stealth and long casts are very important parts to the art of shallow-water fishing when mullet are present. Mullet hear loud noises or mistake a rocking boat for a porpoise and spook. When they leave, so do the predators.

St. Vincent Sound can be thought of as the small end of the funnel, opposed to the big end at East Pass. This western point of water lies behind St. Vincent Island, which is home to the St. Vincent National Wildlife Refuge, and drains westward through West Pass and Indian Pass. This sound can be reached either from Apalachicola's municipal ramp or from the ramp on Indian Peninsula. West Pass stays shoaled much of the time and is generally washed by rough offshore breakers while Indian Pass is more navigable. Both the northern and southern shores of the sound are good shallow-water habitat for inshore species. Oysters line the shore for several miles at the western end of the sound, well into Indian Lagoon, behind Indian Peninsula. There are also good oyster bars to fish along the northern shore of St. Vincent Island at about N29 41.047 W85 10.981 and at the mouth of Big Bayou (N29 40.950 W85 09.115). Anglers wishing to fish a bit deeper will find trout, reds, and Spanish mackerel along the Dry Bar, which extends into the sound off the eastern tip of St. Vincent Island. This bar runs eastward, then south, and almost touches the northern shore of Little St. George Island. It's a shallow reef, subject to movement by extreme weather but a good magnet for fish.

While West Pass is fishy, Indian Pass is fishier. The series of deep cuts and sloughs behind the island carry bait from the sound and from the oyster-rich shorelines out into the gulf. Fishing Indian Pass can be difficult but very productive. Tarpon, sharks, cobia, and king mackerel often lurk in the deep water waiting for whatever washes by, either from the gulf or from the thirty-plus miles of backwaters reaching all the way eastward to Carrabelle. An interesting technique used by some anglers in deep passes is to anchor the boat and drift lipped plugs such as the MirrOlure 111MR or 113MR behind the boat in the current. The combination of the lure's rattle and the push of the tide do all the work—you get to sit back and save your strength for the big strike.

The gulf side of the barrier islands off St. Vincent Sound, Apalachicola Bay, and St. George Sound can best be described with one word—beach. Luckily, this isn't the stretch of beach from Miami's South Beach to Ft. Lauderdale Beach, and it's just not very crowded here. If you use a boat to fish outside the surf line for redfish, tarpon, or cobia, you'll rarely have problems with swimmers getting in your way. Deep water gets close to St. George and St. Vincent Islands and brings with it fish of all species—big reds in the winter, cobia in the spring, and tarpon and sharks in the summer. Pelagics are sometimes found cruising the beaches in all but the coldest weather. If you want to wade-fish from the beach, there's good access from County Road (CR) 300 on more than half of St. George Island. And if you have a four-wheel-drive vehicle, you can buy a permit to fish the eastern end of the island. The $6 fee is a bargain to be able to reach this lonely stretch. Beach-bound fishermen always have the warm weather advantage of casting shrimp-tipped jigs or live sand fleas to pompano in the surf, but be prepared to catch redfish, Spanish mackerel, and nice sea trout at any time during the year.

Offshore Fishing from Apalachicola and Carrabelle

Offshore waters take on a different character west of Carrabelle. The bottom gets less structured but deeper closer to shore. Of course, there is still some natural structure and live bottom, but it's much scarcer than in the eastern gulf waters and it's almost nonexistent past Cape San Blas. Luckily, artificial reefs abound and larger wrecks are found close to shore past this tip of land, making offshore fishing much easier here than on the Big Bend.

That said, fishing for deep-water species such as grouper, snapper, king mackerel, amberjack, and cobia doesn't involve nearly as much wear and tear on boats and motors as it does farther down the coast. It's only about twenty five miles from the sea buoy off Carrabelle (N29 44.518 W84 39.151) to the Air Force V Tower (N29 24.961 W84 20.695) in more than seventy feet of water. Likewise, it's eleven miles from the Bob Sikes Cut through St. George Island (N29 36.180

W84 57.158) to the seventy-foot contour. Despite the slightly longer inshore run from Apalachicola to the Cut than from Carrabelle to East Pass, neither trip is a killer.

The goal of many offshore anglers departing Carrabelle is to fish near the eastern Air Force towers, K, V, and O. K Tower (N29 39.966 W84 22.153) is about fifteen miles east-southeast of the sea buoy at East Pass. Getting to V (N29 24.961 W84 20.695) involves more travel, as it's in almost eighty feet of water, twenty-five miles southeast of the buoy. O Tower (N29 32.127 W84 37.081) is twelve miles south of the sea buoy, but in only sixty-five feet of water. In any case, these towers provide deep-water hangouts for bait and structure for predators such as snapper, grouper, king mackerel, and cobia. And, there are occasional reports of dolphin (mahi-mahi), small tuna, and wahoo being caught near them in warmer months. If you're able to anchor and chum, you'll attract lots of fish to your boat, particularly at night. Trolling big lures, spoons, or live baits also works well, but don't expect these popular spots to be uninhabited by fellow anglers when you arrive, and tangled lines are not good manners.

In addition to the towers, many anglers leaving East Pass and Carrabelle head to the edge of the sixty-foot contour and drag large lipped lures near the bottom. A Mann's Stretch 30 will easily reach fifty-five feet if you use low-resistance super-braid line. Local anglers prefer 30-pound test PowerPro and troll at about five knots. You'll be trolling over live bottom, which you'll occasionally bump, but many times those "bumps" turn into nice grouper, reds, and gags. While trolling this ragged edge, keep an eye on your depth finder for ledges and rock outcrops holding schools of American red or gray (mangrove) snapper. Snapper season is short and the bag limit small. (Please see www.myfwc.com for current rules and regulations.) But snapper are delicious and catching a few makes the cost of any off-shore trip worthwhile. On sensitive depth-finders, schools of snapper sometimes appear as an inverted Christmas tree.

If the Bob Sikes Cut didn't bisect St. George Island and provide direct southerly access from Apalachicola to the gulf, it would be a long trip offshore by way of East Pass. Yes, West Pass is a possible

Deep waters are not far offshore of Carrabelle and Apalachicola. When in season, grouper and snapper make a fair showing at local fish-cleaning tables.

route to the gulf, but it's also littered with wrecks of boats captained by the uninformed or adventurous. Offshore anglers leaving the Cut have plenty of deep-water options. Many anglers travel westward toward the eastern Air Force towers, but others stay closer, fishing near the C Tower (N29 24.706 W84 51.339) and along the sixty-foot contour. C is only twelve miles from the Cut in eighty feet of water. Of particular interest to anglers fishing in sixty feet is the remains of the old St. George bridge. There are two locations at which the rubble was dumped in 2004, N29 30.052 W84 49.937 and N29 30.014 W84 48.178. These reefs have matured rapidly and are now productive havens for bottom fish and pelagics.

Grouper, snapper, and all their little relatives (black sea bass, pink-mouth grunts, b-liners, and white snapper) are all good to eat, but bottom-fishing at great depths involves lots of work. The Cape St. George Shoal is an underwater extension of the southern point of Little St. George Island. It's close to shore, and although not very deep, a haven for baitfish washing around the cape. But it's a more complex bottom than that found offshore and, therefore, has some bottom-fishing potential. There are also a couple of wrecks along the cape and off West Pass that hold smaller grouper and bottom fish in the warmer months. One wreck marked "PA" (position approximate) on several chart sources, at N29 32.503 W85 05.903, is southwest of Cape St. George in about thirty-five feet of water. It's worth investigating. Also, there is a four-mile-long thirty-five-foot-deep trench running eastward from N29 29.281 W85 04.451 toward N29 29.891 W85 00.107 that merits the trolling of a Stretch 25 lure. The expanses of the Cape St. George Shoal can bring lots of surprises—including a military test-firing range that extends four miles out and is closer to shore than the above coordinates. And you won't burn much fuel getting there.

Getting Around Southern Franklin County

Carrabelle, Eastpoint, and Apalachicola straddle US 98, the main east–west route along Florida's northern Gulf Coast. Access from the north and from Interstate 10 is limited. US 319 runs from Tallahassee and intersects US 98 east of Carrabelle and is probably the best north–south route to Franklin County. Alternatively, State Road (SR) 65 runs from I-10, west of Quincy, to Eastpoint. CR 67 splits off of SR 65 at Telogia and heads southward to Carrabelle. If you plan to launch at Indian Pass, CR 30A veers off US 98 west of Apalachicola, eventually turning back toward Port St. Joe. CR 300 leaves US 98 in Eastpoint and crosses Apalachicola Bay to St. George Island, where it dead-ends. To the east, CR 300 enters the St. George Island State Park. There is a $5 fee per car (up to eight persons) to enter the park, and $3 fee to launch at either of the two sound-side ramps. To the west, CR 300 dead-ends into a private gated residential development.

Where to Stay

Carrabelle

Franklin Inn at Carrabelle, 1589 US 98 West (850) 697-4000, www.franklininncarrabelle.com. Thirty-one rooms, built in 2007.

The Moorings, (850) 697-2800. Lodging, adjacent to full-service marina, free dockage, and trailer storage for guests.

The Old Carrabelle Hotel B&B, Tallahassee Street, one block from the City Docks, (850) 697-9010.

Carrabelle Palms Beachfront RV Park, US 98 West, Carrabelle Beach, (850) 697-2638, www.carrabellepalmsrvpark.com. RV park, rental cabins, convenience store, beach access.

Eastpoint

Sportsman's Lodge, 97 N Bayshore, (850) 670-8423. Lodging, kitchenettes, adjacent marina, ramp, and restaurant.

St. George Island

Buccaneer Inn, W Gorrie Drive, (850) 927-2585. Beachfront lodging.

St. George Inn, Franklin Boulevard, (850) 927-2625.

Resort Vacation Properties, (850) 927-2322, www.resortvacationproperties.com. Beach and vacation rental homes.

Apalachicola

Bay City Lodge, Bluff Road, (850) 653-9294, www.baycitylodge.com. Cabins and motel units, lodge available for parties of 12 or more anglers, restaurant, marina. Bay City is a popular destination for larger groups visiting the area and can provide guides, meals, and lodging.

The Gibson Inn, Avenue C, (850) 653-2192, www.gibsoninn.com. Upscale lodging, adjacent restaurant, limited trailer parking. The Gibson is a landmark in downtown Apalachicola. Trailer parking can be a problem.

Best Western Apalach Inn, US 98 West, (850) 653-9131. Lodging. This motel is one of the few around that actually has parking spaces long enough to handle cars with trailers.

Rancho Inn, US 98 West, (850) 653-9435. Lodging. The Rancho doesn't seem to have problems with guests who park boat trailers in the front yard.

Apalachicola River Inn, (850) 653-8139. Upscale riverfront lodging, adjacent restaurant and bar, transient dockage available.

Coombs House Inn B&B, 80 6th St., 1-888-244-8320. Upscale lodging. "A romantic bed-and-breakfast in an elegant Victorian mansion welcomes guests to experience historic charm in an intimate setting." Need I say more?

Anchor Vacation Properties, Franklin County, (850) 697-9000; St. George/Apalachicola. 1-800-927-2625. Rental homes and condos.

Where to Eat

Carrabelle

Miss Brenda's Coral Sea Restaurant, US 98 East, (850) 697-5494. Seafood, pizza, breakfast, lunch, dinner, closed Mondays. Don't miss the seafood or the pies here.

Hog Wild Bar-B-Q, US 98 West, (850) 697-2776. Seafood and BBQ, Lunch, dinner, closed Tuesdays.

Riverview Restaurant, 600 Marine Street, (850) 697-8488. Seafood, adjacent to Wicked Willie's Bar.

Carrabelle IGA Grocery Store, US 98, Full-service grocery, bait and tackle, adjacent Laundromat.

2 Als at the Beach Café, Carrabelle Beach, (850) 697-4576. Casual dining, bar.

Frank's Good Food, US 98, Carrabelle Beach, (850) 545-4909. Barbecue and seafood, lunch, dinner, closed Mondays. Frank's is basically a large catering trailer that spends some of its time here and the rest of the time next door to AMS Marine Supply in Medart, based on the owner's whim.

Eastpoint

Nat's Food Mart & Deli, US 98, Breakfast, lunch, dinner, closed Sundays.

White Eagle Restaurant at Sportsman's Lodge, 97 N Bayshore, (850) 670-8423.

El Jalisco Mexican Restaurant, US 98, (850) 670-5900. Lunch, dinner daily, American breakfasts all day on weekends.

St. George Island

Flamingo's Restaurant. Breakfast, lunch, dinner, open everyday.

Finni's Bayside Grill and Sports Bar, Gunn Street, (850) 927-2600. Casual sports bar, dinner, closed Mondays.

Harry A's Restaurant, 28 W Bayshore, (850) 927-9810. Lunch, dinner, closed Sundays.

El Jalisco Mexican Restaurant, W Gorrie, (850) 927-3496. Lunch and dinner daily, American breakfasts on weekends.

Apalachicola

Bay City Lodge Restaurant, off Bluff Road (12th Street), north of town, (850) 653-9294. Seafood, breakfast, dinner, box lunches available for guests. Call ahead to confirm serving hours.

Boss Oyster, Apalachicola River Inn, (850) 653-9364. Lunch, dinner.

Apalachicola Seafood Grill & Steakhouse, (850) 653-9510. Lunch, dinner, closed Sundays.

Papa Joe's Oyster Bar & Grill, Scipio Creek Marina, (850) 653-1189. Seafood, oyster bar, lunch, dinner.

Tamara's Café Floridita, Avenue E, (850) 653-4111. Latin food, lunch, dinner, open seven days a week.

Steamer's Raw Bar, 518 W US 98, (850) 653-3474. Local seafood. Leashed well-trained dogs are allowed at the outside tables. Kids, too!

Red Top Café, US 98 West, next door to Rancho Inn, (850) 653-8612. Lunch, dinner.

Seafood-2-Go, US 98 West, (850) 653-8044. Steamed seafood, take-out only.

The Gibson Inn, Avenue C, (850) 653-2192, www.gibsoninn.com. Up-scale dining, breakfast, lunch, dinner, adjacent hotel.

Indian Pass

Indian Pass Raw Bar, Indian Pass Road (CR 30A), (850) 227-1670, www.indianpassrawbar.com. Oysters, seafood, sandwiches, beer and wine, lunch, dinner, closed Sundays.

Marinas, Marine Supplies and Service, Bait-and-Tackle Shops, and Launching Ramps

Carrabelle

Dockside Marina, Timber Island, (850) 697-3337. Wet slips, dry storage, $5 boat ramp, trailer storage, ship's store, no fuel.

Parramore Marine Service, at Dockside Marina, (850) 697-3666. Marine service, marine railroad and ways.

Carrabelle Marina, US 98, (850) 697-3351. Boat and motor sales and service, repairs.

C-Quarters Marina, US 98, (850) 697-8400. Wet slips, transient dockage, gas and diesel, live and frozen bait, bulk ice, adjacent to public boat ramp.

The Moorings Marina and Motel, (850) 697-2800. Full-service marina, free dockage and trailer storage for motel guests, launching ramp free for guests, transient dockage with shore power, gas and diesel, frozen bait, showers, laundry.

Hometown BP, US 98, Extensive tackle selection, frozen bait, deli, convenience store, gas.

Frank's Bait & Tackle, US 98, (850) 697-9232. Tackle, live and frozen bait.

City Boat Ramp, US 98. Free paved ramp, adjacent to C-Quarters Marina, adequate parking.

Timber Island Boat Ramp, Timber Island Road. Free, paved ramp, easy access to river.

Eastpoint

Fisherman's Choice Bait & Tackle, US 98, (850) 670-8808. Live and frozen bait, tackle, ice, opens at 6 a.m. seven days a week.

Taylor's Building Supply, US 98, (850) 670-8529. Tackle, trailer parts, marine hardware, supplies.

Wefings Marine, Inc., US 98, (850) 670-8100. Boat and motor sales and service, marine supplies and repair parts.

Sportsman's Lodge and Marina, SR 65 north of Eastpoint. Free ramp for guests, but consider launching your boat at the Ferry Dock Ramp next door as the ramp here is a bit bumpy and steep.

Ferry Dock Ramp, SR 65 north of Eastpoint. Free paved ramp, limited street parking. This ramp is steep, but has a breakwater that makes launching easy here, easier than the Sportsman's Lodge ramp next door.

Eastpoint City Ramp, US 98. Free, unpaved ramp, no parking.

St. George Island

Fisherman's Headquarters and Hardware, West Bayshore Drive, (850) 927-9817. Live and frozen bait, extensive tackle and marine supplies, trailer repairs.

Survivors's Bait & Tackle, West Pine Avenue, (850) 927-3113. Live and frozen bait, tackle, clothing, shoes.

St. George Island Boat Ramp. Shallow sand ramp at southeastern end of bridge. This ramp, used mostly by local commercial oystermen, provides shallow access to Apalachicola Bay. Many St. George visitors prefer launching at Apalachicola's Battery Park ramp.

St. George Island State Park Ramps. $3 to launch at either unpaved ramp, good access to eastern end of St. George Island and St. George Sound.

Apalachicola

Scipio Creek Marina, Market Street, (850) 653-8030. Full-service marina, gas and diesel, bait and tackle, dry storage, paved ramp, dockage, adjacent restaurant.

Apalachicola Miller's Marine, Water Street, (850) 653-9521. Gas and diesel, marine supplies, closed Sunday mornings. Primarily a fuel facility, Miller's is located just inside the bridge on the Apalachicola River.

Bay City Lodge, north of town off Bluff Road, (850) 653-9294. Boat ramp for guests, gas, wet and dry storage, bait and tackle, lodging, restaurant. This is one of Florida's great fish camps. Located a few miles upriver, it offers easy access to the lower river and to the bay.

Battery Park Ramp, downtown. Free paved ramps with easy access to river mouth. There is limited transient dockage available here. The Apalachicola Dockmaster can be reached at (850) 697-9010.

Scipio Creek Ramp, end of Market Street at the St. Vincent National Wildlife Refuge Headquarters. paved ramp, limited parking.

Bluff Road County Ramp, northern end of Bluff Road (12th Street). Paved ramps, adequate parking. This ramp is upriver, but still offers good access to backwater, bay, and Lake Wimico.

Indian Pass

Indian Pass Ramp, CR 30B. Free paved ramp, adjacent to campground, adequate parking. There is also access to the beach for cars and trucks here.

Local Fishing Guides

Carrabelle

Capt. Adam Hudson, Lanark Village and Carrabelle, (850) 566-5599. Light tackle and fly fishing.

Capt. Kamen Miller, (850) 528-1926. Offshore fishing and dive trips for grouper, snapper, king mackerel.

Capt. Chuck Simpson, (850) 219-1144. Inshore, light tackle.

Capt. Robyn Morgan, (850) 697-9690. Offshore trips for grouper, snapper, cobia, amberjack, and king mackerel. Captain Morgan is one of the few female guides on the Big Bend.

Capt. Randy Craft, 1-800-897-7106. Offshore trips for grouper, snapper, king mackerel.

Capt. Scott Luke, (850) 697-2972. Offshore.

Apalachicola

Capt. Alex Crawford, (850) 697-8946, www.topknots.com. Offshore trips for grouper, snapper, cobia, amberjack, and dolphin.

Capt. Tommy Robinson, Capt. Chris Robinson, (850) 653-8896, www.floridaredfish.com. Inshore, nearshore, offshore.

Robinson Brothers Guide Service, Kathy Robinson, (850) 653-8896, www.floridaredfish.com, robinson@flaredfish.com. Kathy represents a number of inshore, offshore, and nearshore professional guides through her agency.

Capt. Dennis Crosby, (850) 653-8055, www.bosscharters.com. In-shore and offshore.

Capt. Jimmy Maxwell, (850) 653-2820, www.backwaterguideservice.com. Bay and backwater fishing.

Capt. Charlie Logue, (850) 927-3351, charleslogue@hotmail.com. Off-shore.

Capt. Charles Wilson, (850) 653-9008, www.captcharlescharters.com. Offshore and bay fishing.

Book Me A Charter Guide Service, (850) 653-2622, www.bookmea charter.com. Inshore and offshore charters.

Many guides from Lanark Village are familiar with the waters at Carrabelle, and Port St. Joe guides frequent Cape San Blas and St. Vincent Sound. Most offshore waters east of Apalachicola are familiar places to guides from St. Marks to Mexico Beach. Please consult the listings for those areas, if necessary. Also the Web site of the Florida Guides Association (www.florida-guides.com) has a complete listing of United States Coast Guard licensed-and-insured fishing guides.

13

Port St. Joe, Mexico Beach, and St. Joseph Bay

On casual inspection of a Florida map, the twenty-plus-mile stretch of coastline from Cape San Blas to St. Andrew Point is unimpressive. There are no harbors or inlets and the only marked geographic feature is the long and narrow St. Joseph Peninsula, which runs northward, almost enclosing St. Joseph Bay. The bottom of the Gulf of Mexico is largely sandy and smooth here, and the inward curve of the peninsula would lead you to believe that bait and predators bypass the area. However, your first fishing trip here, whether poling the backwaters of Lighthouse Bayou, wading the shorelines, or trolling over the many public artificial reefs, will certainly change your outlook.

I don't want to argue with anyone about where Florida's Big Bend ends and the Emerald Coast begins, but I think Cape San Blas is as good a point as any. Traveling from the boat ramp at Indian Pass, there is a distinct difference between the water offshore of St. Vincent Island, where the coastline runs east and west, and that off of the St. Joseph Peninsula. Deeper, cooler, and clearer water does make a difference. Even the inshore waters are different. St. Joseph Bay is generally deeper than any of the Big Bend bays, and due to the fact that there is no influx of fresh water from rivers, it has a different ecology than the oyster-laden estuarine systems to the east. Here, you get miles and miles of sandy inshore grass flats and take few chances of bashing your outboard's lower unit on hard bottom.

Amenities and facilities at Port St. Joe, St. Joe Beach, and Mexico

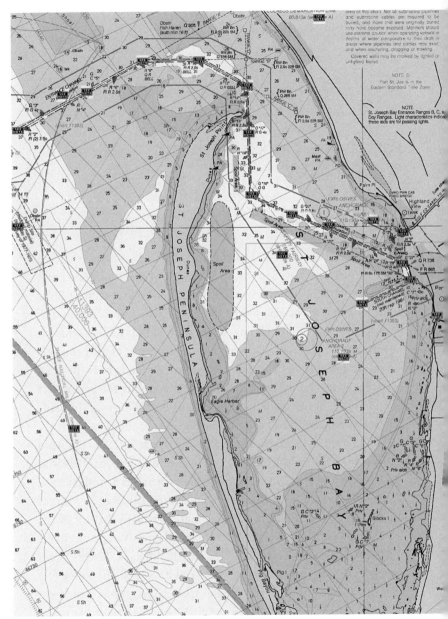

St. Joseph Peninsula, at the western end of St. George Sound, marks the beginning of what many call the Emerald Coast, where beaches are more predominant, as are people, but there are still plenty of fish to be caught.

Beach are excellent, and for the most part oriented toward beachgo-ers. Some motels do have ample parking for boats and trailers, the food choices are good, and the ramps and marinas are both well-maintained and convenient. The campgrounds and RV parks nearer the cape are typically more angler-friendly, as is the St. Joseph Penin-sula State Park.

Inshore and Nearshore Fishing, St. Joseph Bay, and the St. Joseph Peninsula

I'm a sucker for shallow-water and wade fishing, so I'm always im-pressed by the mainland shoreline along US Highway 98 on this stretch of Florida's coast. Visitors should be awed as well. Just south of the town of Port St. Joe, where the highway hits the coastline at Oak Grove, you'll almost always find anglers trudging across the shallow mud flats heading toward the deeper water that comes close here. In the summer, they'll be throwing topwater plugs such as Heddon Su-per Spooks (SS style) or slowly retrieving D.O.A. shrimp (glow style) along the drop-offs. On sunny and cooler afternoons, they'll move closer to shore as the tide rises and throw slow-sinking and slow-moving lures such as D.O.A. Bait Busters, MirrOlure Catch 2000s, and Corky Mullet in hopes of finding big trout and reds warming up and feeding in the shallows. In any season, live-baiters also do well along this shoreline. Live shrimp, pinfish, or mud minnows fished under popping corks are the local choice. A popular rig is made by attaching a 5/0 or 6/0 circle hook (Mustad Ultra Point) to a length of 20-pound-test fluorocarbon leader necessary to keep the bait just above the bottom. Hook your bait through its tail, and wait for your prey to attack and hook themselves on the circle hook. No hook-setting is necessary. The use of circle hooks is becoming popular, as smaller fish are less likely to be gut-hooked. Safely released, these fish can be caught another day after they've grown up.

Wading the shallow flats isn't limited to the short stretch of shore-line between Oak Grove and Port St. Joe. St. Joseph Bay has some of the finest seagrass beds in the state, and while many are too deep to wade, those fringing the bay offer excellent wading, depending on your ability to gain access to them. Live and active seagrass beds extend from Palm Point (N29 50.265 W85 19.607), just north of the Gulf County Canal, all the way around the lower end of the bay to St. Joseph Point (N29 52.500 W85 23.052) on the other side. Some of these areas are accessible from the roads, but others involve using a boat to reach the shallow edges. The grass flats edging the southern end of St. Joseph Bay extend two miles from shore in many places. To protect this fragile environment, take extraordinary care not to scar the bottom with your propeller. The use of a pushpole or trolling motor to maneuver over the seagrass is the best way to reach these areas from deeper water.

While the southern end of St. Joseph Bay is shallow, there are a couple of deep spots that are accessible by most boats and merit attention from anglers. Most of this bay is deep, charted to more than thirty feet in some locations, and there are several sloughs running well south toward Lighthouse Bayou and Pig Bayou. Big full tides flood the lower bay, especially on a new moon, and the subsequent falling tides drain through these channels, taking with them bait of all sorts. Anglers willing to stake out along the edges of the deep channel or slough running from N29 41.937 W85 21.918 to N29 42.967 W85 21.708 in Pig Bayou often find success as falling tides drain the shallows. Depending on the stage of the tide, fish are either near the edges of the channels or holding near the bottom. Topwater plugs, light jig heads rigged with soft-plastic tails, or live or artificial shrimp all attract strikes up on the shallow edges. When the fish move into the depths, staying warm in winter or cool in summer, try a bait that gets down to the bottom. Cut mullet or live shrimp are good choices here for reds, flounder and trout, but you'll have to contend with bites from stingrays, catfish, and other junk fish, particularly in the warmer months. Artificial lures such as deep-running D.O.A. Bait Busters or TerrorEyz jigs seem to do just as well and don't encourage pesky by-catch.

An easier spot to reach is Eagle Harbor (29 46.528 W85 23.641), the location of the state park boat ramp. This backwater is also easily reached from the Port St. Joe boat ramp and the South Channel, about four miles across the bay. Its depths drain the shallow flats much like the channels near Pig Bayou, and its proximity to the upper deeper part of the bay sometimes make it better habitat for schooling fish such as Spanish mackerel and bluefish. From Eagle Harbor to St. Joseph Point, trolling #00 Clarkspoons or Flowering Floreos tipped with FishBites or small strips of mullet belly, at about four knots, is a good way to catch mackerel along the deep edge. The slough inside the big spoil bank about midway up the island can be lively in late summer and early fall, as can the spoils to the south of the North Channel.

St. Joseph Peninsula is nothing but a big attached barrier island protecting the coast from the direct wave action of the gulf. That being the case, the stretch of shoreline that's not protected, including St. Joe Beach and Mexico Beach, is different from the southern shoreline. White-sand beaches and rolling surf are the norm here, and that means a different fishery.

Public beaches, such as the ones at St. Joe Beach and Mexico Beach, mean lots of swimmers. Luckily they don't seem to get out much during the gray, predawn hours of summer when the pompano, bluefish, and Spanish mackerel forage between the surf and the inner sandbars. Just as the sun rises you'll find row after row of rods in beach-style holders waiting for something to eat. Seasoned beach-fishers use 8- to 9-foot spinning rods capable of casting rigs consisting of egg sinkers and 2/0 or 3/0 hooks baited with shrimp or sand fleas toward the inner bars. Many fishermen catch their own sand fleas as they need them with perforated five-gallon buckets; this ensures fresh bait. Also, by locating the bait in the surf, they gain a good idea of the location of the predators nearby. A tried-and-true spot for nice keeper pompano is at the end of 4th Street in Mexico Beach. Just look for the early morning crowds.

If you're not excited about getting your feet wet, or just want to avoid those long casts, try fishing from the Mexico Beach Pier. It's not the longest fishing pier on the Emerald Coast, but it's productive and conveniently located near the center of the Mexico Beach community.

Surf fishermen get to the beach at Mexico Beach early in order to beat the swimmers to the water.

Of course, the beach fishing here is not limited to just the St. Joe Beach and Mexico Beach shorelines. St. Joseph Peninsula's western shoreline is a spectacular fifteen-plus-mile stretch of white sand. Depending on the season, St. Joseph Peninsula beach anglers have the same good fishing as fishermen along the inshore beaches and catch nice pompano, sea trout, reds, and Spanish mackerel. They're also more likely to hook up a king mackerel in the late spring or summer, and anglers wading the surf hook a few tarpon each year. Techniques used here are the same as on the inshore beaches, but access is not quite so easy as from US 98 on the mainland.

The sandy beach on the peninsula falls off almost immediately into depths of twenty to thirty feet. Along its mid-section are close-in fin-

Pompano are a popular species found near many beaches along the Emerald Coast.

gers of deeper water (Approx. N29 43.573 W85 25.237) that attract many species of game fish and a few eager fishermen in boats. The fact that neither the boat ramp at Port St. Joe or at Indian Pass is close can make one feel pretty lonely when fishing this area. That's a good thing—the fish don't know the difference!

Other good spots are along the beaches at the northern and southern tips of the peninsula. Bait washing in and out of the St. Joe Bay keep the predators busy most of the year at St. Joseph Point (N29 52.505 W85 23.042), and the cuts and fingers off Cape San Blas (N29 39.316 W85 20.700) bring deep-water species closer to shore in search of bait washing out of Indian Pass. And, keep in mind the geographic orientation of Cape San Blas and the St. Joseph Peninsula; this point of land is a natural catch-point for just about any fish species you'd care to target.

In the spring, cobia cruise the peninsula's shoreline and are easily sight-fished by boaters using live baits (white bait, pinfish, or eels) or heavy jigs. King mackerel arrive here in the spring as well, following large schools of white bait on their northern migration. Slowly trolled blue runners make excellent king-mackerel baits, but even pinfish or big menhaden work well. Artificial-bait specialists usually pull big Clarkspoons at four to five knots when targeting kings.

Summer brings many species, including fat Spanish mackerel, bluefish, and lots of cruising tarpon. Spanish mackerel and bluefish are usually found attacking large schools of bait, marked by birds wheeling overhead. Take care to not run into the middle of the action but troll small spoons or jigs around the edges of the melee. If you are able to drift with the bait and striking fish, you'll have a great time with topwater plugs or almost any artificial bait. Spanish mackerel and blues are lots of fun on light tackle and good table fare if eaten very fresh. Do take care to rig with light wire leaders, though, as their sharp teeth can make quick work of even 40-pound fluorocarbon leaders. Tarpon are best fished early in the day, before the inevitable sea breezes make sight-fishing impossible. Sub-surface plugs such as the big Yo-Zuri Crystal Minnow in silver and black, the D.O.A. Bait Buster, or even the small TerrorEyz jig attract ferocious tarpon strikes—if the angler has the skill to present the bait naturally in front of the tarpon. Baits should cross above and across a tarpon—never from his rear or below him. This is a perfect place to fish for these silver kings with light tackle or fly rods. There are no snags to contend with and plenty of open water. Many local tarpon anglers are happy with 20-pound-test PowerPro line on their spinning outfits, and all a 12-weight fly-rod angler needs is the skill to present the fly to the fish at fifty to sixty feet. Favorite flies used here have traditionally been cockroach, toad, or destroyer patterns rigged on 20-pound-class-tippet leaders and 80-pound bite tippets.

Summertime action usually continues well into September, when big bull redfish, which spend most of the year offshore, come close to the beaches, where the water is deeper than the nearshore waters of the Big Bend. And, while smaller slot-size reds are found almost year-round in the bays and estuaries, it's the big ones that get catch-and-release anglers excited during the late summer and fall. Taken on a variety of baits and with all sorts of tackle, these over-slot redfish are great fun, and if care is taken to release them properly, a renewable resource. Serious sport fishermen and women often go the trouble of removing the barbs from the hooks of their lures and flies just to make the catch less traumatic for the reds. And recently, the advent of circle hooks has made the use of live or cut bait for these fish practical. J-hooks are more easily swallowed than circle hooks, which almost always pierce only the outer lip of the fish, allowing an easy humane release.

One final inshore comment is appropriate in any discussion of St. Joseph Bay, the westernmost body of water where recreational scalloping is permitted by the state of Florida. Spawning bay scallops require exceptionally clean, salty water and healthy seagrass beds, like those found here. The scalloping season always runs from July 1 to September 10, and while no one area can be counted on from year to year local anglers usually see scallops in early summer and provide reports to local marinas and bait shops. Protecting the seagrass beds by not scarring them should be paramount in the minds of scallopers and all anglers. Light scars heal during the off-season, but prop ditches caused by inconsiderate boaters last much longer.

Offshore Fishing from Port St. Joe and Mexico Beach

There have not always been man-made artificial reefs, but as sailors started losing ships to the sea, the value of structure to fishermen became evident, particularly in areas such as Florida's Emerald Coast, where the sea floor is mostly flat and sandy. No discussion of the offshore fishing from Port St. Joe or Mexico Beach is complete without mention of the Mexico Beach Artificial Reef Association (MBARA). Incorporated in 1997, MBARA has had as part of its mission the task of constructing "artificial reef habitat to enhance sustainable fisheries in the waters of the Gulf of Mexico. The MBARA set a milestone of establishing 1,000 patch reefs, or small artificial reef habitats in the waters off Mexico Beach, Florida. Working closely with the City of Mexico Beach, the Florida Fish and Wildlife Commission, and the United States Army Corps of Engineers, the MBARA is well on the road to achieving that milestone." And what a difference it's made.

Offshore fishing spots here that are not over artificial structure are mainly over small ledges and rock outcrops. It's safe to say that most are south and southwest of Cape San Blas and probably best reached by trailered boats launching at Indian Pass. It's a long run to this area from either Port St. Joe or Apalachicola.

King mackerel, Spanish mackerel, and cobia are likely to be found anywhere from the point of Cape San Blas out to N29 29.290 W85 33.588, along the thirty-foot contour. In some places, the reef gets extremely shallow, a requisite for cobia and Spanish mackerel. Look for birds eating scraps over the top of the reef (N29 38.693 W85 21.105), then troll small Clarkspoons or Flowering Floreo jigs at about four knots for Spanish mackerel. Cobia will be seen cruising the edges of bait pods in the spring and summer, and are fair game for anglers tossing live crabs, live eels, or jigs. There are also several wrecks atop the reef, but their published locations are no longer accurate due to the 2005 hurricanes. It's best to investigate any spot that looks like the shadow of a boat; it may be an old or new wreck worth fishing. Farther offshore and west of Cape San Blas are some deepwater artificial reefs in 100-plus feet that are known to hold grouper, snapper, and other bottom dwellers, particularly the Sandy Reefs at approximately N29 40.009 W85 41.432. The newer Ard Reef (N29 45.339 W85 52.367) and Clift Reef (N29 44.445 W85 52.388) are to the northwest and in about 120 feet of water. Expect a twenty-plus-mile trip to these depths from marker #2 in the entrance channel to Port St. Joe (N29 52.254 W85 28.972).

The thirty-foot contour parallels the beach of St. Joseph Peninsula and is irregular until about midway up the shore, at which point it straightens out. From this point north to Panama City, the bottom is quite barren. However, don't miss any opportunity to troll this or any other contour while en route along the coast, as you'll likely pick up a grouper, king mackerel, or even a cobia. Mann's Stretch lures are a good bet, and a tandem rig is even better. Fishing one near the bottom (a Stretch 30) and one near the surface (a Stretch 15) doubles your chances for a hookup. Consider fishing the shallow-runner with a reel holding lots of 20-pound monofilament line, as a king mackerel can strip hundreds of yards of line from a reel in a matter of seconds after the initial strike.

Man-made reefs, like those constructed by the MBARA, are home to most of the grouper and snapper caught here. Unlike wrecks, these reefs are relatively clean. If they're car bodies, old boats, barges, or railroad cars, they've likely been stripped of rigging or snags and modified to support marine life. Wrecks are not so angler-friendly, and more care must be taken not to foul lines on their rigging. In either case, it's best to anchor away from an artificial reef or wreck and count on the current to hold fish away from the structure. A complete list of the MBARA artificial reefs, with their locations and composition, can be found on the Internet at www.mbara.org. It's quite a list.

Grouper tend to hide inside structure, but are likely to move away from cover in order to attack baits. Understanding this allows anglers to safely put their baits, cut or live, near the edges of wrecks and artificial reefs and still get bites. Begin your grouper fishing by using smelly cut bait such as frozen sardines or squid rigged on dropper rigs. You'll attract bites from other bottom fish, but the grouper will soon become interested. It's then that you bring out the grouper candy—live white bait (menhaden, alewives, threadfin herring) or pinfish. Teasing and taunting grouper to leave their protective habitat is a tried-and-true method.

Most snapper, including American red and gray (mangrove), are more likely to venture above the bottom to attack bait from pods attracted to the structure. Understanding this behavior gives advantages to the snapper fisherman. You'll see them on your depth finder, generally represented as a plume or inverted tree shape, above structure or a natural ledge. And, you don't have to fish all the way to the bottom to catch them. Snapper usually feed above the bottom on alewives, small menhaden, and even shrimp, which are smaller baits than grouper eat. Smaller hooks and lighter tackle are also practical, particularly for night-feeding gray snapper, which seem to be able to see leader material even in the dark. Six-ought and 7/0 circle hooks on multi-hook dropper rigs made with 40-pound-test fluorocarbon leaders work well for snapper, even at depths of 100 feet or more, where they're likely found.

Cobia and amberjacks are less discriminating. They generally cruise the area and will sometimes not allow a grouper or snapper bait to pass without charging it. Either can be a nuisance, however many anglers target them for table fare, especially cobia, which are excellent to eat regardless of size. The flesh from smaller amberjacks is usually less infested than larger amberjacks are with harmless but unappetizing worms. Both AJs and cobia are great fighters, making each species excellent targets for light-tackle and fly-rod sportsmen.

Finally, I'll comment on really deep, bluewater fishing from the Port St. Joe and Mexico Beach area. Heading southward and westward from Cape San Blas, you'll find hard-bottom areas along the 100-foot contour from N29 18.120 W85 24.880 to N29 26.380 W85 46.080, and these areas can attract wahoo, dolphin (mahi-mahi), marlin, and sailfish in late summer. If you have the ability to reach these areas, as well as gain access to sea-surface temperature data, you might have an interesting day fishing the edges of thermoclines. Look for long grass lines formed by winds and upwelling currents as well. Trolling ballyhoo rigged on Iland Sea Star lures and trolled at the surface are a good bet along weedlines. In addition, or in cases where bait pods are within casting range, Mann's Stretch Plus Imitator lures (menhaden design) will cover the middle of the water column at speeds between five and eight knots. Fishing blue water has potential from this area but is not so popular as it is from ports to the west, including Panama City, Destin, and Pensacola.

Getting Around the Port St. Joe and Mexico Beach Area

Navigating the area from Port St. Joe to Mexico Beach, including the St. Joseph Peninsula by either water or land is simple.

US 98 runs from Apalachicola to the east and from Panama City to the west. State Road (SR) 71 begins at US 98 in Port St. Joe and intersects SR 20 at Blountstown. SR 71 is the most direct route to Interstate 10, the main east–west artery in the Florida Panhandle.

SR 30A jogs off of US 98 west of Apalachicola and heads to Indian

Many fishermen enjoy camping near Port St. Joe.

Pass. County Road (CR) 30B makes a reverse turn at Indian Pass and follows Indian Peninsula east toward the boat ramp and campground. Just up the road, SR 30A makes a turn to the north along lower St. Joseph Bay and heads back to Port St. Joe. The beach road is CR 30E, and it runs along the peninsula to Eagle Harbor and the boat ramp there.

The center of St. Joseph Bay is fairly deep, and there are only two channels into Port St. Joe. The unmarked South Channel leads from downtown Port St. Joe into the middle of the bay and about twenty feet of water. The North Channel is dredged, marked, and meanders around St. Joseph Point and well into the Gulf of Mexico. There is also a small channel that leads to the mouth of the Gulf County Canal, which in turn runs inland to the Intracoastal Waterway.

To the north, Mexico Beach has a short channel that cuts through the shallows to twenty-foot depths. Its entrance, at marker #1 (N29

56.924 W85 25.817), is 3.2 miles due north of marker #8 in the Port St. Joe Channel (N29 53.654 W85 25.822).

Where to Stay

Port St. Joe

Mainstay Suites, 3951 E US 98, (850) 229-6246. Lodging, all suites with kitchens.

The Port Inn, US 98 at SR 71, (850) 229-7678. Upscale lodging, adjacent bar. The Port Inn is located just across the street from the St. Joe boat ramp.

Presnell's Bayside Marina & RV Resort, CR 30, (850) 229-2710, www.presnells.com. Full RV hookups, boat ramp, showers, pump station.

Indian Pass Campground, CR 30B, on Indian Pass, (850) 227-7203. Trailer and cabin rental, canoe and kayak rentals. This campground is popular, located just across Indian Pass from St. Vincent Island. It's adjacent to a county boat ramp, the St. Vincent ferry landing, and beach access for vehicles.

St. Joseph Peninsula State Park, CR 30E, St. Joseph Peninsula, (850) 227-1327. Eight cabins, full-facility campground or primitive camping.

Dixie Belle Motel, 3155 W US 98, (850) 227-1443. Lodging. Located between Port St. Joe and St. Joe Beach, near the Windmark Community.

Gulf Sands Motel, 8042 W US 98, St. Joe Beach, (850) 647-8233. Lodging, adjacent restaurant.

Paradise Coast Rentals, 1-888-227-2110. Condo and house rentals.

Mexico Beach

Driftwood Inn, US 98, (850) 648-5126. Upscale lodging.

Gulf View Motel, US 98, (850) 648-5955. Lodging.

El Governor Motel, US 98, (850) 648-5757. Beachside lodging.

El Governor Campground, US 98, (850) 648-4959. Full RV hookups, beach access, showers.

Ocean Breeze Lodge, 4103 E US 98, (850) 648-4800. Lodging.

Paradise Coast Rentals, 1-866-216-3399. Condo and house rentals.

Parker Realty, (850) 648-5777. Condo and house rentals.

Where to Eat

Port St. Joe

Dockside Café, First Street, (850) 229-5200. Lunch, dinner, open seven days a week.

Indian Pass Raw Bar, Indian Pass Road, (CR 30A), (850) 227-1670, www.indianpassrawbar.com. Oysters, seafood, sandwiches, beer and wine, lunch, dinner, closed Sundays.

Sunset Coastal Grill, 602 Hwy 98, (850) 227-7900. Seafood, lunch, dinner, closed Mondays.

Billy Bowlegs Restaurant, First Street, (850) 227-3500. Patio dining, lunch seven days a week, dinner Saturdays and Sundays.

Regan's Pub & Oyster Bar, US 98, St. Joe Beach, (850) 647-2800. Lunch, dinner, open seven days a week.

Mexico Beach

The Fish House Restaurant, US 98, (850) 648-8950. Breakfast, lunch, dinner, open seven days a week.

Toucan's Bar & Restaurant, US 98, (850) 648-8207. Lunch, dinner, open seven days a week.

Beach Pizza . . . And Much More, US 98, (850) 648-4600. Dine in, takeout, delivery, lunch, dinner, closed Sundays.

Marinas, Marine Supplies and Service, Bait-and-Tackle Shops, and Launching Ramps

Port St. Joe

Half Hitch Tackle, 212A US 98, (850) 227-7100. Live and frozen bait, extensive tackle. The Half Hitch chain of bait-and-tackle stores is well-known for good service and reliable local fishing reports.

Bluewater Outriggers, US 98 West, (850) 229-1100, www.bluewater outriggers.com. Tackle, live and frozen bait, clothing, dive gear, fly-fishing gear, kayaks. A fishing, hunting, diving, and kayaking super-store. It's lots of fun.

Port St. Joe Marina, Marina Drive, (850) 227-9393, www.psjmarina. com. Full-service marina, dockage, gas and diesel, live and frozen bait, tackle, restrooms, laundry. This big marina is located near the center of Port St. Joe. It's within walking distance of restaurants, lodging, grocery stores, and tackle shops.

Presnell's Bayside Marina & RV Resort, CR 30, (850) 229-2710 www. presnells.com. $10 boat ramp, RV park, bait and tackle. Presnell's limits boat launches to 50 per day, as trailer parking is limited. The boat ramp closes at 6:30 p.m. daily.

Indian Pass Marine, CR 30, (850) 229-9700. Boats, service and supplies. Located across from Presnell's.

Indian Pass Ramp, CR 30B, on Indian Lagoon, Free paved ramp, adjacent to campground, adequate parking. There is also access to the beach for cars and trucks here.

Port St. Joe City Ramp, 5th Street, on St. Joseph Bay. Double ramp.

St. Joseph Peninsula State Park Ramp, SR 30E, single ramp. Good access to the middle of St. Joseph Bay. The ramp is on Eagle Harbor, on the bay side.

Highland View boat ramp, US 98 at Gulf County Canal. Free, paved single ramp, restrooms. Launching here can be difficult as there is heavy traffic on this section of the canal. However, this ramp offers excellent access to the bay.

Mexico Beach

Marquardt's Marina, 3905 US 98, (850) 648-8900, www.marquardts marina.com. Boat and motor sales, storage, extensive tackle, frozen bait, gas, boat ramp, boat rentals.

City of Mexico Beach Boat Ramp, 3700 US 98. Paved ramp. Using this ramp entails backing across the highway. Parking is available just to the west in some trailer parking lots.

Miramar Boat Ramp, Miramar Drive at Circle Drive. Paved ramp. Located just past the Mexico Beach Canal, this ramp is closer to the trailer parking area. It has no parking whatsoever.

Mexico Beach Fishing Pier, 37th Street, off US 98. Public fishing pier, restrooms.

Local Guides

Port St. Joe

Capt. Gary "Red" Goodrich, (850) 229-3474. Inshore and nearshore.

Capt. Trey Landry, (850) 227-9720, www.captaintrey.com. Inshore.

Capt. Danny Tankersley, (850) 227-1200, www.charismacharters.com. Offshore.

Capt. Jeff Lassiter, (850) 819-8471. Offshore and nearshore.

Capt. Earl Middleton, (850) 229-8034. Inshore and offshore.

Capt. Bobby Burkett, (850) 229-8074. Inshore and scalloping trips.

Mexico Beach

Capt. Chris Wiwi, (850) 258-6359. Inshore and nearshore.

Capt Clint Moore, (850) 229-8039. Inshore and nearshore.

Capt. Chip Blackburn, (850) 527-6272, www.charterboat-missmary.com. Offshore.

Capt. Chuck Guilford, (850) 648-8211, www.charismacharters.com. Offshore.

Many guides from Panama City and Apalachicola are familiar with the waters in and near St. Joseph Sound. Please consult the listings for those areas, if necessary. Also the Web site of the Florida Guides Association (www.florida-guides.com) has a complete listing of United States Coast Guard licensed-and-insured fishing guides.

14

Panama City

Sandy beaches, water parks, miniature golf courses, and rowdy college kids. Where? Panama City, of course. At least, that's how some potential visitors perceive this central panhandle town, located northwest of Cape San Blas between Port St. Joe and Destin. In addition, and of interest to fisher-folk, is the fact that Panama City is one of Florida's premier fishing areas due to its complex estuarine backwaters and proximity to the depths of the northern Gulf of Mexico.

Panama City sits just inside St. Andrew Pass, which leads from the deep gulf to St. Andrew Bay. Panama City Beach is on the western side of the pass, while Tyndall Air Force Base takes up much of the eastern shore. The name of the small bay just inside the pass is called St. Andrew Bay. The balance of the backwaters here comprises three bodies of water, creatively named East, North, and West Bays. Creeks draining lands from the north feed each of these bays, and the combination of fresh water from the north and salt water from the gulf result in some spectacular inshore fishing. And from an offshore-fishing perspective, what's better than having sixty feet of crystal-clear gulf water only two miles from the beach and an excellent artificial reef system?

Yes, the Panama City area can be crowded at times, particularly near the beaches. And please understand that Spring Break is not a great time to trailer a large boat down Thomas Drive in a rush to get

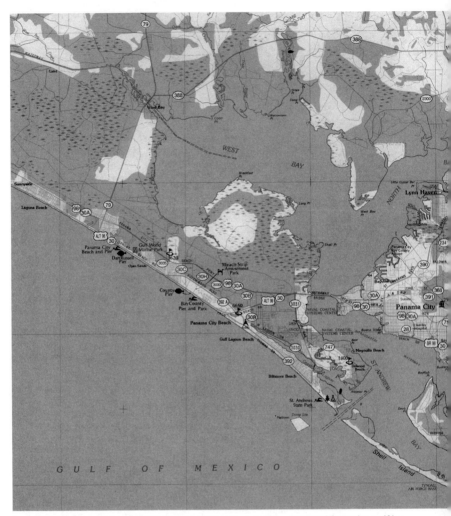

Panama City proper sits between East and West Bays, and is protected from the gulf by well-populated beach islands.

to the St. Andrews State Park boat ramp on the Grand Lagoon. On the other hand, there are many other less-stressful options for fishermen here.

The folks at Panama City understand the needs of fishermen as well as those of beach bunnies, and provide both with appropriate amenities and services.

Inshore and Nearshore Fishing at Panama City

Where to fish, where to fish? First, consider what fish species you're likely to find in the inshore and nearshore waters of the bay system and the Panama City beaches. Consider what the areas looks like, from a bird's-eye view.

On close inspection of a marine or fishing chart you'll likely be awed by the complexity of the bays and feeder creeks here. Where creeks along much of Florida's peninsula feed into relatively shallow water, here they feed into bays that are structured much like deep rivers. For example, the necks between East Bay or North Bay and St. Andrew Bay have depths in excess of fifty feet. As one of only a few deep passes along the Emerald Coast, St. Andrew Pass offers excellent access to the gulf for anglers willing to leave the protection of the bays and wishing to fish the deep water near the shoreline. What all this means is that there are few species *not* found in any of the bays or along the beach shorelines. Yes, slot-sized redfish, flounder, sheepshead, and trophy sea trout are often found in the brackish upper reaches of North Bay. Yes, cobia and bull reds are caught all along the beaches from spring to fall. Yes, Spanish mackerel are found throughout the inshore bays, particularly in late summer. And while you'll not find red snapper, marlin, or sailfish close to shore here, understand that offshore species such as gray snapper (mangrove snapper), grouper, and king mackerel are sometimes caught in the deep waters of St. Andrew Bay. Anglers even find lots of pompano in the late summer in the bay and on the beaches.

Panama City's East Bay stretches (unofficially) from Long Point (N30 06.137 W85 36.184) to the mouth of Wetappo Creek, the eastern entry point of the Intracoastal Waterway (N30 01.615 W85 23.484). The significant fisheries are the creeks and bayous on the northern side and the shoreline along the southern side. East Bay is primarily known for its redfish, flounder, and sea trout. Sheepshead are also found along the pilings of the DuPont Bridge at Long Point during the cooler months. Be on the lookout for active bait, mostly mullet, along the entire length of this fifteen-mile bay. If there are big mullet, there are likely to be redfish underneath them searching the stirred-

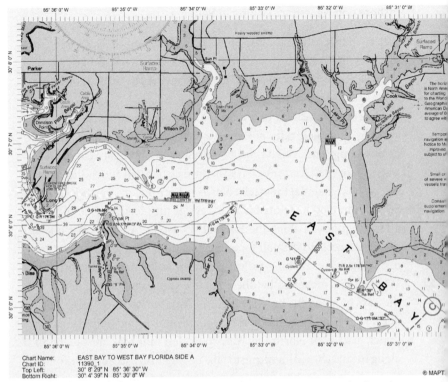

Chart Name:	EAST BAY TO WEST BAY FLORIDA SIDE A
Chart ID:	11390_1
Top Left:	30° 8' 29" N 85° 36' 30" W
Bottom Right:	30° 4' 39" N 85° 30' 8" W

© MAPT

East Bay at Panama City is more than a muddy backwater. Fed by a multitude of creeks and littered with shell bars, it offers a variety of fishing opportunities.

up water for crustaceans. If there are smaller mullet, you may notice big sea trout or reds actually striking them. If there are finger mullet or small schools of killifish (mud minnows), expect to find a flounder, especially if you're near the edge of a deep drop-off or alongside a bar. On the southern side, concentrate your efforts during a rising tide along the shore between Goose Point (N30 04.464 W85 31.564) and Strange Point (N30 02.060 W85 29.906). The combination of creeks and bays, some with oysters, along this shore make perfect habitat for game fish.

On the northern side of East Bay, count on the outflow of creeks to carry baitfish toward the bay on falling tides. Finding the narrow spots in the creek channels will give you a good chance of finding reds and trout in the creek mouths during the colder months when they hunker down to stay warm on overcast days. On sunny winter days, expect them to chase bait up onto the banks as both the air and water temperatures increase. Both Laird Point (N30 07.229 W85 31.498) and the mouth of California Bayou (N30 05.192 W85 29.690) have deep sloughs bordered by shallow flats. Little Sandy Creek's marsh grass edges also provide good forage grounds for predators waiting just outside the creek's mouth (N30 03.356 W85 26.226).

West Bay and the smaller North Bay are similar to East Bay, but not quite as deep in their middle grounds. These bays do, however, hold expanses of shallows that make them excellent for trout, reds, and flounder in almost any season.

The northern shore from West Bay Creek (N30 17.218 W85 50.927) past Coon Point (N30 17.138 W85 47.539) to the mouth of Burnt Mill Creek (N30 17.942 W85 45.697) is a good one to drift or pole in search of mullet schools. Depending on the season, Warren Bayou (N30 16.436 W85 44.578) and the power-plant hot-water discharge

Inexperienced anglers are often pleased after a professionally guided trip to West Bay at Panama City.

can also be productive. In cold weather, there may be fisheries regulations in force regarding the keeping of fish from the discharge. Following a big winter frontal system, many inshore species are attracted to the warm water here, and despite the prohibition of taking fish home, catching them is still fun.

The southern shore of West Bay has a couple of places that act as eddies for moving water, trapping bait and predators. The shoreline between Botheration Bayou's mouth (N30 13.980 W85 49.723) and Breakfast Point (N30 15.348 W85 48.032) is shallow and can be especially active on sunny winter afternoons. Another good cool-weather spot is the deep cut that runs into the center of Harrison Bayou (N30 13.597 W85 45.799), just north of Shell Point, around the corner from the Hathaway Bridge boat ramps.

North Bay resembles a large river and is navigable to the Deer Point Dam (N30 16.038 W85 36.323), about six miles northeast from West Bay Point (N30 13.967 W85 43.198). West Bay Point marks the natural divide between West Bay and North Bay. The southern shore of North Bay is fairly populated, but there's good fishing year-round for trout and reds around structure, including the pilings of the power lines at Little Oyster Point (N30 15.036 W85 40.860). These pilings also hold lots of sheepshead during cold weather. On the northern shore, the mouths of Newman Bayou (N30 15.888 W85 40.330) and Gainer Bayou (N30 16.334 W85 37.482) are also worth investigating—and stopping to fish should there be baitfish present.

There are several successful techniques for fishing a mixed shoreline such as the ones at Panama City. If you're not accustomed to lots of casting, consider using live shrimp, D.O.A. shrimp—root beer is a good color to use here—and mud minnows or pinfish under popping corks. Hook your bait to a leader of 20-pound-test fluorocarbon so that it hovers just above the bottom. After casting, give the cork a pop every twenty or thirty seconds, then wait for the strike. If you're using live bait, try using a 4/0 or 5/0 circle hook and you won't even have to set the hook.

If you don't mind the work, casting topwater plugs will probably catch bigger fish, especially trout. Also, there's nothing quite like the thrill of seeing a fish eat a topwater lure in the early morning or late afternoon. You'll find the combination of light spinning tackle, 10-pound-test PowerPro line and a Heddon Super Spook Jr. is hard to beat as your go-to outfit for inshore species almost anywhere. Remember that long casts are important when tossing artificial lures, as is a stealthy approach to the area. Don't motor to these spots at full speed and expect to start catching fish right away. Push poles, trolling motors, kayaks, and canoes all make stealth easier to accomplish.

If you're bottom-fishing along the edges of the deep channels, you'll do well with a simple slip-sinker rig or knocker rig made with a fluorocarbon leader and a circle hook. Use a 4/0 or 5/0 hook for trout, flounder, or slot-sized reds. The same rig will also work for sheepshead, but J-style hooks seem to work better on these toothy critters. Each style of hook holds cut bait, live shrimp, and pinfish well. Another option for sheepshead is a light jig baited with a live shrimp or small crab. Tear the tail off a live shrimp and thread it upward to the jig head or simply hook a fiddler crab through the body. Start fishing and neither will last very long.

The most difficult part of the Panama City inshore fishery to explain is St. Andrew Bay, and any discussion of the bay will leads to techniques for fishing any of the deep water in any of the local bays. Of course, there are shallow edges at places along all of St. Andrew Bay, but fishermen need to be aware that this is a busy waterway and small boats and large ones don't necessarily mix. If you fish a smallish inshore boat, remember that it takes a big boat a long while to slow and stop, so don't dilly-dally or anchor in channels or main waterways. There's plenty of water to fish in the three other bays and a lot more leeway.

I'm a sucker for trolling any deep channel that's fed by both the gulf and the backwaters. When the Spanish mackerel start to feed on bait pods swept inshore by the currents, it's hard to resist getting out the light tackle. Expect to find mackerel from spring through fall in St. Andrew Bay and even around Camelback Shoal (N30 06.610 W85 41.262) toward East Pass (N30 03.795 W85 37.112), an access point to the gulf that's usually silted in and not navigable. Either #00 Clarkspoons tipped with a small strip of synthetic bait (FishBites) or mullet belly or Flowering Floreo jigs are a good choice for Spanish mackerel. Remember to troll around the bait pods rather than through them.

Other possible targets for anglers wishing to troll these channels in the summer months are grouper and king mackerel. My choice for a trolling lure would be a Mann's Neptune 4D Stretch 25+ or one of the smaller, shallower-running 20+ models in the blue-herring color. These brilliantly colored plugs run deep but not so much as to foul the bottom in these channels. Pulled at about four knots and rigged with wire leaders on 20-pound PowerPro, they should interest both species. Trolling a live blue runner (hard tail) on a stinger rig would also work well for king mackerel, but you might have to cruise a bit more slowly or even use a planer to get the bait down deep.

Nearshore fishing along the beaches can be sporadic, depending on the amount of activity ashore. (Swimmers can be a nuisance.) The highlight of the fishing year is the spring cobia run, which usually starts in late March and lasts several months. They usually come close to shore at St. Andrew Pass and migrate westward. Cobia are usually sight-fished along the beaches with 30-pound-class spinning tackle and colorful bucktail jigs or live eels. Spanish and king mackerel are also plentiful off the beaches during the warmer months—the larger of each species are caught in the fall after fattening up all summer. Trolling spoons or jigs for either works well, but be sure to use wire leaders. Big spawning redfish always begin to show up around the pass and its jetties in late summer. Many say the time of the big full moon in September marks their arrival. Cut bait, finger mullet, pin-fish, and live shrimp are all excellent natural baits, but light-tackle anglers wishing to cast to the jetties often use sinking D.O.A. Bait Busters (chartreuse or gold) or larger versions of the D.O.A. Glow Shrimp.

Finally, there's no disadvantage to being a shore-bound angler in Panama City. Actually, those having access to beaches and private shorelines sometimes have an advantage, in that they're fishing less-pressured waters. Wading is popular along beaches, but care needs to be taken near some creeks, as muddy bottoms are not fun to tread. There are also public marinas that allow anglers to fish from docks and seawalls as well as a several good fishing piers. The Dan Russell Pier is an excellent long pier with a full-service tackle shop, located west of the pass. The two smaller piers within the St. Andrews State Park are nearer St. Andrew Pass. There is also good access to beach wading and jetty-fishing in the state park.

Offshore Fishing at Panama City

I generally assume nothing. But, in the case of the existence of live bottom west of Cape San Blas, I'll assume that there's very little to be found. Most of the offshore fishing along the Emerald Coast takes place over wrecks, artificial reefs, seamounts, thermal edges, or weed lines created by winds and waves.

Given those possibilities, Panama City is a pretty good place to begin an offshore adventure. The deep waters of the gulf don't come as close to shore here as they do at Destin or Pensacola, but thirty-five miles isn't a bad run to find 200-foot depths, and some great artificial reefs and wrecks. If you're bound and determined to troll the blue

Man-made reefs are the basis for much of the offshore fishing at Panama City. This tugboat is bound for deeper, silent waters.

water for marlin and tuna at the 600-foot contour, you'll need to run toward the southwest at least fifty miles from Panama City.

Artificial reefs and wrecks are nothing more than homes for bait-fish and the predators that follow them around, seeking an easy meal. In the eastern Gulf of Mexico, chunks of upturned rocky bottom provide that structure, as do big sponges and sea grass beds. In the western gulf, it's been up to man to provide housing for fish, intentionally or unintentionally.

Since men started using boats to travel or fish, there have been wrecks. Those wrecks attracted fish, then fishermen. When the wrecks became over-fished or simply fewer in number, someone had the bright idea of building artificial reefs. The concept moved quickly from old refrigerators, washing machines, and junked cars to thoughtful (and more ecologically sound) structures such as reef balls, fish haven modules and towers, and even stripped-down ships and barges.

No better reef system exists than that sponsored and built by the Mexico Beach Artificial Reef Association (MBARA). Although their reefs are located to the southeast of Panama City, they're still worth the trip. The MBARA reefs are not in great depths, but their deployment and style has made them an excellent example of a true artificial reef system. MBARA's goal is to place at least 1,000 reefs, and they're well on track to do so. A complete listing of the MBARA reefs is available on the Internet at www.mbara.org.

For the most part, artificial reefs are not placed in water that's too distant or too deep. The concept is to provide fishing that's accessible and safe for the average angler. For example, MBARA placed a 195-foot steel barge on the bottom in seventy-one feet of water in 2001. This wreck, at N29 53.195 W85 32.850, is just three miles from the entrance to the Port St. Joe channel and sixteen miles from the Panama City Sea Buoy (N30 05.597 W85 46.191).

Another popular wreck, also sunk as a reef but not by MBARA, is the *Accokeek*, a 143-foot Navy tugboat. The *Accokeek*, located at N29 58.475 W85 51.915, is in about 100 feet of water just ten miles off the beach at Panama City. Other placed wrecks are the USS *Strength*

(N30 01.860 W85 42.670) and the USS *Grierson* (N30 00.000 W85 40.500). Some of these ships are popular with divers, but for anglers, they're worth investigating in hopes of finding more transient game species such as cobia, king mackerel, and amberjack.

There are other good reef areas closer to Panama City. Try the fish havens just to the north of the *Accokeek* at about N30 00.462 W85 52.157 or those due west of St. Andrew Pass at about N30 06.830 W85 49.530. These reefs are conglomerations of bridge rubble and more sophisticated reef materials, and are popular areas for bottom-fishing as well as trolling.

Plan to make the far offshore run into the deep blue waters of the northern gulf if you're in search of wahoo, dolphin (mahi-mahi), tuna, sailfish, or marlin. The Squiggles (approximately N29 30.000 W86 25.000) is about fifty miles from Panama City and in 600 feet of water. This general area is known for its massive weed lines and upwelling cool water, and is a good starting point for a bluewater trip. The Spur (N29 28.000 W86 53.000), at the top of DeSoto Canyon, is even farther—and three times as deep. A fishing expedition to the heart of the gulf is neither for weekend anglers nor the faint of heart. If you're either, hop aboard a charterboat with a professional captain and crew.

Surprisingly, the tackle and gear needed for fishing in sixty-five feet of water is just about the same that you'd use in 2,000 feet, only smaller. Also, there's not much bottom-fishing other than at the artificial reefs and wrecks, and they're relatively shallow. If you're bottom-fishing, it's important to have tackle with the power to handle not only the weight of the fish, but to move him quickly away from structure and get him to the surface.

Fishing for snapper is usually done over structure rather than beside it, and it requires less hefty tackle than does fishing for grouper. Long rods, six to seven feet long, and trolling reels (Shimano TLD20s and 30s) spooled with 30-pound-test PowerPro line make snapper fishing fun. Big spinning rigs work well for snapper, too. Good snapper rigs require two or three 5/0 to 8/0 circle hooks tied with 50-pound fluorocarbon leader material. Adjust your sinkers based on depth and current, but always have some 8-ouncers in your tackle box if you plan to fish in 100-foot depths. Snapper are pickier about what they eat than grouper are, making live bait your best choice. Chumming with commercially produced chum blocks can also help entice them nearer the surface.

Grouper are generally larger than even the biggest snapper and have a decided tendency to take your bait back into the structure, leaving you tugging against the reef rather than the fish. Bottom fishing for grouper is best done along the edges of structure. The object of the angler is to tease the fish away from its hiding place and to tackle him away from the reef or wreck. Begin the teasing process with frozen or cut bait such as squid, white bait, or even mullet. Then, once the frenzy starts, generally aided by smaller fish, get out the live bait—pinfish, menhaden, or alewives. Live bait is less likely to be eaten by smaller fish and usually will attract bigger grouper. Tackle for grouper doesn't need to be fancy. Simple one-speed 4/0 or 6/0 Penn Senator reels are fine, mounted on stubby six-foot boat rods. Having a fine-tuned drag system isn't important—many anglers tighten their star drags with hammers. Terminal tackle for grouper isn't pretty, either: An 80- to 100-pound monofilament leader is fine, as is heavy 50- to 80-pound PowerPro. Dropper rigs can be made with single or double 8/0 to 15/0 circle hooks. Many serious grouper fishermen make dozens of leaders in advance of an offshore trip, knowing they'll lose many during the course of the day.

Deep jigging, termed *butterfly jigging* by Shimano, has recently become a popular technique for fishing depths up to 300-feet. There are many versions of these relatively expensive jigs, which seem to be nothing more than bars of highly reflective metal to which you attach the hooks of your choice. Deep jigging is surprisingly effective on many species and successful when most other methods and baits, including live ones, don't interest game fish. As is the case with most high-end fishing gear, there are special rods, hooks, and leaders available at your local tackle outfitter.

Offshore trolling tackle is usually more sophisticated than that used for bottom fishing. Smooth-running drags are very important, as is trolling speed and the choice of baits. Unless you're trolling very shallow, which doesn't happen offshore of Panama City, you'll have plenty of time to get your inactive lines back to the boat and then concentrate on the hooked fish. This is where owning those relatively expensive high-speed and multi-speed reels such as the Shimano Tiagras and Trinidads pay off.

Most trollers in the deep gulf concentrate on the water column above structure and work the edges of bait pods holding there. King mackerel, dolphin, and wahoo are popular species, especially in the warmer months. Try different lure depths while trolling over wrecks or artificial reefs. Mann's Neptune Stretch 4D lures are flashy and have good swimming action. They are available in a variety of sizes, colors, and pre-set depths, and can be used with lighter 30-pound-class tackle. Use your Stretch lures to fish the water column from fifteen to forty feet (deeper if you use braided line such Power-Pro) and then use ballyhoo or cigar minnows rigged with skirted feather-style lures on the surface. Seven-inch Iland Tracker lures are good rigged to the nose of a frozen ballyhoo, and Iland's five-inch Sea Star lures are appropriate with smaller cigar minnows, live or dead.

Trolling the deep deep water is a matter of finding either the right temperature or structure in the form of weed lines. The same method of using carefully rigged ballyhoo or mackerel trolled along the surface will raise fish from amazing depths. If you're fishing here, expect your rods and reels to cost as much as an inshore boat. Fifty- and 80-class Tiagras and Penn International reels are *de rigueur*, as are satellite TVs, satellite phones, and on-board ice-makers.

Getting Around the Panama City Area

From the eastern end of East Bay to the western end of West Bay, there's about forty miles of marked Intracoastal Waterway (ICW). St. Andrew Pass intersects it about midway, forming St. Andrew Bay. North Bay wraps around the city and heads northeast for about ten miles. Using the bays, the marked channels (including the ICW), and St. Andrew Pass as references, navigating Panama City by water is easy.

Getting around by land isn't so easy. Blame all those creeks and points and beaches and islands that make local inshore fishing so good. US Highway 98 is the main east–west corridor through the Panama City area. From the east, you enter Panama City just north of Tyndall Air Force Base. Traffic can be congested before you reach the western side of town and the Hathaway Bridge over St. Andrew Bay. From the west, unless you have a beach destination, stay on US 98 rather than County Road (CR) 30, which is the crowded beach road. Thomas Drive, the main road from town to the beach, St. Andrews State Park, and the Grand Lagoon area, intersects US 98 just west of the Hathaway Bridge.

US 231 is the major highway heading northeast toward Marianna, Interstate 10, and Georgia. SR 77 heads more northerly from town and hits SR 20, as does SR 79 to the west. SR 20 is an excellent east–west artery from Tallahassee to the Ft. Walton Beach area. It's south of I-10 and surprisingly easy to travel.

Where to Stay

There's no shortage of lodging at Panama City and Panama City Beach. I've listed a few places to stay that are of interest to anglers in terms of convenience and location. True fisherman-friendly lodging is disappearing as the Panama City area grows and becomes more beach and resort-oriented. If you're trailering a boat to the area and plan to stay on or near Panama City Beach, I encourage you to call ahead and be sure there's suitable parking for your rig.

Lagoon Motel, 5915 N Lagoon Dr., Panama City Beach, (850) 235-1800, www.lagoonmotel.com. The Lagoon Motel has a dock on the lagoon, but trailer parking is very limited. It's conveniently located just off Thomas Drive before you reach Panama City Beach.

Hampton Inn, Panama City Beach, 2909 Thomas Dr., (850) 236-8988, www.hamptoninn.com. This hotel is near the beach and has adequate parking for trailers.

Quality Inn & Suites, 3602 W US 98, (850) 522-5200.

Comfort Inn, 4128 W US 98, (850) 763-0101.

Econo Lodge, 4411 W US 98, (850) 785-2700.

Sleep Inn, 5126 W US 98, (850) 763-7777.

These chain-style motels are all in Panama City near the Hathaway Bridge, Sun Harbor Marina, Carl Gray Park Ramp, the Hathaway Bridge Ramp, and Thomas Drive, which is the main route to Panama City Beach.

St. Andrews State Park, (850) 233-5140. Full facilities, camping, two fishing piers, beach and inshore access for fishermen, nature trails. Be sure to call ahead for reservations. This park is popular.

Where to Eat

Capt's Table Restaurant and Oyster Bar, 1110 Beck Ave., Panama City, (850) 767-9933. Fresh local seafood, lunch, dinner, closed Sundays. This restaurant, located just up the street from St. Andrews City Marina, is a local favorite. Don't miss this one.

Hunt's Oyster Bar, 1150 Beck Ave., Panama City, (850) 763-9645. Fresh local seafood, lunch, dinner, closed Sundays. Another local favorite not to be missed.

Thomas Drive Waffle & Omelet House, Thomas Drive, Panama City Beach, Breakfast, lunch, weekdays 6 a.m. to 2 p.m., open twenty-four hours on weekends. Located near the entry to St. Andrews State Park, this is a popular breakfast spot on weekends.

Flamingo Joe's Grill & Seafood, Thomas Drive, Panama City Beach, (850) 233-0600. Lunch and dinner Monday through Saturday; lunch Sunday. Call-ahead and drive-through service is available.

Captain Anderson's Restaurant, Lagoon Drive at the Grand Lagoon, Panama City Beach, (850) 234-2225. Dinner seven days a week. A Panama City Beach institution for more than 40 years, serving fresh local seafood.

Dock O' The Bay, 5505 Sun Harbor Rd., near the eastern end of the Hathaway Bridge, Panama City, (850) 913-8555. Seafood, lunch, dinner. Located at Sun Harbor Marina.

Marinas, Marine Supplies and Service, Bait-and-Tackle Shops, and Launching Ramps

Half Hitch Tackle, 2206 Thomas Dr., Panama City Beach, (850) 234-2621. Live and frozen bait, extensive tackle. The Half Hitch chain of bait-and-tackle stores is well-known for its service and accurate local fishing reports. This is their flagship store. Rod and reel repairs are done on the premises. An added attraction is the Twice-The-Ice ice-vending machine in the parking lot.

Howell Marine Supply, 3100 W US 98, three-miles east of the Hathaway Bridge, (850) 785-8548. Live and frozen bait, extensive tackle. Howell's is an excellent source for current local information. They also offer consolation to not-so-lucky anglers.

Pier Tackle at Dan Russell Pier, 16101 Front Beach Rd., Panama City Beach, (850) 230-5936. Live and frozen bait, tackle, pier-fishing gear. The pier has been undergoing renovation and may close for 2008. Pier Tackle is part of the Half Hitch Tackle chain of stores.

Panama Marine, 202 W. 6th St., (850) 785-4661. This is a *real* marine supply that sells parts, electronics, and repair supplies. There is also a Panama Marine store on Thomas Drive at Panama City Beach, but it's more consumer-oriented.

West Marine, 1338 W 15th St., Panama City, (850) 763-1844. Marine supplies, fishing tackle.

West Marine, 2225 Thomas Dr., Panama City Beach, (850) 234-2717. Marine supplies, fishing tackle.

Carl Gray Park Ramp, at Gulf Coast Community College, eastern end of Hathaway Bridge. Single shallow ramp, adequate parking, and picnic area. A good ramp for smaller boats.

Hathaway Bridge Ramp, southwestern end of Hathaway Bridge. Paved double ramp, limited parking. This ramp is steep and access involves a U-turn on US 98 if you're headed south.

St. Andrews State Park Ramp, inside park in Grand Lagoon. paved double ramp, ample parking, security, $5 park entry fee. This ramp offers the best access to St. Andrew Pass and to offshore fishing grounds.

West Bay Ramp, SR 79 at the southern end of the bridge. single ramp, adequate parking. This ramp affords good access for smaller boats to the upper reaches of West Bay and North Bay.

Leslie Porter Park Ramp, southeastern end of SR 77 bridge at Lynn Haven. Four paved ramps, good parking. Launch here to fish the upper reaches of North Bay.

Marina Civic Center Ramp, behind civic center at the end of Harrison Street, Panama City. Free paved double ramp. A relatively steep ramp, it does have a nice protective breakwater and plenty of parking nearby.

St. Andrews City Marina Ramp, W 10th Street, Panama City. Paved double ramp. A busy ramp, maneuvering your rig may be difficult.

Dolphin Avenue Ramp, off Thomas Drive on Grand Lagoon.

Safari Avenue Ramp, off Sunset Avenue on Grand Lagoon, Panama City Beach, free, paved single ramp. These residential ramps have no parking. If you have a place to store your trailer, they are very convenient.

Earl Gilbert Park Ramp, northwestern end of DuPont Bridge. Paved single ramp, adequate parking. The current can make launching difficult here, but there is good access to the ICW and East Bay. The ramp is convenient to Tyndall Air Force Base.

There are two excellent public marinas in the area, Panama City Municipal Marina and St. Andrews City Marina. Each can handle craft of all sizes and have good launching ramps. Most commercial boats, including the charter fleet, are based at St. Andrews Marina. Both are conveniently located and offer easy access to St. Andrews Pass, the gulf and the ICW.

Panama City Municipal Marina, end of Harrison Street, Panama City, (850) 763-4696. Dockage, fuel, bait, convenience store, showers, restrooms, boat ramp, adjacent to downtown and civic center)

St. Andrews City Marina, W 10th St., Panama City, (850) 872-7240. Dockage, fuel, bait, convenience store, restrooms, boat ramp, adjacent to local restaurants.

Treasure Island Marina, Thomas Drive on Grand Lagoon, Panama City Beach, (850) 234-6533. Twenty-four-hour gas and diesel service, dry storage, dockage, convenience store, marine supplies, tackle, sanitary pump station, adjacent restaurants. This beach marina offers good access to St. Andrews Pass and the gulf.

Several excellent marinas are located at Panama City, including two municipal operations.

Charter boats abound at Panama City.

Lighthouse Marina, Thomas Drive on Grand Lagoon, Panama City Beach, (850) 234-5609. gas and diesel, dry storage, dockage, parts and service, bait and tackle, adjacent restaurants. This beach marina offers good access to St. Andrews Pass and the gulf. There is also a sizeable charter-boat fleet located here.

Sun Harbor Marina, at Hathaway Bridge, Panama City, (850) 785-0551. Dry storage, dockage, fuel, restaurant. Good access to the ICW.

Local Fishing Guides

Capt. Pat Dineen, (850) 376-0400, flyliner@cox.net, www.flyliner. com. Inshore and nearshore, light-tackle and fly fishing.

Capt. Chris Wiwi, (850) 258-6359, chriswiwi@yahoo.com. Inshore and nearshore, light-tackle.

Capt. Gjuro Bruer, Santa Rosa Island, (850) 685-5756, shallowwater expeditions@hotmail.com, www.shallowwaterexpeditions.com. Inshore and offshore, light-tackle and fly fishing.

Capt. David Mangum, Santa Rosa Island, (850) 496-0594, shallow waterexpeditions@hotmail.com, www.shallowwaterexpeditons.com. Inshore and offshore, light tackle and fly fishing.

Capt. Carroll Lamb, Capt. Charles Lamb, (850) 625-4047, www.bay watchcharters.com. Inshore, nearshore, light-tackle and fly fishing.

Capt. Kyle Pitts, (850) 258-6602, kp4747@aol.com, www.hightide guide.com. Inshore and nearshore, light-tackle.

Capt. Bob Zales II, (850) 763-6242, bobzales@att.net, www.fishpc. com. Offshore, bluewater.

Capt. Todd Jones, (850) 819-5829, www.backbayadventures.com. Inshore, light-tackle, and fly fishing.

Capt. Keith Page, (850) 596-4491, www.pcbfishing.com. Offshore, blue water.

Capt. Mike Williams, (850) 265-6856. Offshore.

Capt. Shawn McGowan, (850) 235-2781. Offshore.

Capt. Jim Crowell, (850) 819-4625. Offshore.

Capt. Anderson's Deep Sea Fishing, 1-800-874-2415, www.captandersons marina.com, captanders@aol.com. Party-boat fleet fishing from Panama City Beach.

Jubilee Deep Sea Fishing, (850) 236-2111, www.jubileefishing.com, deepseafishing_2000@yahoo.com. Party-boat fishing from Panama City Beach.

Many guides from Mexico Beach, Port St. Joe, and Destin are familiar with the waters at Panama City. Please consult the listings for those areas, if necessary. Also the Web site of the Florida Guides Association (www.florida-guides.com) has a complete listing of U.S. Coast Guard licensed-and-insured fishing guides.

15

Destin and Fort Walton Beach

The communities of Destin and Fort Walton Beach bustle—as do the upscale beachside "neo-villages," such as Santa Rosa Beach, along County Road (CR) 30A—especially during tourist season, which never seems to end. Amenities such as lodging and restaurants are abundant here, and in many cases, excessive. The beach crowd never seems to tire of miniature golf, fudge parlors, or quaint shopping areas with an up East flair. Luckily, the area's fishing heritage and importance as one of Florida's great fishing destinations hasn't been overlooked by the people who promote its development and advancement—its popularity as a fishing destination is usually ranked higher than its popularity as a beach destination.

Inshore and Nearshore Fishing at Destin, Fort Walton Beach, and Choctawhatchee Bay

At first glance, you'd think that Choctawhatchee Bay is a large, slow-moving backwater. However, its depth, combined with its numerous feeder creeks, eastern rivers, and a huge volume of water from the Gulf of Mexico that's pumped through Destin Pass, make the bay an excellent inshore fishery.

The shallow eastern end of the bay is made up of several river estuaries. The Intracoastal Waterway (ICW) from Panama City also enters the bay here at N30 22.812 W86 07.062. The outflow from Black

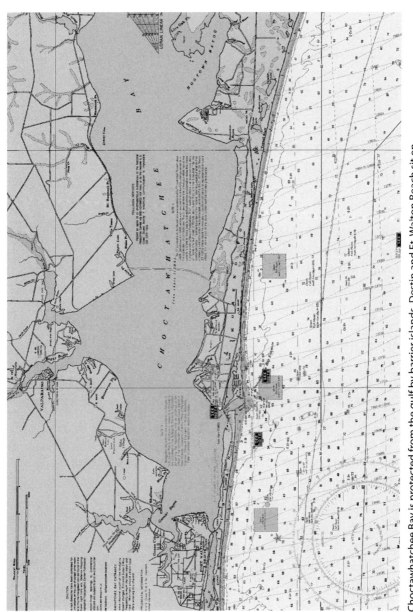

Choctawhatchee Bay is protected from the gulf by barrier islands. Destin and Ft. Walton Beach sit on either side of Destin Pass, the only outlet to the Gulf of Mexico.

Creek and the rivers (Mitchell, Indian, Cypress, and Choctawhatchee) dump fresh water into the bay. This area, including the eastern side of the US Highway 331 bridge, is good habitat for trout, redfish, and flounder, which is the predominant species in Choctawhatchee Bay. The bridge structure and causeways make for good fishing, as does the spoil bank that runs diagonally across the back of the bay. The entire eastern shoreline from Jolly Bay (N30 25.377 W86 08.541) to Bunker Cove (N30 23.364 W86 07.141) is a good location for throwing topwater lures in summer or slow-sinking lures in winter.

To the west of the US 331 bridge, both the southern and the northern shores of the bay are fringed by shallow grass flats. On the northern shore, there are a few spots with good access for wade-fishermen, including the Bay Flats Recreation Area just east of Choctaw Beach off State Road (SR) 20. Canoe and kayak fishermen are also successful along this shoreline, as well as in Alaqua Creek and along the shoreline toward and into LaGrange Bayou (N30 26.911 W86 11.337). On the southern side of the eastern bay, Hogtown Bayou offers some pretty good action year-round. It's also protected from the winds, and its boat ramp is popular with folks staying at the beachside communities on CR 30A. The deep center channel, beginning at N30 24.468 W86 16.524, is good for trout and reds in the winter when the fish seek refuge from the cold. In late summer, expect schools of jack crevalle to be crashing bait along the edges, and reds and big trout to be hunting along the grassy points. The grassy edge along Alligator Point (N30 25.137 W86 16.030) is home to some pretty nice fish, many ending up in the coolers of visiting fishermen.

As you move westward in Choctawhatchee Bay, the bottom deepens and there's a better chance your fishing will be influenced by the gulf waters flowing through the pass. Sheepshead are frequently caught on live shrimp near the pilings of the Mid-Bay Bridge, which runs from White Point (N30 27.112 W86 25.293) southward to the heart and soul of Destin's commercial district—the Bass Pro Shops store. In the deeper water here, and toward Fort Walton Beach and Eglin Air Force Base, numerous wrecks can be found on the bottom if you understand how to patiently read the display on your depth sounder. Some of the wrecks are small, but most hold baitfish as well as jacks, Spanish mackerel, bluefish, gray snapper (mangrove), and big redfish during the fall. The closer the wreck to the pass, the more likely it will hold several species of game fish. You'll also notice that the closer you get to Destin Pass, the more likely you'll find sea grass beds fringing the shoreline.

The entire northern shore from Boggy Point (N30 28.750 W86 28.769) to Black Point (N30 25.789 W86 33.485) at Shalimar has good grass flats with hard bottom suitable for wading. The channels of Boggy Creek and Rocky Bayou are good for wintertime deep-water fishing, as each offers protection from the elements for both anglers and their prey. These channels also funnel lots of the backwater into the bay during almost any falling tide in any season. Try the deep spots at N30 25.789 W86 33.485 in Boggy Creek or at N30 29.597 W86 26.912 in Rocky Creek, for starters.

If the water's too cool for swimmers, there's some pretty good fishing just inside Destin Pass along the inshore side of Okaloosa Island. Nice grass flats stretch from the middle of the pass all the way to the shore, and redfish are frequent sight-fishing targets for light-tackle and fly-rod anglers. Once the water warms, however, forget the fishing here, as the big sandbar (Crab Island) inshore of the Destin Pass bridge will be covered with boats, their occupants partying day and night. In general, Destin Pass and its surrounding waters are best on falling tides, when lots of bait washes out into the gulf. Depending on the crowds, try trolling big plugs for shore-bound gag grouper and king mackerel, or chum up some sharks just outside the pass.

A final inshore fishing destination is Santa Rosa Sound, which extends the entire gulf coastline from Fort Walton Beach to Pensacola. With only two entrances, Destin Pass and Pensacola Pass, this 40-mile-long backwater has some excellent fishing, particularly along ruined docks, dredge islands, and grass flats (usually found closer to the passes). Try fishing at night from any of the newer docks that have lights, especially in the summer. Trout and flounder love to hang out under docks and in the deep troughs formed when boats back in and out of slips. Look for boats on lifts or davits, and carefully pitch

Crab Island, just inside Destin Pass, is often crowded with partiers. Some anglers, however, just never give up.

shrimp (live or artificial) or jigs (D.O.A. TerrorEyz, root beer color) under them or across any lighted edges around the dock itself.

Since Destin Harbor is actually outside the Destin Pass bridge, I'll consider beach fishing here to be nearshore fishing. The beaches are deep, but when species such as redfish, cobia, and tarpon, on their east-to-west migrations, come ashore west of the pass, they become excellent targets for anglers in smaller craft.

In Destin Pass itself, the shoals are almost fluid, and at many places the outside channel gets shallow. Also, be aware that a falling tide

The flats in Choctawhatchee Bay and the beaches at Destin and
Santa Rosa are excellent places to sight-fish for redfish.

bucking a big summer sea breeze can create rough seas and surf. Expect cobia to arrive in spring and stay along the beaches for a few months. Sight-fishing, using bay boats with high towers, is popular and productive. Big cobia are caught here using big flashy jigs, live eels, or crabs, often rigged to 30-pound-class spinning gear.

Fall is bull redfish season along the coast here and westward to Pensacola. These big fish come in from the deep gulf and cruise the beaches, eagerly feeding on just about anything in their paths, including schools of white bait. It's mostly sight-fishing, but lots are caught at the jetties around Destin Pass and at the Okaloosa Island Fishing Pier using live shrimp, live pinfish, or cut bait. Most sight-fishermen prefer topwater plugs such as MirrOlure Top Dogs (chartreuse or hot pink) or slow-sinking lures such as D.O.A. Bait Busters (#372 color, pearl-and-black, black-and-red chin). Depending on the surf activity and the need for more noise, a MirrOlure Popa Dog chugger will also attract strikes from these big fish. If you don't have a boat but have access to the beach, don't hesitate to try for big reds in the surf. They are sometimes so close as to be seen silhouetted in the cresting waves. Expect to find Spanish mackerel and bluefish along the beaches, too. Just keep your eyes peeled for birds wheeling over schools of baitfish. Cast small jigs (Flowering Floreos) to the edges of the bait pods, or troll small #00 ClarkSpoons attached to short lengths of wire leader material.

Inshore fishing techniques for most of Choctawhatchee Bay are straightforward and fairly simple. In warm weather, expect the shallow water bite to be best early, before the water and the weather get uncomfortably hot for game fish—and anglers. Look for baitfish along the shorelines, and work the area thoroughly with quickly re-trieved topwater lures, such as the Heddon Super Spook, Jr. If you're not an accomplished caster, try live or artificial shrimp (D.O.A. glow version) under popping corks. Attach your bait with just enough fluorocarbon leader to keep it just above the bottom and give it a hard *pop* every so often. The noise from the cork will give an impression that baits are being struck and will increase interest by predators in whatever you're offering.

In cool or even cold weather, expect the predators to be sluggish and not necessarily aggressive. Don't even try to entice them on overcast days, but if the sun shines and the tide is rising in the afternoon, try slow-sinking lures such as MirrOlure Catch 2000s or Corky Mullet fished over the shallows. Move them just enough to keep them from getting snagged, as wintertime fish are not anxious to expend much energy in order to catch a meal.

If you fish the deeper drop-offs along bridge causeways or deep channels, try using a lure that will get near the bottom, where the fish are huddling to keep warm in the winter or cool in the summer. MirrOlure TTs (red holographic) or almost any variety of soft bait attached to a jig head will do. Tipping the jig head with a piece of FishBites or frozen shrimp will improve your chances for trout, reds, and even flounder. If you're a serious meat fisherman, try live shrimp, fiddler crabs, or cut mullet chunks on 5/0 or 6/0 circle hooks rigged knocker-style—then sit back and enjoy the fishing.

Offshore Fishing from Destin and Fort Walton Beach

If inshore fishing here is good, offshore fishing here is off the charts—in a manner of speaking. Yes, while most offshore anglers in Florida are happy to fish in water measured in hundreds of feet, it's hundreds of fathoms that bring smiles to the faces of Destin's deep-water fishermen and women.

Destin's close-in offshore fishing is all about structure, most of it artificial. To the west of Cape San Blas and Port St. Joe, the gulf's floor is mostly flat and devoid of natural or live structure. Offshore anglers along this stretch of coast rely on artificial structure, ranging in size from small concrete reef balls to sunken aircraft carriers that attract bait and the predators that follow them.

If you're fishing in less than 100 feet, you probably aren't too far offshore of Destin. The Timber Hole (N30 10.100 W86 55.000) is a popular bottom-fishing spot in about 100 feet of water. A good general area for red and gray snapper, grouper, amberjack, bonito, and even a random king mackerel, the Timber Hole is only about twenty-five miles southwest of Destin Pass. In the summer, expect reefs such as this one to attract stray wahoo or dolphin (mahi-mahi) away from their usual deep bluewater hangouts.

Another popular spot is the wreck of the *Hayward*, a WWII-vintage Liberty Ship. Located at N30 18.270 W86 36.240 in less than ninety feet of water, the *Hayward* is only seven miles from Destin Pass. With lots of relief, it attracts as many bottom-dwelling species as the deeper wrecks and reefs. Three popular local wrecks and artificial reefs are the *Miss Janet* (N30 15.750 W86 23.750, ten miles southeast of the pass in ninety feet), the Eglin #1 Reef (N30 15.920 W86 23.160, near the *Miss Janet*), and the *Walton Hopper* barge (N30 19.690 W86 22.900, a bit closer to shore in seventy feet). Other close-to-shore fish havens are two artificial reefs located just a mile or two off the beach. These reefs (N30 21.814 W86 29.908 or N30 22.054 W86 35.577) sit in about fifty to seventy feet of water but are busy with anglers and fish, particularly king and Spanish mackerel in the summer and cobia during the spring run. Or, try the wreck of the *Miss Louise* at N30 22.340 W86 25.340 nearer the beach in sixty feet.

Trolling deep-diving plugs such as Mann's 4D Stretch 30+ near the bottom is a good method for the bigger species, including gag grouper, in water less than 100 feet deep. You might also try covering several parts of the water column over these structures, as other species hang out above structure rather than inside it. Pull a 4D Stretch 15+ mid-column and a live (or frozen) cigar minnow rigged on a feather near the surface. Trolling for bottom fish requires heavier tackle than does trolling for pelagic speedsters. Experienced grouper fishermen use shorter rods rigged with 4/0 and 6/0 Penn boat reels and sometimes adjust their star drags as tightly as possible. 30- to 50-pound-test PowerPro braided line will help pull the fish away from structure, too. The upper reaches of the water column is probably better fished with lighter gear, such as Shimano's TLD-30 level-wind trolling reels spooled with as much 20- to 30-pound line as they'll hold. Many anglers use monofilament line for this application, using the line's stretch to avoid pulling the hook prematurely. Drags are best set moderately, allowing the initial burst of speed from a king mackerel or wahoo to give you time to clear your other lines from behind the boat. Never put all your trolled baits at the same depth or all your eggs in one basket!

Bottom-fishing the waters just offshore of Destin to depths of about 100 feet is a straightforward process. Big rods and reels are required, and high-speed retrieve systems are handy. Spend a day aboard a head boat and learn how much work is involved in hours of winding up 100 feet of line with an eight-ounce sinker. Use 50- to

80-pound line. Super braids such as PowerPro are more sensitive to a fish's bite at these depths. Use 8/0 to 11/0 circle hooks on the terminal end of a 100-pound-test monofilament leader for good results. Make up several spare multiple-hook dropper rigs, and use as much weight as is necessary to quickly reach the bottom. The deeper you fish and the more rapid the current, the more weight is needed. Two- and three-ounce sinkers are just too small for 100-foot depths. Use baits that are seasonally available. Many local anglers prefer to start fishing the perimeter of a wreck or reef with cut bait, such as squid or threadfin herring. They don't break out the live pinfish, alewives, or cigar minnows until the bigger fish come out of hiding onto the edges of the reef area. Of course, the bigger the species, the bigger the bait you'll need. Grouper will eat big pinfish and porgies. Snapper seem to enjoy small white bait (alewives, cigar minnows, sardines) and even live shrimp.

The big show at Destin is bluewater fishing for marlin, tuna, dolphin, swordfish, sailfish, and wahoo. On almost any day during the warmer months, big sportfishing boats leave Destin Harbor and head southwest toward the upper canyons of the gulf. If the twenty-five-mile run to the Timber Hole intimidates you, don't even think of heading toward the depths routinely fished by these big boats.

Of course, there's no bottom fishing out here. The Squiggles (N29 30.000 W86 25.000), about fifty miles due south of Destin Pass, is along the edge of the 100-fathom contour; that's 600 feet down and one of the closer spots routinely fished by Destin anglers. To the southwest, and well into waters south of Pensacola and Mobile, Alabama, other popular bluewater areas are the Spur (N29 28.000 W86 53.000, a 2,000-foot trench running eastward into 1,400 feet of water), the Wall (N29 14.040 W87 00.000, along the 2,000-foot contour, and the Steps (N29 14.000 W87 35.000, a canyon wall falling off into 4,000 feet). And then there's the granddaddy of them all, the Nipples, at N28 57.100 W87 35.000, in about 6,000 feet of water and about 100 miles from Destin Pass.

Trolling the contours, the upwelling thermal currents, and the weed lines that accumulate above them, is the way fishing is done out here. Fifty- and 80-pound-class rods and reels that rival the costs

A family trip on an offshore charter boat can be the adventure of a lifetime for a young angler.

of small inshore boats are the status quo aboard these big boats. In advance of the trip, ballyhoo and mackerel are rigged by the dozens to trolling feathers (blue-and-white Iland Lures' Sea Star or Cruiser series) and 10/0 to 12/0 hooks, just in case there's a feeding frenzy. Some captains troll bare feathers alongside the rigged baits, just to increase the odds of a strike. Noise isn't an issue, as diesels turn constantly and loud teasers and arrays of fake baits are pulled close to the boat to attract the interest of big fish.

In blue water, many hours of boredom often end with just a few minutes of absolute pandemonium. Fish strike, inactive lines are quickly reeled out of the way, and the angler is strapped to the fighting chair. What follows is work, and more work, ending with a gaff or a tag and a release—and a photo. And it's not even breakfast time!

Getting Around The Destin–Fort Walton Beach Area

Fort Walton Beach and Destin are located at the western end of Choctawhatchee Bay, between Panama City and Pensacola. The two communities are separated by a short section of Okaloosa Island–Santa Rosa Island, which actually runs from Destin Pass (East Pass) all the way to Pensacola, some forty miles to the west. Santa Rosa Sound runs behind the barrier island system to Navarre and on to Pensacola.

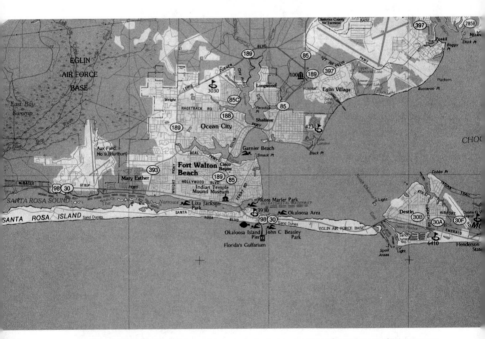

Ft. Walton Beach is at the eastern end of a long stretch of Intracoastal Waterway, which runs west to Navarre and then on to Pensacola and Perdido. Reprinted with permission from the full-color *Florida Atlas & Gazetteer*. Copyright DeLorme.

The main east–west throughway is US 98. Traveling from Panama City, you have the option of taking CR 30A through the congested but scenic beachfront communities of Seaside, Rosemary Beach, and Grayton Beach. If you're in a hurry to get to Destin or Fort Walton Beach from the east, stay on US 98. Fort Walton Beach has a quaint downtown and has been shaped by the existence of Eglin Air Force Base. The city has excellent amenities, and it's much cheaper to eat and stay there than at Destin, Okaloosa Island, or Santa Rosa Beach. After passing through Fort Walton Beach, US 98 follows Santa Rosa Sound to Navarre, Gulf Breeze, and Pensacola.

The main north–south arteries between this section of the Gulf Coast and I-10 are SR 85 from Fort Walton and US 331 from Santa Rosa Beach and the eastern end of Choctawhatchee Bay. Both intersect SR 20, which is an excellent east–west route through north Florida.

The ICW represents the main east–west channel through this area. It enters along the eastern edge of the bay and continues inland past Fort Walton Beach on to the Alabama line at Perdido. Expect some

Destin Pass can be quick moving—and crowded.

commercial traffic in the waterway. Destin Pass, also known as East Pass, is the only entrance to Choctawhatchee Bay from the Gulf of Mexico. Despite frequent dredging, it has a tendency to shoal, making access dangerous on lower tides or in stormy weather.

Where to Stay

There's no shortage of lodging at Destin, Okaloosa Island, and Fort Walton Beach. I've listed a few places to stay that are of interest to anglers in terms of convenience and location, but true fisherman-friendly lodging is disappearing as the area grows and becomes more beach and resort-oriented. Remember that the closer you stay to Destin or Okaloosa Island, the more expensive the lodging. And, if you're trailering a boat to the area and plan to stay on or near the beaches, I encourage you to call ahead and be sure there's suitable parking for your rig.

Destin

Comfort Inn, 19001 Emerald Coast Pkwy., (850) 654-8611. Lodging.

Holiday Inn Destin, 1020 E US 98, (850) 837-6181. Lodging.

Days Inn Destin, 1029 E US 98, (850) 837-4667. Lodging.

Hampton Inn, 1625 E US 98, (850) 654-2677. Lodging.

Extended Stay America, 4615 Opa Locka Lane, (850) 837-9830. Lodging, efficiencies.
This hotel is located on the eastern end of Destin, close to the eastern end of Choctawhatchee Bay.

Best Western Summerplace Inn, (850) 650-8003. Lodging.

Destin Harbor Inn & Marina, 500 E US 98, (850) 837-6171. Boat slips, adjacent marina, convenient restaurants.
Located on Destin Harbor.

Southern Resorts, 1-800-737-2322, www.southernresorts.com. Upscale condo and house rentals.
If you plan an extended stay at Destin or have a large party, consider

renting a condo. Southern Resorts represents a full range of excellent lodging.

Fort Walton Beach

There are several motels along US 98 in Fort Walton Beach that are convenient to the Liza Jackson Park and Ramp. They also have adequate parking for cars with trailers.

Fairway Inn, (850) 244-8663.

Quality Inn Bayside, (850) 275-0300.

Bayside Inn, (850) 243-6162.

Regency Inn, (850) 302-0460.

Hampton Inn Santa Rosa Island, 1112 Santa Rosa Blvd. (US 98), (850) 426-7866. Lodging.

Hampton Inn, Mary Esther, (850) 243-7700.
West of Fort Walton, but convenient to Liza Jackson Park and Ramp. Limited trailer parking in adjacent dirt lot.

Where to Eat

Destin

Donut Hole, two locations, Destin and Santa Rosa Beach, breakfast, lunch, dinner.
Don't drive by one of these places without stopping. The food is excellent, and the donuts are superlative. The Destin shop is open twenty-four hours.

Another Broken Egg, Baytowne Wharf at Harbor Boulevard (US 98). Breakfast, lunch.

AJ's Seafood & Oyster House, 116 E US 98, (850) 837-1913. Lunch, dinner, open seven days a week.

Lucky Snapper Restaurant, on Destin Harbor, (850) 654-0900. Lunch, dinner, open seven days a week.

Jim 'n Nick's Bar-B-Q, Baytowne Wharf, (850) 351-1991. Lunch, dinner, open seven days a week.
Decent 'cue from a national chain of restaurants.

Destin Diner, US 98 at Airport Road, (850) 654-5843. Breakfast, lunch, dinner, open seven days a week. Good solid food.

Fort Walton Beach

Original Waterfront Crab Shack, 104 Miracle Strip Pkwy. (US 98). Lunch, dinner, adjacent to yacht basin. Good seafood, relaxed atmosphere, a local favorite.

Hightide Restaurant & Oyster Bar, southern end of Brooks Bridge, Okaloosa Island, (850) 244-2624. Lunch, dinner, fried and grilled seafood, closed Sundays.

Sealands Restaurant, 47 Miracle Strip Pkwy., (850) 244-0044. Lunch, dinner, seafood, steaks, pasta.

Staff's Seafood Restaurant, 24 Miracle Strip Pkwy., (850) 243-3482. Lunch, dinner. Florida's oldest seafood restaurant.

Brooks Bridge Bar-B-Que and Café, 240 Miracle Strip Pkwy. (US 98), (850) 244-3003. Lunch, dinner, homestyle daily specials. A local favorite.

Rick's Crab Trap, 203 Brooks St., (850) 664-0110. Lunch, dinner, seafood—broiled, grilled, and fried.

Marinas, Marine Supplies and Service, Bait-and-Tackle Shops, and Launching Ramps

Destin

Half Hitch Tackle, 621 Harbor Blvd., (850) 837-3121. Live and frozen bait, extensive tackle. The Half Hitch chain of bait-and-tackle stores is well-known for good service and accurate local fishing reports.

Bass Pro Shops World Wide Sportsman, US 98 at Mid Bay Bridge

(CR 293) in Destin Commons Mall. Not as big as the chain's megastores but still a great source for tackle and fishing supplies.

West Marine, 862 E US 98, (850) 269-0636. Tackle, marine supplies.

Destin Harbor Inn & Marina, 500 E US 98, (850) 837-6171. Fuel, bait and tackle, boat slips, fishing dock, adjacent lodging, food. On Destin Harbor

Destin Marina, 7 Calhoun Ave., (850) 837-2470. $10 ramp, gas and diesel, frozen bait, overnight dockage available. Just across Destin Pass from Crab Island, this family-run marina is an anomaly when compared to the mega marinas in the area.

Joe's Bayou Ramp. Double ramp, $10 fee, adequate parking. This ramp is considered by many to be Destin's municipal ramp. It can be very crowded during the summer when partiers invade nearby Crab Island.

Choctawhatchee Bay

Choctaw Beach Ramp, SR 20 at Mullet Creek on the northern side of Choctawhatchee Bay. Single ramp, adequate parking. Access to Hammock Point flats and the Mid-Bay Bridge.

Basin Bayou Ramps, SR 20 at Basin Bayou. Limited parking. Good access to the Basin Bayou flats and the northern shore of the bay.

Gannon Park Ramp, SR 20 on Rocky Bayou at Niceville. Open dawn to dusk, adequate parking.

Niceville Public ramp, SR 20 at the upper end of Boggy Bayou. Good parking. Access the upper bay, Boggy Bayou, and Rocky Bayou from these ramps.

Black Creek Lodge, on Black Creek at the eastern end of Choctawhatchee Bay, (850) 835-2541. Boat ramp, bait, gas, dockage. The eastern end of Choctawhatchee Bay is shallow and estuarine. Launch here for good access.

Santa Rosa Beach

Many anglers visiting resorts at Santa Rosa Beach (Sandestin) and south Walton County (Grayton, Seaside, Seagrove, Alys, Seacrest, and Rosemary Beaches) find it convenient to hire a professional fishing guide rather than to bring their own boat. The closest access to the gulf for large boats is at Panama City or at Destin, but the Cessna, Wheeler Point, and Grayton Beach ramps are relatively close and convenient.

Charles Cessna Ramp, on Hogtown Bayou, CR 393 off US 98. Paved single ramp, adequate parking

Wheeler Point Ramps, on the northern causeway of the US 331 Bridge. Two ramps, adequate parking on the shoulder of the highway.

Grayton Beach State Park Ramp, in the state park. Small canoe and kayak ramp. Access to gulf unpredictable due to shoaling.

Fort Walton Beach

Fort Walton Beach Yacht Basin, 104 Miracle Strip Pkwy. (US 98) on Santa Rosa Sound, (850) 244-5725. Dockage, fuel, sanitary pump station, showers, adjacent to Original Waterfront Crab Shack.

Brooks Bridge Bait & Tackle, under the southern end of the Brooks Bridge, Santa Rosa Island, (850) 243-5721. Gas and diesel, $7 launching ramp, pontoon boat rentals, live and frozen bait, overnight trailer storage available.

West Marine, 4 SE Eglin Pkwy., (850) 244-9005. Marine parts, fishing tackle, clothing. One of the most complete West Marine stores on the Emerald Coast.

Auer Marine, 33 Beal Pkwy. NE, (850) 243-7163. Boat sales and service, marine supplies.

Okaloosa Island Fishing Pier, open 24/7, bait and tackle, rod rentals. See the Pier's Web site at www.okaloosaislandpier.com for up-to-date fishing reports.

Liza Jackson Park Ramp, 318 US 98. Restrooms, double boat ramp, near motels. This ramp probably offers the best access to the eastern end of Santa Rosa Sound and the Fort Walton section of the ICW.

Seaway Boat Ramp, Cinco Bayou. Double ramp, limited parking. Good access to the western end of Choctawhatchee Bay.

Shalimar Boat Ramp, Poquito Bayou Park on Hand Cove. Limited parking. Just north of Fort Walton, this ramp offers access to upper Garnier Bayou.

Local Fishing Guides

Capt. Pat Dineen, (850) 376-0400, flyliner@cox.net, www.flyliner. com. Inshore and nearshore, light-tackle, and fly fishing.

Capt. Rob Cochran, (850) 621-6956, rob6956@aol.com. Inshore and nearshore, light-tackle.

Capt. Leo Collins, (850) 654-1106. Light-tackle and fly fishing.

Capt. Alan Steele, (850) 217-1395, alan@bluebayoutfitters.com, www. bluebayoutfitters.com. Inshore, light-tackle, and fly fishing.

Capt. Gjuro Bruer, Santa Rosa Beach, (850) 685-5756, shallowwater expeditions@hotmail.com, www.shallowwaterexpeditions.com. Inshore and offshore, light-tackle and fly fishing.

Capt. David Mangum, Santa Rosa Beach, (850) 496-0594, shallow waterexpeditions@hotmail.com, www.shallowwaterexpeditons.com. Inshore and offshore, light-tackle and fly fishing.

Capt. Donnie Dineen, (850) 376-8399. Offshore, bluewater, and bottom fishing.

American Spirit Deep Sea Fishing, (850) 837-1293, www.newflorida girl.com, newflagirl2000@aol.com.

Party boats leaving from Destin are a good way for a shore-bound angler to experience the deep sea.

Many guides from Panama City, Navarre, and Pensacola are familiar with the waters near Destin and Fort Walton Beach. Please consult the listings for those areas, if necessary. Also the Web site of the Florida Guides Association (www.florida-guides.com) has a complete listing of U.S. Coast Guard licensed-and-insured fishing guides.

16

Navarre to Perdido, Including Pensacola

It's about the same distance from Jacksonville to Miami as it is from Jacksonville to L.A.—Lower Alabama, that is. And, while Pensacola's location at the western end of Florida's panhandle can make its residents feel detached—both geographically and politically—from the rest of the state, be assured Pensacola is a serious player in terms of inshore and offshore fishing.

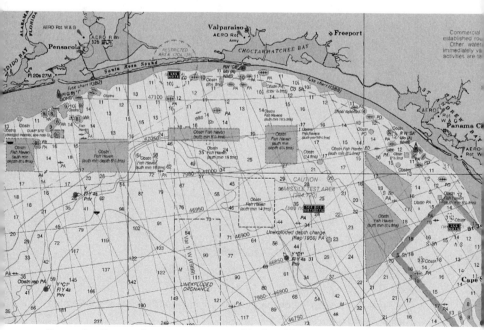

Pensacola offers excellent access to some of the best blue water fishing in Florida.

The Pensacola area actually extends from Navarre to Alabama and the Perdido River. Atop some of the Gulf of Mexico's deepest waters, Pensacola has a long history as an active port city. The city itself sits aside Pensacola Bay, which is protected from the gulf by both Santa Rosa Island and the peninsula forming Gulf Breeze. Pensacola Bay includes Escambia Bay to the north, Blackwater Bay to the northeast, and East Bay to the east. These three shallow bays are fed by rivers and creeks, making their upper reaches good habitat for many inshore game-fish species.

Santa Rosa Sound runs from Ft. Walton Beach, forty miles to the east, and enters Pensacola Bay at Gulf Breeze. Santa Rosa Island extends westerly to Ft. Pickens, and on to Pensacola Pass. Both Pen-

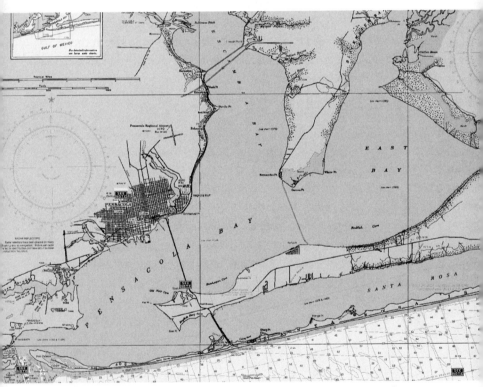

Pensacola Bay is deep—probably deeper than many offshore areas in the eastern Gulf of Mexico.

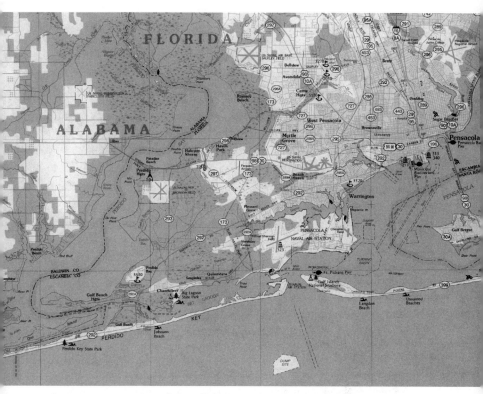

There are a variety of possibilities for fishermen from Pensacola to Perdido and the Alabama Line. Beach fishing is good, but many anglers prefer the backwaters and areas near the mouth of the Perdido River. Reprinted with permission from the full-color *Florida Atlas & Gazetteer*. Copyright DeLorme.

sacola Bay and Santa Rosa Sound's western stretches are regularly flushed with clean gulf water and even attract some deepwater species as well as the usual inshore inhabitants. Likewise, Big Lagoon, Old River, and Perdido Bay to the west, all are similarly affected by the gulf's proximity.

Amenities appealing to anglers are excellent at this established city, although the 2005 hurricanes ravaged the region. And, while Pensacola, Perdido, and Navarre Beaches attract hordes of sun-worshipers, the powers-that-be haven't forgotten that fishing is an important part of the area's appeal.

Inshore Fishing, the Pensacola Area

The waters from Pensacola Bay, Santa Rosa Sound, Big Lagoon, and the deep northern Gulf of Mexico mix at Pensacola. As a result, inshore and nearshore fishing is excellent from the headwaters of Blackwater Bay all the way to the beachfront.

The popular species found in East, Blackwater, and Escambia Bays are sea trout, redfish, and flounder. As you cross the imaginary line between these bays and deeper Pensacola Bay, you're more likely to find cleaner gulf water as well as Spanish mackerel, sheepshead, and in late summer, an occasional king mackerel.

The backwater of East Bay, known as Miller Bay and formed by the relatively small East Bay River, can sometimes be muddy. But it does have a shallow channel that is known to attract trout, redfish, and flounder year-round. On warm days, flounder hang out along the channel edges, and reds and trout cruise the shoreline searching for unsuspecting baitfish, primarily mullet. On a falling tide, expect the channel to funnel bait out of the backwaters only to be ambushed by predators that are then ambushed by anglers. The shoreline of East Bay is fairly shallow, but the center of the bay can be as deep as ten feet, making approaches to the edges easy and safe. The shallow northern shore between Miller Point (N30 27.409 W86 56.253), at the mouth of the Miller Bay, and Escribiano Point (N30 30.223 W87 01.210), at Blackwater Bay, is a good place to toss slow-sinking lures for trout on a cold afternoon. The mud warms and soon attracts baitfish. You know the rest of the story.

The southern shoreline of East Bay is fringed with docks and dock ruins. This structure is attractive to big trout and reds seeking refuge from either hot summer days or cool winter water. When it's warm, trouts and reds lay in the shade of the docks; when it's cold, they enjoy the deep holes formed by docking boats. There are hundreds of docks from Miller Point westward all the way past Redfish Cove (N30 23.919 W87 03.536) and the southern end of the Garcon Point Bridge, at Gulf Breeze. Don't bypass the bridge abutments close to the southern shore, as the pilings and cover hold trout—flounder and reds, too. Live shrimp, live mud minnows (killifish), and finger mullet all work well along the docks. However, there's nothing like the sight and sound of a big trout or red crashing a topwater lure at twilight. In the summer, get there early; in the winter, fish later in the day.

Blackwater Bay is really the estuary of the Blackwater River, which drains from the north. Even though the upper reaches are brackish, expect trout, reds, and flounder to be plentiful well above the Interstate 10 Bridge. On high tides, concentrate your efforts close to the shorelines and docks. On falling tides, watch the western edges of the channel and look for predators striking schools of white bait from deeper water. Work the entire western shoreline of Blackwater Bay from Bay Point (N30 34.198 W87 00.095) all the way to White Point (N30 26.872 W87 03.884), near the northern end of the Garcon Point Bridge. This shoreline makes a nice protected drift on cold days when the wind's howling out of the northwest, but generally only when the sun's shining and the tide's rising. The eastern side of the Blackwater River is a bit more wild and woolly, and is lined by marshes created by the smaller Weaver and Yellow Rivers. Each of these river channels is a good spot for trout and reds, particularly in cool weather.

On warm mornings, drift the front of the marsh from Pine Bluff (N30 33.776 W86 59.622) down to Grassy Point (N30 31.214 W87 00.806) and throw topwater lures along the grassy edges. As the sun gets higher in the morning sky, switch from topwaters to either live or artificial shrimp or mud minnows free-lined to the edges of the grass. Even though you may see mullet jumping or schooling along the shoreline, don't hesitate to use baits such as shrimp, crabs, or smaller fish (mud minnows or white bait). Remember that mullet are not always the prey; sometimes they serve only as the mechanism to stir up other bait from near the bottom.

Escambia Bay is fed by the Escambia River from the northwest and by a few smaller creeks, locally called bayous, from the east. The western shore, from Rock Point (N30 30.552 W87 09.746, at the western end of the I-10 bridge) to the mouth of Bayou Texar (N30 25.106 W87 11.113, at the northern end of the Pensacola Bay Bridge), is fringed with high bluffs. The shallow shoreline up to the bluffs is best fished by drifting along docks, generally located just north of the Bayou

Texar entrance and into the bayou itself. The bars near the bridge and crossing the bayou hold reds and flounder in the summer, and trout in cold weather. Also, if you're interested in cast-netting bait, be on the lookout for schools of menhaden along the shore outside Bayou Texar in the summer.

Redfish and sea trout are popular targets for anglers fishing the upper reaches of Escambia Bay. From the mouth of the Simpson River (N30 34.599 W87 10.599), near the US Highway 90 bridge, and down the shoreline to the Escambia River channel (N30 32.473 W87 09.845) is a rich, marshy environment for these species. Trout and reds are usually abundant in cooler weather, cruising the shoreline and sometimes moving into deeper holes or sloughs right after a severe cold front. Slow-moving and slow-sinking lures are highly effective for catching these fish. Flounder are also present along the marshes in summer, eating mostly small mullet or mud minnows. These voracious feeders will eat almost any bait, live or artificial, that get within their range, but mud minnows are the hands-down favorite.

The combination of an irregular muddy bottom studded with some wrecked pilings off the shoreline south of Avalon Beach, on the eastern side of Escambia Bay, make for some good redfish and flounder action too. Start near the mouth of Indian Bayou (N30 31.293 W87 06.291) and work your way southward past Trout Bayou (N30 30.444 W87 05.828). Stay between the pilings and the shore and work topwater lures around structure in the summer, especially at dawn. If you fish a diving lure or use live bait under corks set to depths of four feet or so, you might hook a nice flounder, too. As you get closer to Garcon Point (N30 26.587 W87 06.131), near the north end of the bridge, keep your eyes peeled for schools of Spanish mackerel, chasing bait pods in the deeper water. If you see them here, or anywhere in any of the bays, work the perimeter of the school with bright jigs or spoons.

Pensacola Bay is an active body of water that is relatively deep and bisected by the main ship channel and some deep spoils. Its bottom is also peppered with wrecks and even some private structures—reefs placed by local anglers. (This practice is no longer legal.) While there is certainly good fishing along the shoreline, particularly near the mouth of Bayou Grande (N30 22.690 W87 15.822, along the western shore near the Navy base), the best bet is to fish over deep structure, the Pensacola Bay Bridge, and near bait pods. Using your depth sounder, look for irregularities along the bottom of the bay. In warm weather, you'll likely find gray (mangrove) snapper inhabiting wrecks and structure in the bay. You'll also find king and Spanish mackerel chasing baitfish all over the bay. As the weather cools, big bull redfish will wander into the bay waters that are closest to the pass, as will sheepshead. Both can be caught around structure, including the pilings of the Pensacola Bay Bridge. In the cold winter months, expect gag grouper to move inside the pass, fair game for folks trolling deep-diving plugs along the channel edges. There are a number of wrecks, spoils, abandoned piers, and old bridge abutments stretching across the Pensacola city waterfront. If the wind's howling out of the north or northwest, stay close to shore and explore the moderate depths from the mouth of Bayou Chico (N30 23.533 W87 13.732) eastwards toward the north end of the Pensacola Bay Bridge. Also, remember that in times of war or increased national security, access may be limited to some areas in Pensacola Bay. Local tackle shops and outfitters will usually have specific and timely information available for the asking.

Despite its almost forty-mile length, and the fact that it's fed at only two places by the gulf, Santa Rosa Sound is a great inshore fishery. Its middle, near Navarre and Navarre Beach, has enough water movement to sustain nice grass flats and to attract bait and schools of Spanish mackerel. The Navarre Bridge is a popular spot for redfish in the fall and for sheepshead in the early winter months.

For trout and reds, fish the shallow northern shoreline and docks from Woodlawn Beach (N30 23.198 W86 59.369) to Oriole Point (N30 22.364 W87 05.235). The residential canals at Oriole Beach are also popular with winter trout fishermen, especially on cold days when the fish are seeking shelter. Big Sabine Point (N30 21.602 W87 02.490) and the very shallow cove to its east are known to hold sea trout throughout the year and bait-crashing bull reds in the fall. Also,

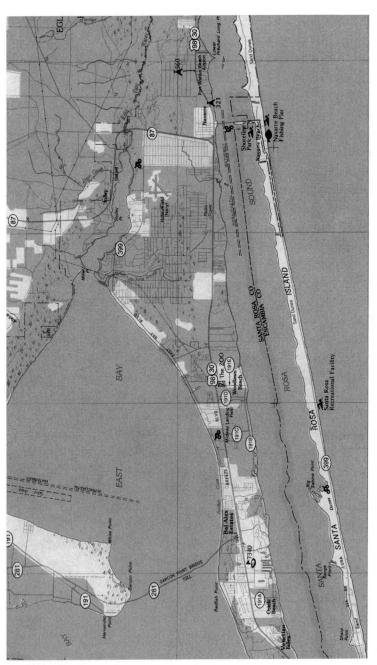

The Intracoastal Waterway runs behind the barrier islands at Navarre, protecting anglers from both northerly and southerly winds. Reprinted with permission from the full-color *Florida Atlas & Gazetteer.* Copyright DeLorme.

the thirty-foot depths reaching from the point to the Intracoastal Waterway (ICW) channel marker 130 will often attract bait schools and Spanish mackerel in the late summer and early fall.

The ICW crosses the ship channel just inside Pensacola Pass and heads westward through Big Lagoon and Old River to Perdido Bay. Like Santa Rosa Sound, this stretch of water holds mostly trout and redfish, but also attracts Spanish mackerel schools near Pensacola and Perdido Passes. In Big Lagoon, fish the docks and wrecked dock structures along the northern bank between markers 10 (N30 19.439 W87 21.086) and 12 (N30 19.053 W87 23.553). Also, the Langley Point–Redfish Point spur (N30 19.073 W87 21.324), on the Big Lagoon side of Perdido Key, is worth fishing on an early morning trip in the summertime. The southern side of Big Lagoon is shallower than the northern side and topwater lures are effective here for both trout and reds.

From the Perdido Key Bridge westward, you'll find water that's surprisingly clean and fishable. Be sure to fish the docks on the northern and southern sides of Innerarity Point (N30 18.888 W87 29.896) and the close shoreline on its western end. To the north of Innerarity Point, and up into Perdido Bay, the entire shoreline from the mouth of Bayou Garcon (N30 19.369 W87 26.707) to Tarkiln Bay (N30 20.809 W87 25.598) and DuPont Point (N30 21.957 W87 26.719) is usually active with trout and redfish. If you can, ease your boat along the edges here and work the shoreline structures and edges with topwater lures (in summer) and live or artificial shrimp.

Every angler wants to catch huge fish, but it's important to realize that it may not happen in certain areas. Huge, over-slot redfish are not likely to appear in the bays and sounds, except near the passes. And, while there are likely to be a few 8-pound sea trout roaming the estuaries, it's mostly the fish that are just big enough to keep that you'll be catching. For this reason, use light tackle unless you absolutely know you'll need the big guns for those bull redfish in autumn or king mackerel in late summer.

Six- to eight-foot medium-action spinning rods, matched with light reels are a good choice, as are lightweight baitcasting outfits.

Ten-pound braided line, such as PowerPro, is an excellent choice for fish up to 10 pounds, so long as it's paired with the appropriate leader material. I recommend 20-pound fluorocarbon leaders for most applications, but you may want to upsize to either 25- or 30-pound line if you're fishing near docks, ruins, or oyster bars. The trick to catching many inshore species is stealth. Long casts, quiet anglers, and virtually invisible terminal rigs are all necessary.

Trout, redfish, and most other inshore species react well to topwater lures, providing the light levels are low. Noisy plugs such as Heddon's Super Spook, Jr. and MirrOlure's Top Dog are good choices. Many anglers start with dark colors early and later move to brighter fluorescent pinks or chartreuse colors. The topwater bite is best in warm weather and will typically last from daybreak for a few hours. When the topwater action slows, or when the fish start missing the topwater lures, it's time to change tactics and maybe use a D.O.A. BaitBuster in chartreuse or gold or slow-sinking Corky Mullet. Another good choice for trout, reds, and flounder is either a live shrimp, pinfish, white bait, or mud minnow on a jig head or 4/0 to 6/0 circle hook rigged under a popping cork. Use just enough leader material to keep the bait off the bottom or over the top of the sea grass. This is an excellent way to fish an artificial shrimp (D.O.A.) or a soft-plastic-and-jig-head combination. Be sure to pop the cork occasionally, mimicking the action of a predator striking a baitfish. If you wish, eliminate the cork. Free-lined baits are extremely effective, as they allow a truly natural presentation.

Spoons are also another effective way to catch backwater redfish. The traditional gold Johnson spoon is weedless and works well around oysters and structure. This is also a great way to introduce someone to artificial-lure fishing, as fishing with a spoon is as simple as winding it in. Spinner baits also work well for reds in shallow water. Their bulk makes them more difficult to cast long distances, but their noisy action is useful when the water's surface is choppy or rough, or along deeper drop-offs.

To fish for sheepshead near old wrecks, rocky shores, and jetties, or around bridge pilings, use live shrimp or fiddler crabs on either jig heads or on knocker rigs made with a 40- pound leader and small strong J-style hooks. Use cut pieces of shrimp for smaller sheepshead, but when the big ones arrive in January or February, use whole shrimp, threaded backward on your hook. Big sheepshead don't peck at bait like the little ones.

Many locals fishing the bays use MirrOlure medium or deep-running lures such as the 52M or TT series, especially in cold weather. These classic lures also work well around rocky shorelines, but care must be taken, as they're not inexpensive and they have lots of hooks with which to snag the bottom. And, if the big reds are biting, increase your tackle to 30-pound class rods and reels and troll a couple of Mann's 4D Stretch 25+ lures alongside the bridge pilings or the deep mid-bay channel. Spanish mackerel, usually spotted crashing schools of white bait, are an easy-to-catch delicious fish. If you see birds wheeling over striking mackerel or bluefish, don't run your boat into the thick of the battle. Troll Flowering Floreo jigs or #00 ClarkSpoons, attached to your running line with wire leader, at about five knots around the perimeter of the action. Light spinning tackle works fine for Spanish mackerel, but when the bigger fish appear in the late summer or early fall, you might need tackle with more backbone.

Near shore fishing can have several interpretations when you're in the upper gulf. In the eastern gulf and along the Big Bend, it means less than five to ten miles. Here along the Emerald coast, at five to ten miles, you'll likely be at eighty to 100 feet depths, fishing over the wreck of a battleship. So, I'll qualify nearshore by saying it includes beach fishing from boats, piers, bridges, and from shore and fishing in the stretch of the Pensacola Pass out to its marker 1 at N30 16.256 W87 17.548.

With the exception of the busiest beachfront, the beaches from Navarre to Perdido offer excellent opportunities for the beach-bound angler. Trout and redfish are found closer to the passes, jetties, and fishing piers. The interaction of backwater and gulf influences action at the passes. The pilings and structure of the Navarre Pier ruins and the active Pensacola Beach Fishing Pier attract bait, which is followed by pelagic species. You'll be more likely to find Spanish mackerel, king mackerel, and bluefish near structure.

Pounding surf along the nearly barren sections of beach uncovers sand fleas, making summer angling for pompano popular for wading anglers. If you fish from the beach or pier you'll need to fish with rods long enough to make extended casts. Here, 9-foot rods with medium to heavy spinning reels are popular. Braided PowerPro line will extend the distance you can cast. Pompano fishermen prefer live sand fleas hooked with small hooks or short, heavy jigs, fished on the bottom in the backwash of the surf. If the mackerel or blues are running the beach, topwater lures attract lots of action, but be sure to use a wire leader, as they'll cut monofilament with their teeth. For big reds, use finger mullet, white bait, or large topwater plugs. Noisy topwater lures are great fun to throw toward schools of reds cruising the beaches in late summer or early fall.

The big event along this coastline is the cobia run in the spring, when the annual migration of these great sport fish carries them close to shore. Live eels and brightly colored jigs, rigged on the same 20- to 30-pound spinning gear used for big redfish, are popular with sight-fishermen, many using boats with high towers to spot cruising cobia. Tarpon cruise the beaches here, too, but usually follow the cobia later into the summer. In fact, many are hooked but rarely landed by anglers fishing from the Pensacola Beach Fishing Pier. Others are targeted by fly-rod or light-tackle fishermen sight-fishing from boats just off the surf line.

The Pensacola Ship Channel extends about three miles into the gulf. It's dredged and is a controlled fairway for big ships. Take care to avoid any shoaling or breaking waves, particularly on the western side of the channel nearshore, and troll deep-diving lures for grouper, king mackerel and big redfish along the channel edges. Start at Ft. Pickens (N30 19.905 W87 18.168) or Ft. McRee (N30 19.534 W87 18.688) in Pensacola Pass, and fish south toward marker 1. Although scuttled in 1921, the wreck of the battleship USS *Massachusetts* (N30 17.810 W87 18.710) sits just west of the channel and is still an active fishery. Watch out for divers, but be prepared to catch cobia, king

The old Navarre fishing pier was destroyed by a hurricane, but still acts as an attractant to fish.

The "retired" beach bridge from Gulf Breeze to Pensacola Beach has become a popular fishing pier.

mackerel, amberjack and small snapper over the wreck. Also, the jetties along Pensacola Pass are excellent for big redfish in the late summer or early fall.

If you plan to troll the channel and its environs for grouper, redfish, or kingfish, you should consider heavier tackle. Boat rods with 30- to 50-pound-test line are adequate for trolling lures such as the Stretch 30+ at these depths for grouper. Kings and reds are likely to be higher in the water column and a Stretch 15+ or 25+ is appropriate. Use lighter spinning or level-wind-style tackle, such as Shimano Spheros 8000 spinning reels or Shimano TLD-20 level-wind reels, for kings. If kings are your quarry, spool your reels with lots of monofilament line, as kings can easily take several hundred yards off a spool in seconds The built-in stretch of monofilament line helps keep them hooked. Kings also respond well to live baits, especially blue runners (hard tails), either slowly trolled on stinger rigs or free-lined with spinning gear.

Offshore Fishing from Pensacola

Offshore fishing along the western Florida Panhandle is generally categorized as *deep* or *really, really deep.*

With the exception of a few natural rock piles, most of the deep fishing is done over artificial reefs or wrecks in less than 100 feet of water. For the most part, these shallow inshore spots are reachable with smaller boats and, in the tradition of artificial reefs sponsored by governments, accessible to the general fishing public. One newer wreck is the aircraft carrier USS *Oriskany,* scuttled in 2006 in 200 feet of water at N30 02.555 W87 00.397, about twenty miles from Pensacola Pass marker 1. Still reachable by smaller craft, this wreck attracted many game-fish species almost immediately. Sitting upright with it's deck 134 feet above the gulf bottom, the ship has also become a popular destination for recreational divers and spearfishers.

There are certainly other wrecks much closer to shore. The *Tex Edwards* (N30 16.140 W87 10.160) and the *Joseph Meek* (N30 16.380 W87 09.570) both lie about three miles to the southeast of Pensacola Pass. Most of the close-in offshore fishing here is based around catching American red snapper, gray (mangrove) snapper, grouper, amberjacks, and king mackerel. Smaller pelagics such as bonito and Spanish mackerel do show up over deeper structure, but mostly are regarded as bait. In late summer, an occasional wahoo, tuna, or even a big billfish will sneak over the 200-foot contour and find its way to the inshore reefs and wrecks.

Depending on the range of your boat and the length of your visit to the area, try trolling the area south of the barge *Minnick* (N30 13.220 W87 13.990) toward the tugboat *Phillip* (N30 07.970 W87 13.320). This area is peppered with wrecks and a few reefs, making it a popular trolling spot for king mackerel. While shared by anglers from Destin, the area called the Timber Hole (N30 10.100 W86 55.000) is popular with Pensacola fishermen, too. Bottom fishermen also find snapper and grouper inhabiting the spots in less than 100 feet. You could easily fish a full week over these shallow reefs and not completely exploit their potential.

Venturing out a bit more, but not to the 600-plus bluewater depths, you'll find a couple of reefs worth trying. The Antares Reef (N30 00.600 W87 07.800) and the Tenneco Rigs (N29 59.700 W87 05.100) regularly hold snapper and sometimes attract big wahoo from deeper waters.

To fish in these relatively shallow waters for the variety of species found there involves using a several different types of tackle. Trolling deep-diving plugs, such as Mann's 4D Stretch 30+, near the bottom is a good method for bigger species in water less than 100 feet deep. Try trolling different ranges within the water column over wrecks and artificial reefs, as pelagic species such as kingfish and Spanish mackerel, and amberjacks hang out above structure rather than inside it. For example, pull a 4D Stretch 15+ mid-column, and a live or frozen cigar minnow rigged on a feather such as an Iland Sea Striker near the surface.

Trolling for bottom fish requires heavier tackle than does trolling for pelagic speedsters. Experienced grouper fishermen use shorter rods rigged with 4/0 and 6/0 Penn boat reels and sometimes adjust their star drags as tightly as possible. Non-stretching 30- to 50-pound-test PowerPro braided line will help pull the fish away from structure, too. The upper reaches of the water column is probably best fished with lighter gear, such as Shimano's TLD-20 and TLD-30 level-wind trolling reels spooled with lots of 20- to 30-pound-test line. Drags are best lightly tensioned, in the two- to three-pound range, allowing the initial burst of speed from a king mackerel or wahoo to give you time to clear your other lines from behind the boat. Never fish all your trolled baits at the same depth, as you're likely to miss finding the depth at which the fish are holding. Once you find the proper depth, and the species you seek, match the rest of your gear to what was successful. "If it ain't broke, don't fix it!"

Bottom-fishing these waters, just offshore of the beach to depths of about 100 feet, is straightforward. Big rods and reels are required, and high-speed retrieve systems are convenient on those days when you need to wind lines all day. Use 50- to 80-pound line. Super Braids such as PowerPro are more sensitive to the fish's bite at these depths. Use 100-pound monofilament leaders and 8/0 to 11/0 circle hooks for good results. Snapper can be caught with less-substantial gear, including big spinning rods and reels. Make up as many multiple-hook dropper rigs as you'll need for the day, and rig the necessary weights depending on the depth. The deeper you fish and the more rapid the current, the more weight you'll need to keep your bait near the bottom. Eight- and 16-ounce sinkers are appropriate for these deep drops. Use baits that are seasonally available. Many local anglers prefer to start fishing the perimeter of a reef or wreck with cut bait, such as squid or threadfin herring, and don't break out the live pinfish, alewives, or cigar minnows until some bigger fish come out of hiding on to the edges of the reef area. Of course, the bigger the species, the bigger the bait you'll need. Grouper will eat big pinfish and porgies. Snapper seem to enjoy smaller baits such as white bait (small alewives, cigar minnows, sardines, etc.), and even live shrimp. Deep-jigging techniques, using weighted butterfly jigs, have recently become popular in deep gulf waters to 300 feet for snapper, grouper, king mackerel, and wahoo. Shimano, Williamson, and others offer extensive lines of deep jigging lures and accessories.

Big fish mean big tackle is needed. Many offshore reels cost more than some inshore boats.

Blue water means really deep water and a whole new style of fishing. Overnight trips in million-dollar boats to fish depths in excess of 6,000-feet for swordfish are not unusual. Nor are catches of blue marlin, big wahoo, tuna, and sailfish. Nor are rods and reels that are each worth more than a '68 Volkswagen.

When the bottom gets to about 300 feet, there's not much bottom fishing, unless you've got electric reels and can find a wreck or some structure. At depths much greater than 600 feet, bluewater anglers troll the contours, the upwelling thermal currents, and the weedlines that accumulate above them. The Squiggles (N29 30.000 W86 25.000) is along the edge of the 100-fathom contour; that's 600 feet down and one of the closer spots routinely fished by Pensacola

Floating grass lines, some many miles long, are the targets of offshore fishing boats. This grass attracts bait, which attracts game fish such as dolphin, wahoo, and marlin.

anglers. The Spur (N29 28.000 W86 53.000, a 2,000-foot trench running eastward into 1,400 feet of water), the Wall (N29 14.040 W87 00.000, along the 2,000-foot contour, and the Steps (N29 14.000 W87 35.000), a canyon wall falling off into 4,000-feet) are within seventy miles of Pensacola Pass. Anglers making overnight swordfish trips or just overnighting during periods of nice weather often frequent the Nipples, at N28 57.100 W87 35.000 in about 6,000 feet of water and eighty miles offshore.

Fifty- and 80-pound-class rods and reels are standard gear aboard these big boats. Ballyhoo and small mackerel are rigged to trolling feathers, such as blue-and-white Iland Lures' Sea Star or Cruiser series) and 10/0 to 12/0 hooks. Many captains troll bare feathers alongside the rigged baits, just to increase the odds of a strike. Since too much noise isn't an issue, loud teasers and spreads of fake baits are pulled close to the boat to attract the interest of predators.

Bluewater fishing isn't for everyone—or everyone's budget. However, it is the top of the sport of offshore fishing and certainly worth trying if you're given the opportunity.

Getting Around The Pensacola Area

As is the case with the entire Florida Panhandle, US 98 is the historical east–west route, linking Pensacola and Navarre with Fort Walton Beach to the east, and with Alabama to the west. I-10 has become a popular westbound link in recent years, as it's faster and convenient to the bigger towns, such as Mobile. It is, however, not scenic. If you're heading to Perdido Key, take US 98 from downtown Pensacola. US 29 and US 90 are alternative north- and westbound routes to and from Pensacola, but neither is more convenient than I-10. SR 87 runs north from Navarre, at the bridge, and intersects I-10 near Milton.

Gulf Breeze is located on the western tip of the mainland just before you reach the Pensacola Bay Bridge. The Pensacola Beach Bridge also comes ashore at Gulf Breeze. Pensacola Beach is located a few miles from the western end of Santa Rosa Island. Since the hurricanes of 2005, road access to Pensacola Pass and Ft. Pickens on Santa Rosa Island has been restricted.

From a marine standpoint, Pensacola Bay is easy to navigate. The bays are generally deep and well marked with navigation aids, however their shorelines can be shallow and muddy. Charts issued before 2005 may have errors and may not show all obstructions, therefore it's a good idea to inquire at local marinas or marine suppliers about updates. The ICW runs behind Santa Rosa Island, across Pensacola Pass, and behind Perdido Key. Care should be exercised within the channel or when crossing it, as it is usually busy with commercial and recreational boat traffic.

Where to Stay

The stretch of Emerald Coast from Navarre to Perdido was pretty much scraped clean in 2005 by Hurricane Dennis and is still rebuilding. In many cases, condominiums have taken the place of motels, and in other areas, the pace of rebuilding is just plain slow. I've listed a few places to stay that are of interest to anglers in terms of convenience and location. True fisherman-friendly lodging is disappearing as the area grows and becomes more beach and resort oriented.

Many motels along the Emerald Coast offer good parking for trailer boats.

If you're trailering a boat to the area and plan to stay on or near the beaches, I encourage you to call ahead and be sure there's suitable parking for your rig.

Navarre

Comfort Inn Navarre, 8700 Navarre Pkwy., (850) 939-1761. Lodging. On US 98, near the Navarre Bridge.

Best Western Navarre, 8697 Navarre Pkwy., (850) 939-9400. Lodging. On US 98, soundside, at Navarre Bridge.

Gulf Breeze and Pensacola Beach

Quality Inn, US 98 at the southern end of the Pensacola Bay Bridge, Gulf Breeze, (850) 932-2214. Lodging. This motel is adjacent to a large public boat ramp and convenient to both Pensacola Bay, Santa Rosa Sound, and the beaches. There is adequate parking for boats on trailers on the premises.

Comfort Inn, Pensacola Beach, (850) 934-5470. Lodging. Conveniently located just across the street from the Pensacola Gulf Fishing Pier.

Pensacola

Days Inn, Pensacola Downtown, 710 N Palafox, (850) 438-4922. Lodging. Located in the historic district, this hotel offers good value, but maneuvering boat trailers in the parking lot may be difficult.

Harbor Inn, 200 N Palafox, (850) 432-3441. Lodging. Ditto the parking.

Perdido

Holiday Harbor Marina, River Road, (850) 492-0555. Rental apartments.

Where to Eat

Navarre

East River Smokehouse, SR 87 north of US 98, Navarre, (850) 939-2802. Lunch, dinner, open seven days a week.

Cracker Jax Buffet, 8147 Navarre Pkwy., (850) 939-5441. Breakfast, lunch, dinner, open seven days a week.

Sailors' Grill & Bakery, Navarre Beach, (850) 939-1092. Breakfast, lunch, dinner, open seven days a week. This is a great place to grab a meal at Navarre Beach. It's next to the boat ramp at the southern end of the bridge. Breakfast starts late, though, at 8 a.m.

Gulf Breeze and Pensacola Beach

Billy Bob's Beach BBQ, 911 Gulf Breeze Pkwy., (850) 934-2999. Lunch, dinner, catering, take-out available, closed Sundays. Their slogan is "Mouth Slobberin' Good Barbeque."

Pensacola

Chet's Seafood, 3708 Navy Blvd., (850) 456-0165. Lunch, dinner, open Thursdays, Fridays, Saturdays only. According to Capt. Wes Rozier, this is *the* place for seafood in Pensacola!

The Shrimp Basket, 709 Navy Blvd., (850) 455-1926. Lunch, dinner, open seven days a week. Don't miss their shrimp slaw or the all-you-can-eat popcorn shrimp.

Skunked? There's always Joe Patti's Seafood in Pensacola. Stop by anyway—you'll be impressed.

Rooks Marina Oyster Barn, 505 Bayou Blvd., (850) 433-0511. Lunch, dinner, seafood, closed Sundays and Mondays, adjacent to Bayou Texar boat ramp.

Skopelos on the Bay Seafood Restaurant, 670 Scenic Hwy., (850) 432-6565. Dinner weekdays, seafood, closed Sundays.

Joe Patti's Seafood Co., foot of A Street. Pensacola, (850) 435-7843. Retail seafood market. Anyone visiting Pensacola should visit this market just to see the incredible selection of locally caught seafood.

Sam's Seafood Restaurant, 420 S A St., across from Joe Patti's, (850) 432-6626. Lunch Mondays, Tuesdays; lunch, dinner Wednesdays–Saturdays; closed Sundays.

Hub Stacey's Sandwiches, 321 E Government St., (850) 469-1001. Eleven a.m. to 1 a.m. daily, closed Sundays.

Hall's Seafood, 920 E Gregory St., (850) 438-9019. Lunch, dinner, open seven days a week.

Perdido

The Shrimp Basket, 14600 Perdido Key Dr., (850) 492-1970. Lunch, dinner, open seven days a week. Great fried shrimp!

The Reef Restaurant, 13595 Perdido Key Dr., (850) 492-9020. Seafood, breakfast, lunch, dinner, open seven days a week.

Sunset Grill Restaurant, at Holiday Harbor Marina, (850) 492-1063. Lunch, dinner, dockage, open seven days a week.

Hub Stacey's at the Point, Galvez Road, off Innerarity Point Road, (850) 497-0071. Opens at 4 p.m. each day. This great sandwich spot is next to the Galvez boat ramp.

Flora-Bama Lounge, 17401 Perdido Key Dr., (850) 492-0611. Just because you've never seen anything quite like this place.

Marinas, Marine Supplies and Service, Bait-and-Tackle Shops, and Launching Ramps

Navarre

Half Hitch Tackle, 8711 Navarre Pkwy. (US 98), Navarre, (850) 230-5936. Live and frozen bait, extensive tackle. The Half Hitch chain of bait-and-tackle stores is well-known for good service and accurate local fishing reports.

Boater's World, Navarre, US 98 at SR 281, Oriole Beach and Tiger Point, (850) 932-0812. Tackle and marine supplies.

Woodlawn Beach Ramp, Woodlawn Beach Road, on Santa Rosa Sound midway between Gulf Breeze and Navarre.

Navarre Beach Ramps, southern end of Navarre Beach Bridge. Three paved ramps, adequate parking, restrooms, showers, adjacent restaurant.

The boat ramp at Navarre Beach is typical of the nice facilities along the Emerald Coast.

Holley Ramps, on East Bay north of Navarre. Two single ramps, limited parking.

East River Ramp, SR 87 north of Navarre. Single paved ramp, adequate parking.

Gulf Breeze and Pensacola Beach

Gulf Breeze Bait & Tackle, 825 Gulf Breeze Pkwy., Gulf Breeze, (850) 832-6789. Live and frozen bait, tackle, complete fishing supplies, custom rods, rod and reel repairs. If you're near Gulf Breeze or Pensacola Beach, this *the* place to shop for bait and fishing gear. Eels and fiddler crabs are available during cobia and sheepshead seasons. And there's a twenty-four-hour Waffle House right next door.

Pensacola Beach Marina, 655 Pensacola Beach Blvd., (850) 932-0304. Dockage, fuel, adjacent restaurant. On Little Sabine Bay near the

Anglers atop the Pensacola Beach Pier make the long walk easy by packing their needs on rolling coolers and trolleys.

southern end of the Pensacola Beach Bridge. Many of Pensacola's charter boats run out of this marina.

Pensacola Beach Gulf Pier. Daily $6.50 fee, yearly permit available, adequate parking. One of the few big piers left on the Emerald Coast, this one is more than 1,400 feet long and busy every day—all year long.

West Marine Express, 3483 Gulf Breeze Pkwy., Gulf Breeze, (850) 932-4404. Tackle and marine supplies.

Wayside Park Ramp, southern end of Pensacola Bay Bridge. Paved ramp, adequate parking, adjacent small fishing pier.

Woodlawn Beach Ramp, Woodlawn Beach Road on Santa Rosa Sound midway between Gulf Breeze and Navarre.

Pensacola

West Marine, 7160 N Davis Hwy., Pensacola, (850) 476-2720. Tackle and marine supplies.

West Marine, 3500 Barrancas Ave., Pensacola, (850) 453-0010. Tackle and marine supplies.

Outcast Bait & Tackle, 3520 Barrancas Ave., Pensacola, (850) 457-1450. Live and frozen bait, tackle, complete fishing supplies. Outcast is without doubt the best tackle shop in Pensacola. Eels are in stock during cobia season, and they usually have fiddler crabs during the winter months.

Bahia Mar Marina, 1901 Cypress St., Pensacola, (850) 432-1561. Gas and diesel, dockage, dry storage, marine supplies. On Bayou Chico.

Bayou Chico Marina, off US 98 at the end of Myrick Street, (850) 439-1708. Double ramp, $5 daily fee, tackle, frozen bait, no fuel, adequate parking.

Jim's Fish Camp, northeastern end of US 90 and Escambia River Bridge, Pace, (850) 994-7500. Single paved ramp, bait and tackle. Access to upper Escambia Bay.

Navy Point Ramp, Sunset Avenue, on Bayou Grande. Paved triple ramp, adequate parking. Good access to the pass and offshore.

17th Avenue Ramp, near northern end of Pensacola Bay Bridge. Two small ramps, limited parking.

Bayou Texar Ramp, Stanley and Cervantes Streets. Double ramp, adequate parking.

Floridatown Ramp, CR 197, south of US 90, Pace. Single ramp, adequate parking. Good access to upper Escambia Bay.

Perdido

Holiday Harbor Marina, River Road, (850) 492-0555, holidayharbor @bellsouth.net. Gas and diesel, dry storage, transient dockage, bait and tackle, lodging, restaurant. There is a boat ramp here, but it's only available to residents and guests.

Gray's Tackle, 13019 Sorrento Rd., (850) 492-2666. Live and frozen

Facilities, including boat ramps, are good along the Intracoastal Waterway near Perdido.

bait, rod rentals, tackle, fly-tying supplies, ice. Gray's is a fine tackle shop where one can get local up-to-the minute fishing reports.

Big Lagoon State Recreation Area Ramp, on Big Lagoon. Daily $4 car fee plus $4 ramp fee, paved ramp, adequate parking.

Galvez Landing Ramp, Galvez Road, off Innerarity Road. Two free paved ramps, adequate parking, adjacent restaurant. This nice park is just across Old River from Holiday Harbor Marina. Be careful of boat wakes, as this ramp is directly on the ICW.

Coronada Boulevard Ramp, on Perdido Bay. Paved single ramp. This is a neighborhood ramp with no parking and limited turning space.

Local Guides

Capt. Wes Rozier, (850) 982-7858. Inshore, nearshore, and bay charters.

Capt. Baz Yelverton, (850) 261-9035, www.gulfbreezeguideservice.com. Inshore fly fishing.

Capt. Victor Wright, (850) 501-1675, captvictorw@aol.com. Inshore and nearshore.

Capt. Chris Phillips, (850) 255-7288, hotspotsfishing@hotmail.com, www.hotspotsfishing.com. Inshore and nearshore.

Capt. Corey Maxwell, (850) 450-7840, coreyinshore@cs.com, www.hotspotsfishing.com. Inshore and nearshore.

Capt. Rick Harris, (850) 994-5100. Inshore.

Capt. Bob Quarles, (850) 437-3169, www.blueheronguideservice.com. Inshore, light-tackle, and fly fishing.

Capt. Jeff Moore, (850) 554-1484, www.moorebetter.com. Inshore, nearshore, bay charters.

Capt. Eddie Woodall, Navarre, (850) 936-8203, www.fullnetcharters.com. Inshore, nearshore, bay charters.

Capt. Rob Cochran, Destin to Navarre, (850) 621-6956, rob6956@aol.com. Inshore, nearshore, light-tackle.

Capt. Mike Newell, Capt. Eddie Lively, Capt. Ronnie Hogue, Capt Jerry Jacobs, (850) 932-0304. Offshore, bluewater. These guides are booked through Pensacola Beach Marina.

Chula Mar Deep Sea Fishing, (850) 492-1099. Deep-sea party-boat fishing out of Pensacola Beach Marina.

Many guides from Destin are familiar with the waters near Navarre, Pensacola, and Perdido. Please consult the listings for those areas, if necessary. Also the Web site of the Florida Guides Association (www.florida-guides.com) has a complete listing of U.S. Coast Guard licensed-and-insured fishing guides.

2

Practical Matters

17

It's All About the Fish . . .

Popular Inshore and Nearshore Fish Species

Inshore and nearshore fishing along Florida's Gulf Coast has as much to do with economics as it does with species. Of course, all inshore fishermen long to be aboard a big Luhrs sport fisherman trolling the depths for fish of mammoth proportions. The reality, however, of a roundtrip that has fuel costs the equivalent of a new outboard motor in 1968 is staggering to many anglers. Inshore fishing, which includes small-boat, bridge, bank, beach, and pier fishing, is much more democratic than the offshore option. Most game species come near enough to Florida's gulf shoreline that most anglers need only expend a minimum effort in catching dinner on a low-impact low-cost outing.

Flounder

An inshore fisherman friend once commented, "It's easier to catch a flounder than to clean one." That's a pretty good assessment, as flounder are easily targeted and attack both live and artificial baits enthusiastically. Found all along the Big Bend and Emerald Coast, these flatfish lay along the edges of rock piles, shell bars, and channels, and in sandy holes on the flats waiting for passing prey. Small baitfish, shrimp, soft plastic jigs, topwater lures, and suspending plugs all catch flounder. If a tasty treat passes overhead, flounder will eat it.

Not great fighters, flounder are renowned for holding on to the end of a soft plastic lure only until the angler approaches with a landing net. They do have the unfortunate habit of dropping immediately to the bottom after they let go of the bait and will usually strike a second time.

Flounder are plentiful and excellent table fare. Stuffed with shrimp or crabmeat, fried as filets or fried whole, it's hard to beat its firm white flesh. And they're not really that hard to clean—just imagine a trout that's been run over by a pickup truck and you'll figure it out!

Pompano

While pompano inhabit the entire range from Homosassa to Pensacola, it's the beaches from Dog Island westward that get the attention of pompano specialists.

Pompano seem to enjoy feeding where there's water churning up the edges of white sand, uncovering small crabs and sand fleas. They do feed along nearshore sand banks, such as Crystal River's spoil banks and the big sandbars off Steinhatchee, but the rolling surf along the Emerald Coast beaches brings more bait into the open. The attraction of pompano to the surf also makes them an attractive target for shore-bound anglers.

The trick to catching pompano is to get the bait to the bottom and to bounce it along very slowly. Small jigs like the ¼-ounce D.O.A. TerroEyz in bright colors or stubby white Flowering Floreos do well, but the best bait seems to be live sand fleas rigged on simple jig heads. While sand fleas are available at some bait shops on the western panhandle, many anglers prefer to catch their own, using a variety of rakes and strainer baskets. Live shrimp work well, but they're no comparison to sand fleas.

Given their choice of fish to eat, many anglers put pompano at the top of their list. Fresh filets, simply broiled with olive oil and salt and pepper or grilled whole, are unbeatable at the table.

Redfish

Red drum, puppy drum, channel bass, and redfish—they're all the same—it just depends on where you live. When you're on the Big

Bend and Emerald Coast, call them redfish. They are prized by all inshore anglers, not only for their table appeal, but also for their great fighting ability. The redfish population in Florida was almost decimated by the culinary craze for blackened redfish in the 1990s, but has rebounded since then. A statewide one-fish-per-angler-per-day bag limit is currently in effect. Many professional guides and conservation-oriented anglers practice catch-and-release when fishing for reds in the hopes of increasing fish stocks for future generations of fishermen.

More finicky eaters than spotted sea trout, legal-size redfish cruise the shallower waters all along Florida's Gulf Coast, devouring everything from crustaceans to small baitfish. Their downward-facing

Redfish are one of the most popular species found along the Gulf Coast. They are found in the backwaters as well as along rocky shorelines and beaches.

mouths give the impression that they feed only on the bottom of the oyster bars, rock piles, and grassy flats. Crabs and shrimp are certainly part of their everyday diet, but make no mistake; small baitfish and commercial imitations attract quick and upward-oriented strikes. There's nothing like the sight and sound of a big red turning upside down in two feet of water to inhale a noisy topwater plug.

With the exception of wintertime fish found in deep-river channels and big spawning fish found well offshore, reds, sometimes in schools, generally cruise edges of flats, grassy shorelines, and rocky shell bars in search of food. On lower tides, they can be found on sun-drenched shallow flats with their tails and backs out of water, nudging dinner from grass patches or rocks. These tailing fish are prime targets for sight-fishing anglers using light tackle or fishing with fly rods.

While many anglers insist that live bait is essential to catch large redfish, others believe that the smell of cut pinfish or mullet attracts them. Smell seems to be important, but slashing surface lures do well, too. Shrimp, stinky in its natural live condition, is a statewide favorite. Before hooking a whole shrimp, tear off the tail and push the hook up through the body toward the head. This will enhance the scent and attract more fish. Plastic jigs, sometimes sweetened with a small piece of fresh or frozen shrimp or synthetic bait, bounced slowly across the bottom near oyster and shell bars, is also a sure way to catch reds. The use of a super-strong invisible leader, such as those made of fluorocarbon, is important, particularly in clear waters. These fish have a second sense when it comes to recognizing lures and for rubbing leaders ragged across sharp rocks and oysters.

Redfish can be wary prey if found on the flats in very clear water. Any loud noises aboard the boat or from wading anglers can signal to reds that predators are nearby. Many professional captains argue that undue rocking of the boat by casters, particularly fly fishermen, pushes a wave of water out toward redfish and makes them move off. Movement by boats, splashing wade fishermen, or hungry dolphins, the reds don't know the difference.

No discussion of redfish is complete without mention of their close cousins, the black drum. Many an angler swears they've seen redfish tailing on top of oyster bars and along rocky Big Bend shorelines, only to have encountered big black drum. They're also seen along beaches toward the panhandle and in river estuaries. Black drum feed on crustaceans and are wary to bite artificial baits. Smaller, juvenile fish fight well, but not with the enthusiasm of the redfish. Big ones simply lumber off with the hook in their mouths and need to be tugged rather than played by the angler. Black drum have limited table appeal. Smaller ones are edible—if you're really hungry. Larger ones, sometimes as big as 50 pounds, are wormy and tasteless, so catch them for sport—and release them.

Sharks

No matter where you fish along the Big Bend or Emerald Coast, you'll encounter sharks. Whether they're to be considered an inshore or an offshore species gets some argument, but I think most are seen and caught in shallower waters. However, no matter where you find them, they're definitely fighters, and big game on any tackle.

There are many species of shark found throughout the gulf, but the ones you'll likely come across are hammerheads, bonnetheads, blacktips, spinners, bulls, and an occasional big tiger shark or nurse shark.

Big hammerhead sharks are notorious for eating big tarpon boatside and are ferocious. Their smaller cousins, the bonnethead sharks, are mainly found roaming the shallow flats, and will bite cut bait or jigs. Rarely getting bigger than ten pounds, these fish are entertaining on light tackle.

Also found on the flats and in deeper channels, are blacktip sharks, which will steal live shrimp or pinfish from trout anglers and cut bait fished along the bottom. They also will attack topwater plugs or flies, provided the presentation is accurate. These sharks are lots of fun as they are great jumpers. Many anglers confuse blacktips with spinner sharks. Both are aggressive and acrobatic, but the spinner shark is usually narrower across the body and has less distinct black-tipped fins than the blacktip.

Bull sharks are not to be messed with. They are aggressive and rumored (with some substantial facts) to be responsible for many fatal attacks on swimmers and wade fishermen. They stay close to shore, and even move into freshwater rivers in search of prey. They will strike topwater lures and any sort of cut or live bait. Hundred-pound-plus bulls are good reason to not drag a stringer of fish behind you if you're wading. If you see a bull shark, and you're wade fishing, get out of the water.

Nurse sharks are sometimes found by offshore anglers around wrecks and rocky outcroppings, and until landed, are mistaken for goliath grouper. They are fun to catch but tiring. The same goes for tiger sharks. Big, very big, and generally found in deep water, these are caught on big tackle, big baits, and hooks the size of gaff hooks.

Just as there's argument whether sharks should be considered sport fish, there's argument as to their edibility. Many veteran fishermen, including Richard Bowles and Vic Dunaway, consider shark flesh highly edible. Most shark-eaters admit that the flesh smells of uric acid (urine) unless the fish is bled and iced immediately. That's more than I want to know. Besides, sharks have generally been over-fished by commercial fishermen, and it wouldn't hurt to practice catch-and-release for their survival.

Sheepshead

Sheepshead, found all along Florida's western coast, are legendary bait stealers. During most of the year, these small-mouthed fish inhabit coastal oyster and rock bars, dock pilings and rock jetties searching for their favorite prey—crustaceans, including small crabs, shrimp, and even barnacles. It's these smaller fish that are very difficult to catch, as their ability to crush bait, swallow the meat, and spit out the exoskeleton (with the hook) is unrivaled. Small hooks and small baits, such as fiddler crabs and cut shrimp pieces, are the key to catching sheepshead close to shore. Patience helps, too. Learning to feel the signature bite of a sheepshead takes time, and you'll likely miss a few before you get into their rhythm. And, while the size limit on sheepshead is twelve inches, a fish that size yields very little meat upon cleaning.

It's the bigger spawning sheepshead, usually found during the late winter or early spring, that excite gulf anglers. These fish, found mostly in deeper water and around structures such as rock piles and old navigation markers, sometime reach weights of 10 pounds or more. When their spawning ritual begins, mature sheepshead will mill around the structure and seemingly eat any bait presented them. Chumming with crushed crabs, oysters, or shrimp heads will increase the feeding frenzy, but don't over-chum. They're hungry, but they do get full. Spawning fish are mature larger fish and their mouths are bigger. Most anglers rely on whole live shrimp as bait. A simple knocker rig and a sturdy size 2 hook is sufficient, but many anglers simply thread a shrimp, tail-first, onto a ⅜-ounce jig head. The advent of braided line has certainly hurt the sheepshead population in the last few years, allowing anglers a better feel for what's going on down below. Many sheepshead experts agree that you have to set the hook on a sheepshead *before* he bites, or you'll miss the hookup.

Sheepshead are delicious to eat but as difficult to clean as they are to catch. Big boned and heavily scaled, the meat-to-total-weight ratio of sheepshead is low, and most anglers opt for electric knives at the cleaning table. And, no matter how good the meat, cleaning the unrealistic legal limit is a chore. Take what you can eat that night and *not* the fifteen-fish limit, remembering that big spawning sheepshead represent the future of the fishery.

Snook

The biggest complaint I hear about inshore fishing north of Homosassa is that there are few snook. This voracious eater and superb fighter has pushed its range northward in recent years and can now be found in the southern reaches of the Big Bend. If global warming trends continue, I expect their range to push northward; if colder winters reappear, they will stay south.

Snook can be found along channel edges, under brushy mangrove roots, and around docks and snags. They are comfortable in warmer fresh, brackish, or salt waters, and they eat almost any bait, including fish, crabs, shrimp, and look-alikes.

Snook are unparalleled fighters and jumpers. Pound-for-pound they rival tarpon for action—and they're edible. Pay particular attention to a bizarre closed-season schedule, and don't forget to always buy a snook permit for your fishing license. There's nothing worse than not being able to keep a legal snook because you didn't spend a dollar on the permit!

Good snook gear includes a stiff rod with at least 30-pound braided line and 40- to 50-pound-test fluorocarbon leaders. Fly rodders generally get out their 9- or 10-weight gear for snook. Good bait choices for snook are usually light-colored or white. Big D.O.A. shrimp or TerrorEyz in natural or glow colors are effective artificials, as are light-color topwater MirrOlures. Big white Clousers or Norm Zeigler's Schminnow flies are effective on snook in most situations, including early evening around mangrove roots.

Spanish Mackerel and Bluefish

You can either target Spanish mackerel and blues—or they can target you. During the warmer months, finding these species is as easy as finding seagulls wheeling over bait schools on the deep flats. That's seagulls—not pelicans. Gulls tend to eat scraps left behind by predators attacking baitfish, while pelicans tend to dive into schools of small fish and swallow them whole. If you see pelicans diving over bait, there may or may not be predatory fish there.

When you find gulls scavenging near bait schools, look for fish striking the surface and get ready. Preparing for toothy Spanish macks and blues almost always means getting rigged with wire leader—40-pound fluorocarbon might work, but Spanish and blues can rough it up pretty quickly. Learn to attach short wire leaders to a swivel and a snap with a haywire twist and keep a few 12- to 24-inch leaders in the bottom of your tackle box for the occasion you find striking Spanish mackerel or blues. Some anglers prefer to toss lures, including topwater plugs, to striking fish, but most fishermen like to troll. Popular trolling baits are the #00 Clarkspoon or a ½-ounce Flowering Floreo with its tail trimmed back to the end of the hook shank.

The fluorescent orange Floreo is particularly effective, and will work even better if you put a narrow two-inch strip of belly meat cut from the first fish you catch on it. Strips of mullet belly work well too, and can be cut, heavily salted, and frozen in advance of a fishing trip for Spanish mackerel or bluefish.

Spanish mackerel and bluefish can also appear out of nowhere, in water as shallow as one foot. Many a jig or topwater plug simply disappears and it's usually the fault of one of these fish foraging the edge of inshore rock piles or sandbars. However, if you're lucky, the fish will strike the bait and not your line and you'll have an extra bonus for that day's fishing.

Spanish mackerel and bluefish are both good to eat, but neither freeze well. Blues should be eaten the same day they're caught, and Spanish will freeze for a few days. Both are oily and smoke well on home smokers. You'll catch larger versions of both species in the fall, after they've had a chance to eat and fatten up all summer, but the smaller springtime fish are good eating too.

Spotted Sea Trout

Spotted sea trout, sometimes called speckled trout, are the mainstay of inshore fishing along Florida's Big Bend and Emerald Coast. Relatively easy to catch, plentiful, and mild tasting, these fish are primarily found on shallow grass flats in the spring, summer, and fall. During cold overcast winter days, trout move into deep river channels, creek holes, and freshwater springs along the Gulf Coast, providing easy catching on windy, nasty days.

Most trout caught on the grassy flats are within the 15- to 20-inch regulatory slot. Gator or trophy trout are usually caught in shallower close-to-shore waters and don't school up as do the smaller fish. Spotted sea trout in the 7-pound range have become more common catches since Florida's gill-net ban went into force in the 1990s. Many experts reason that smaller trout are prey for larger ones. Checking the stomachs of big trout at the cleaning table will sometimes reveal smaller versions of the same species. In fact, a favorite wintertime deep-water plug is the MirrOLure TT Series—TT stands for *tiny trout*.

Trout are voracious eaters, and big cold-water fish sometimes eat

Sea trout are certainly the most popular fish targeted by inshore anglers
fishing the Gulf of Mexico. They're easy to catch and good table fare.

out of sheer instinct even when they're probably not hungry. This
species can resist few types of bait. Natural forage includes pinfish,
pigfish, shrimp, crabs, mullet, and all varieties of minnows, generically known as white bait. Based on this fish's eating habits, there
are hundreds, probably thousands, of lures manufactured to attract
spotted sea trout. Weighted jig heads with soft plastic tails, synthetic
shrimp look-alikes, hard and soft-bodied plugs made to swim at various depths, and a variety of topwater lures crowd the shelves at marinas and bait shops all along the coast. Most lures and techniques

work on trout, and I suggest finding a few you like and learn to fish them in different situations. Your tackle box will thank you.

Depending on air and water temperature, sunlight or clouds, and time of year, trout will hold at specific depths. Moving water, whether rising or falling, is best. Slack or slow neap tides, usually occurring during the between the full and new moon phases, make trout less eager to eat. Ambushers, they prefer to attack baits that wash into sand holes on grass flats or along the edge of bars.

Wintertime trout in deep-water rivers and creeks are the exception. I think they bite because they're bothered by baits hitting them in the head and attack out of frustration at the attempts to hook them by the dozens of anglers above.

In general, big trout are spookier than smaller ones. Stealth becomes more important the shallower and clearer the water. No slamming cooler lids or loud talking necessary!

Many anglers assume that tactics for sea trout are the same in cold as well as warm weather. Warmer months find trout moving from the shallows during the days to cooler deeper flats. If you plan to target trout early on a warm summer, spring, or fall day, start early and fish close to shore. As the day warms, you'll notice schools of mullet or white bait moving out toward deeper waters. Many trout will move with them. Big summertime high tides do hold trout closer to shore longer in the mornings. Conversely, trout don't get too close to shore on an extreme low tide, no matter the air temperature. However, sometimes rather than moving offshore, they move inside creeks or the river and wait for the rising tide inside deep holes, easy prey for anglers with shallow-draft boats, kayaks, or canoes. Typically, winter fishing for trout on the Big Bend and Emerald Coast is best in the river holes, inside creeks, or on warm sunlit rock piles at creek entrances.

Each year on the Big Bend and Emerald Coast, sea-trout season goes through a mandatory one-month closure in February but reopens March 1. The weather is usually moderate, but the water can still be cold. A drift with a river's current while slowly bouncing live shrimp threaded onto jig heads, Gulp! Shrimp or D.O.A. TerrorEyz jigs off the bottom can be productive.

Take plenty of extra tackle for trout fishing in a river as the same rocks providing hiding spots for the fish will cut lots of line and snag lures. Another cold-weather option for trout is to fish the shallows outside creeks or rocky points on sunny cold afternoons, preferably on a rising tide. A word to the wise—don't get caught up close to shore on a cold winter day with the tide falling, particularly with an offshore wind howling. You *will* get to spend the night, your boat high and dry, and that *won't* be fun. If you're lucky enough to have a boat that will allow you to float in a foot of water, you'll find this type of fishing very productive and the trout oversized. Try to make long casts over rocks and bars, and to be as stealthy as is possible. Local gator-trout experts usually use slow-sinking plugs such as MirrOlure's MirrOMinnows or Catch 2000s, and B&L's Corky Mullet.

As water temperatures reach a temperate 70 degrees, sea trout become more predictable. The warm water attracts a greater stock of pinfish, mullet, white bait, and shrimp, and the trout spread out on the flats, chasing them. The depth you'll find trout depends on water temperature. A successful tactic is to make a drift over mixed grass and sand flats, preferably from inshore to offshore. When you start catching fish, note the depth, toss a marker buoy or hit the "Man Overboard" button on your GPS. Typically the trout will hold with a comfortable amount of water over their backs, allowing you several drifts over active fishing areas before the tide changes the depths.

Silver, or sand, trout are also found in gulf waters and are close relatives of spotted sea trout. These smaller fish tend to school up in sandy or shelly sloughs or holes. They are easy to catch with small jigs and are very good to eat, although each fish yields very small filets. They're great fun for kids and less-active anglers.

Tarpon

It's important that I mention tarpon, the silver king, in the context of inshore species, as you might be lucky enough to hook up with one on almost any warm-weather inshore trip.

In late April, tarpon begin a northward migration along the Big Bend. In addition to these traveling fish, there are resident tarpon found year-round in most of the rivers along Florida's Gulf Coast.

Tarpon eat almost anything. Mullet heads on the bottom, topwater lures, jigs, live pinfish or white bait, and flies—it makes no difference. It's all about the individual fish's mood.

Tarpon are specifically targeted by anglers in the lower reaches of the Big Bend at Homosassa and Crystal River and west of St. Marks along beaches and sand shoals. In between, it's more a matter of having a pod of fish cruise past your boat and being prepared. Most flats anglers carry a heavy spinning rod rigged and ready with a heavy 80-pound fluorocarbon leader and a simple eel-like jig. Tarpon love eels, making this is a good choice for the random encounter.

If you're interested in targeting tarpon and are new to the game, I recommend you hire a professional guide for your first trip or two. Guides will have better knowledge of the specific fishery and what's working in terms of bait and tackle. Also, tarpon fishing involves certain etiquette regarding fighting fish, landing them, and handling them for photos. This species deserves the greatest care, as civilization has encroached upon them and they have become more endangered than ever. Careful catch-and-release is essential for the future of these great fish.

Tripletail

Always, always, always look around floating debris, crab-trap floats, and channel markers for tripletail. These goofy-looking fish are found floating or drifting near the surface and eat a variety of baits, including live shrimp, jigs, and plugs such as the MirrOlure 52M. They inhabit the entire range of gulf shoreline. If you find one, spend the time needed to entice him to bite, and hang on. They're notorious for wrapping lines around structure, and you want to be prepared to pull the fish toward your boat. Sometimes tedious to clean, tripletail are some of the best tasting fish you'll take from the gulf.

Popular Offshore Fish Species

What exactly is offshore fishing? Personally, I consider it fishing in any water that's over my head in depth. Many others, though, think it's silly to have a perfectly fine outboard motor aboard a boat and elect to push it along the shallows with a big stick. The National Weather Service delineates *inshore*-weather forecasts from *offshore*-weather forecasts at twenty nautical miles off the coastline, but that's extreme in parts of Florida where depths may only be 20 feet at that distance.

Depth might be a better descriptor, with any depth that regularly holds offshore species, such as grouper, considered *offshore*. Rules are made to be broken (by fish, of course) and plenty of keeper grouper are caught in river channels and big king mackerel move onto the shallow flats at times. So, you define offshore for yourself, and I'll go with species as my guide.

Amberjack

AJs can be good and AJs can be bad. First, the bad news. If you try fishing a wreck or big rock pile anywhere in the gulf, you're likely to have amberjack hovering somewhere between you and the grouper or snapper you're targeting. And they're always hungry. Getting a live bait past them is usually an exercise in futility. Many anglers sacrifice a few baits on one side of the boat in order to let their buddies get baits to the bottom fish on the other.

The good news is that AJs are fun to catch and pound-for-pound offer a mighty struggle. They hit hard and fight up until the bitter end. They also taste pretty good, at least the smaller ones. As they grow older and larger, they tend to have more worms than in their youth, but many anglers overlook this distribution of parasites in their flesh, claiming, "They cook up just fine." Many claim that amberjack is the best fish for smoking and for dips.

While amberjack are hard fighters, a soft approach will make the task easier for fishermen. Don't jerk them around, pull them up slowly and steadily, and they'll come right to the landing net or gaff.

Barracuda

In the northern gulf, including the Big Bend and Emerald Coast, large barracuda are seldom seen inshore. Mostly large specimens hover over and around wrecks and reefs, seeking an easy meal, which could easily be the fish you're pulling into your boat.

Great fighters and suckers for bright flashy lures, these big northern 'cudas are great fun on light tackle with steel leaders, but care should be taken to release them as carefully as possible. They are not really fit to eat, as they may carry the *ciguatera* toxin, a poison you don't want to experience.

Cobia

Are cobia an inshore or an offshore species? I certainly don't know, as I've seen huge ones taken within sight of shore and also off of wrecks in a hundred feet of water.

These crab-eaters spend their winters in the southern gulf and migrate northward in spring, finally ending up all along the Emerald Coast in huge numbers. Northern gulf anglers can think of little else in April and May but cobia.

Structure interests cobia, as do the shade and shelter provided by big rays. Many inshore anglers make it a habit to carry a big spinning outfit rigged with an eel-like jig during the summer months, and most never miss the opportunity to check out big channel markers or passing rays for cobia. Deep offshore reefs, springs, and rock piles also interest cobia, as they're good spots to ambush passing bait, including crabs, small fish, eels (a cobia favorite), and shrimp.

Cobia can bite enthusiastically or not at all. Many anglers complain when cobia swim around their boat, nibble at chum bags, and eye the crew—but don't bite. That's just the way cobia are.

It's hard to prepare for a cobia bite, but most fishermen use large spinning rods with enough backbone to pull the fish away from structure. Cobia know their neighborhoods, and will wrap a line around a marker in seconds. 30-pound-class reels and braided lines help with the fight. If you're lucky enough to find cobia in open water or along northern gulf beaches, lighter tackle is fun and practical. Ultra-clear fluorocarbon leaders help too, as cobia will back away from visible line or leader, although corks or balloons floated above free-lined pinfish or crabs don't seem to spook them. Finally, don't put a green cobia in your boat. These fish are very strong, and although you take a chance of losing one the longer you fight him, they will break cooler tops, rods, and even human limbs if brought into the cockpit of a boat too soon. Gaffing a big cobia can be dangerous, too, if he's not tired and not ready to give up the fight.

Cobia are popular game fish for their sport and for their food value. Their firm clean flesh cuts nicely into steaks for the grill, and they are very good smoked. And big cobia taste as good as smaller ones, an unusual quality found in few fishes.

Dolphin

The fish, not Flipper, is also known as dorado or mahi mahi, and they are found throughout the northern gulf and sometime come surprisingly close to shore, especially along the deeper Emerald Coast than along the Big Bend. Offshore, they hide under weedlines or around

Dolphin (the fish) are often caught while trolling colorful lures in deep offshore waters.

structure, and smaller fish will travel in large schools. Great fighters, mahi can be caught on all sorts of lures and baits, live or artificial, trolled or pitched. In deep water, especially, have a hooked-up mahi in the water and grab another rod. Mahi are schoolies, and will hang around their buddy instead of disappearing on you.

Birds wheeling over the surface of the water can help you spot schools of dolphin, and try chumming to keep them nearby. Once chummed close to the boat, smaller peanut-size fish are lots of fun on fly rods or light spinning gear. Whatever size mahi you boat is the size you can expect to catch, as these fish travel together in schools the same age and size.

The flesh of the mahi is some of the best around, and it takes well to grilling or smoking.

The Groupers

Gag Grouper

Found all along the Big Bend and Emerald Coast, gags are probably the most sought-after offshore species along the Emerald Coast and Big Bend. Delicious table fare and easy to catch, they are targeted by

Any offshore angler would be proud of this cooler filled with snapper and grouper.

anglers at varying depths along the coast. Fish as large as forty pounds are caught well offshore, but the bulk of gags taken are just above the legal size minimum. Frankly, these smaller fish are better eating and provide great action without having to invest in oversize tackle.

Gag grouper tend to prefer structure, including rock outcroppings, offshore springs, and artificial reefs. Juveniles, known as grass grouper, inhabit inshore flats, channels, and creeks. While they're not legal to keep, small grouper can provide fun on light tackle and surprise many an angler looking for inshore species, but special care should be taken to safely release juvenile fish of all species. Avoid using gaffs or landing nets on small fish. Mechanical fish grippers and dehookers ensure safe releases, as do circle hooks. Learn to vent the air bladders of all groupers that are suffering from decompression due to a quick trip to the surface at the end of a fishing line. Your local tackle supplier will demonstrate the use of a venting tool, an item now required on all boats fishing for reef fish. Rocky outcroppings and wrecks don't necessarily appear just in deep water. With the onset of cold weather, larger gags move closer to shore, particularly in the lower Big Bend, and many are taken with live bait or diving plugs in as little as eight feet of water.

Gags are omnivorous but moody. Many successful grouper diggers begin fishing a spot with frozen baits, such as squid, Spanish sardines or threadfin herring, and move on to live baits only when the action picks up. Pinfish, pigfish, large shrimp, menhaden, spots, or cigar minnows are tried-and-true live baits for grouper. Large jigs and deep-jigging techniques work well over rocky live bottom, attracting strikes primarily as the lure falls toward the bottom from an upward stroke of a long rod. Imitation shrimp and mullet baits are also deadly, and like jigs, don't smell up the boat or require constant attention and baiting. While bottom-fishing has its advantages in that several anglers can fish at one time, anchoring safely and accurately in rough seas can be difficult. Many grouper fishermen prefer to troll large lures all day; others use them only to prospect for new fishing spots. Large diving plugs with treble hooks trolled at four to five knots and fished deep on modern braided line are a fun way to catch lots of nice gags, but fuel consumption can be a consideration. These big lures are sold in many size and depth configurations, and can be trolled directly or used with downriggers or planers. Simply put, gags love to eat, a statement bolstered by the stories of stomachs inspected at the cleaning table containing leftover chicken bones tossed overboard by anglers.

Tides affect a gag's willingness to eat, with action falling off as the flow slacks. Even the slightest tidal change will affect not only the bite, but also the location of gags. Slow movement will hold the fish close to structure, while strong tides draw them away from cover to nearby sandy flats where they prey on bait washed toward them. Be sure to take tidal strength and direction into consideration when fishing bottom structure, whether it be artificial reef balls, wrecks, ledges, or lone rock piles. At the time of the full moon—or just after—you will probably notice a decrease in the grouper bite. The big boys fill up with the visibility of a full moon—especially in cooler weather.

Red Grouper

Red grouper are probably served in more restaurants than any other fish from the northern gulf. They roam the underwater plains and prairies in the central and northern gulf. Deep, live coral and grass bottom are their preferred habitat. Highly detailed structure is not necessary for the average red grouper. Notorious eating machines, undersize specimens will beat gags to anglers' baits and empty a live well or bucket of cut bait quickly. Reds also eagerly attack large plugs trolled over grassy knobby bottom. Solid advice from experienced grouper fishermen is to move to another spot should nothing but short red grouper start coming to the surface.

Other Groupers

While gag grouper and red grouper make up the bulk of grouper caught by anglers along the Gulf Coast, they are not the only species in the habitat.

The most-noticed other grouper is certainly the goliath grouper, formerly known as Jewfish. These mammoths, some upwards of 500 pounds, have fooled many anglers into thinking they've hooked Mother Earth. Adults of the species are found all along the Big Bend and Emerald Coast inside wrecks, under offshore ledges, and around artificial reef structures. It is illegal to take or possess a goliath grouper, and that includes hoisting one into the boat for photos should you find yourself fortunate enough to get him to the surface. I mention the species as they have become more numerous and pesky since becoming a protected species in 1990. The sight of a fifteen-pound gag grouper being swallowed whole at your boat's gunwales is a startling experience for any angler. Don't even try sharing a rock pile or wreck with a bunch of goliaths—just move along to another spot.

Other important but less available gulf groupers are the snowy grouper, speckled hind grouper, Warsaw grouper, and the tasty scamp. Pesky at times, black sea bass can entertain frustrated anglers or kids. They're small, ferocious, and their delicate white meat is excellent. The bottom that holds black sea bass may also hold their grouper cousins. But, if you're pulling in a lot of sea bass, they're likely getting to your bait before the grouper. That means you're in a good area for black sea bass, but on the wrong spot for grouper. It's time to move the boat.

The Mackerels

King Mackerel

King mackerel, or kingfish, are found all along the Big Bend and Emerald Coast, making an annual migration northward in spring, summering in the deep water off the panhandle, and returning south in the fall. While most of these aggressive speedsters school up, it's the larger versions that come closer to shore in search of food. Fifty-pound fish are not unusual, and their ability to empty a reel of 400 yards or so of line and burn up a drag is legendary—hence their nickname: smokers.

Tactics for kings vary. Slow-trolling large feathers, spoons, dusters, hooded ballyhoo, or live bait is a preferred method for schoolies during the big spring and fall runs. Blue runners are a favorite king mackerel bait throughout the gulf. During the summer, fishermen working the bottom for grouper and snapper will sometimes put out a free-lined live bait rigged with a stinger rig consisting of a pair of

4X-strong treble hooks. The sight of a 40- or 50-pound king skyrocketing with your bait in his mouth is always exciting, but remember to keep your reel's drag set lightly and it's spool well-filled. Fish hooked on a stinger rig are most-often lightly hooked, many times snagged, and require lots of finesse and patience to land.

There are a number of opinions about eating kingfish. Many feel only smaller ones should be eaten, and those grilled quickly after the catch—never frozen. Others enjoy the fish smoked. Some medical experts claim the oily flesh valuable for its vitamins; others claim it a health issue due to high levels of mercury, usually in larger fish.

Wahoo

Wahoo are deep-water cousins of the kingfish and members of the mackerel family. They usually are found well offshore and generally while trolling at high speeds for billfish. They sometimes will attack a bait on the surface and skyrocket, like a king, but usually strike deep. Their clean, white meat makes excellent table fare.

Sailfish, Marlin, and Swordfish

Sailfish, swordfish, and blue and white marlin are collectively known as billfish, and they are game of choice for bluewater anglers.

Sailfish are usually found in the northern gulf during the warmer months, and some will roam into shallow coastal waters along the Big Bend. This species is a small billfish, rarely exceeding 100 pounds, but is a ferocious fighter and can be taken on lighter trolling tackle, including spinning gear.

White marlin are great jumpers and fighters, and are found in the depths of the gulf. Like sailfish, however, they sometime come inside of the Continental Shelf toward the shore. One-hundred-pounders are considered sizeable, and like sails, they readily attack slow-trolled live baits or rigged ballyhoo and squid.

I don't know any angler who would object to catching a 500-pound blue marlin and having a replica mount on his family room wall. These are the fish that dreams are made of, and the opportunity to catch one is a once-in-a-lifetime experience. These deep-dwellers are found in the northern gulf and are the target species of many Emerald

Coast charterboat captains and crews. Some captains are so serious, in fact, that they subscribe to online services that predict water temperature and current flow based on real-time satellite information. Blue marlin are fond of weedlines and temperature thermoclines, and success or failure can be measured by simply not trolling an active area and the bait it holds. It takes big tackle and big bait to catch big blue marlin. Live bonito or whole rigged mullet or mackerel are good baits to troll, as are artificial lures. Eighty-pound-class tackle is usually considered appropriate for the fight of a lifetime.

Big and powerful, swordfish are finally making a comeback in the very deep gulf waters. Usually caught at night using squid or illuminated lures at extreme depths off the Continental Shelf, a few swordfish are taken in waters as shallow as 300 feet. Big tackle, big boats, and an experienced crew are all essential in the quest for this species.

In general, billfish have good food value, but stocks are dwindling. Extreme care should be taken to safely release these fish into their habitat.

The Snappers

American Red Snapper

American red snapper are prime targets for northern gulf anglers. Usually found in depths exceeding sixty feet, red snapper are tasty and relatively easy to catch. Fished hard commercially and recreationally and nearly destroyed by shrimp trawls, strict seasonal limits exist.

Red snapper gather over structure, and their preference seems to be ledges over which they can gather to snag passing baits. A depth finder showing an inverted Christmas-tree shape over a ledge is usually showing a school of red snapper.

More finicky about their food than grouper, red snapper prefer live baits such as pinfish, cigar minnows, and pogies (menhaden), if available. Frozen sardines and shrimp work well, but it's the live baits these fish love.

Fishing at night for red snapper in depths well below 100 feet is common practice in the upper gulf. Consider extending an offshore

American red snapper are excellent to eat and require lighter tackle than grouper.

day trip and do some night-fishing for snapper. Try using underwater lights, such the Hydro-Glow Light stick, to attract various baits to the side of the boat. You'll be able to catch small live baits using a Sabiki rig and will soon replenish your live well.

Gray or Mangrove Snapper

Mangos are another favorite of northern gulf reef anglers—and folks lucky enough to find legal juveniles in inshore waters. Offshore, they usually inhabit the same structure as American red snapper but are bigger and, like reds, provide lots of action at night. Live bait, such as cigar minnows, is the key to catching these fish, which reach 6 or

8 pounds. Inshore, they can be found in deep river holes or in cuts through bars, and are lots of fun to catch on very light tackle. All sizes of this species are excellent at the table.

Other Snappers

While fishing for red or mangrove snappers, you'll likely hook up on either Lane snappers or vermillion snappers (also called beeliners), both of which inhabit the same waters in the northern gulf. Both are smallish, and the meat is fragile, needing quick icing aboard the boat. Hogfish, or hog snapper, are also found on very deep reefs, and are usually taken with shrimp rather than with baitfish. In fact, many hogfish taken offshore of the Big Bend seem to come up at the end of a diver's spear gun, as they're sometimes hard to entice with hook and line.

Finally, I would be remiss not to include Florida snappers or Cedar Key snappers, both the same fish. There's no doubt that reef-fish populations—and snapper numbers in particular—have dwindled over the years. So, imagine trying to make your living as an offshore fishing guide, unable to keep fish that are caught during a closed season, yet having to satisfy the appetites of paying anglers. Creative marketing by guides, chambers of commerce, and marinas is the process, and re-naming of fish generally called "grunts" to Florida snapper or Cedar Key snapper is the outcome. Easy to catch, generally plentiful, excellent to eat and sometimes growing to a pound or more, white grunts or Key West grunts just have unappetizing names. They range throughout the central and northern gulf, and are usually found over structure such as live bottom, rocks or wrecks.

Triggerfish

If you've ever read the menu in a fine restaurant and seen *turbot* listed, and wondered what it was, the answer is probably triggerfish. Common in three varieties (gray, queen, and ocean) throughout the gulf, these flattish small-mouth bait-stealers are some of the best eating you'll find.

Usually not taken in great quantities on hook and line, most are by-products of searches for grouper or snapper.

Extremely difficult to clean, even in comparison to sheepshead or flounder, most anglers are happy to have only one or two of these fish to clean at the end of the day.

Tuna

Yellowfin and blackfin tuna roam the depths of the gulf and are usually targeted from Emerald Coast ports, as deeper water is closer. Some do appear at docks on the Big Bend, but usually after a boatload of anglers has returned from an extended trip to the northern canyons or to the towers offshore of Carrabelle. Tuna fishing is big-boat work and good reason to hire a professional boat and crew. This is long exhausting fishing and local knowledge is invaluable. In the northern gulf, popular methods are trolling multiple offshore lures and/or rigged baits.

Both yellowfin and blackfin tuna are excellent to eat—seared, grilled, or even raw. Their dark red flesh, sometimes shaved off a still-flopping specimen and splashed with tamari-style soy sauce, is a popular offshore raw lunch.

Junk Fish

What constitutes a junk fish? Is there such a thing?

If you're hungry enough you'll eat almost any species. Many consider mullet a baitfish, but others would rather eat mullet than grouper. Mediterranean fish markets display elaborate arrays of sardines, scad, and herring that we regularly use for bait. And, during 1930s and the Great Depression, fried fish patties made of tarpon flesh was the highlight of many a Sunday dinner in certain areas of Florida.

Jacks, including blue runners, jack crevalle, and horse-eyes, are the great sport fish of the junk-fish category. That said, never miss an opportunity to tackle any of these fish with light tackle and flashy lures. Pound-for-pound, they're the best fighters you'll find and have saved the day for many fishing guides. Even little blue runners that many anglers consider only bait for king mackerel put up a valiant struggle. The food value of these fish is suspect, and although I try to eat a smoked jack crevalle every couple of years, the news gets no better.

Bonito (Atlantic bonito and little tunny) are also great sport fish and always worth the effort to catch, although finicky sometimes. You'll likely see schools of them offshore bashing baits and waiting for you to toss a small spoon or jig into their midst. Despite being cousins to the delicious tunas, bonito suffer the same fate as jacks when it comes to their table value: they're basically cat food.

While jacks make drag-screaming runs, ladyfish are the great jump-

There's really no such thing as a junk fish—as long as the angler is having fun!

ers. Considered by many to be poor-man's tarpon, these sleek and voracious fish rarely make it to the boat, as they're experts at head shaking and lure tossing. Many are caught by accident by inshore flats fishermen, but you'll just as likely find them mixed into fast-traveling schools of Spanish mackerel, jack crevalle, and bluefish. They are terrific targets for fly rodders and will eat almost any fly tossed to them and worked quickly. They are bony, their flesh is mushy, and they're really not fit for human consumption. They do, however, make wonderful tarpon bait.

On the subject of good tarpon bait, it's not surprising that the saltwater catfish—hardhead and gafftopsail—are a favorite of anglers fishing cut bait. It's soft and smelly, and catfish don't move all that quickly. Tarpon and cobia have no problem with the cats' sharp spines and bones. They're used to eating crabs and crushing them quickly in their jaws and consider them prime targets. Catfish are mostly pests but can provide lots of entertainment for kids on a flats fishing trip. Care should be taken in handling them, as their spines are sharp and carry a potentially infectious bacterial slime.

The list of junk fish goes on and on, as do the arguments about their sport or table value. Some are simply not fit to eat. Pufferfish are considered poisonous, and alligator gar just taste bad. But croakers, silver perch (butterfish), sand perch (squirrelfish), and the entire porgy clan all come to mind when thinking about fish with nice white meat and the willingness to fight on a hook and line. Given the right situation, any of these species can be fun to catch and will occupy easily distracted kids or adults. And, if you're hungry for fish, there's no such thing as junk fish.

Bay Scallops and Scalloping

Scalloping is the Big Bend and eastern Emerald Coast's alternative to South Florida's lobster season. It's a combination of complete madness at boat ramps and marinas, motels filled to capacity, family fun, and some of the best eating around.

Bay scallops are legal in the gulf from July 1 to September 10 of each year from the Pasco–Hernando County line to the western bank of the Mexico Beach Canal in Bay County. That's a shorter season than the one for lobsters, but while it lasts, it's just about as much fun as you and your family can have.

Scallops seem to be predictable, and there are generally reliable preseason reports as to their availability from flats anglers as well as from researchers at the Florida Fish and Wildlife Research Institute. It seems that with the increased development of the Gulf Coast that the best spots to scallop are in the least populated areas, in particular the coastline between Homosassa and Carrabelle, including Crystal River, Steinhatchee, Keaton Beach, St. Marks, and Lanark Village. Water quality and salinity is an issue with scallops, one convincing example being that there are few to be found near the mouths of the brackish and turbid Suwannee and Withlacoochee Rivers, both located in the geographic middle of other scallop hotspots. Skip the

Bay scalloping is a popular family activity between the Pasco–Hernando county line and the Mexico Beach Canal.

mouth of the Apalachicola River as well, but look for good scalloping grounds toward the west at Indian Pass and St. Joe Bay.

Scallops move, too. One day they'll be found in the clear water next to shore; the next they'll be in eight feet of water on banks far offshore. No matter the depth, scallops are not hard to find, and the more they gather in one spot (a part of their reproduction cycle), the better catches folks bring back to the dock.

If you're the first boat out of port on the first day of scallop season, you probably need to pay attention to reports from marinas and local newspapers or television as to the location of the best potential areas. If you're out on July 2, which is day two of the season—just look for the flotilla!

Once you're in the scallops' neighborhood, you'll need to do a little bit of searching, just to make anchoring worthwhile. Hopefully the water will be clear—scallops like it this way—and you can position a couple of spotters to look for scallops turned light side up. While most scallops are found with their dark sides upward to the surface of the water, a few tend to settle on the bottom flipped over, making it easy for boaters to spot them. If you see a few light or colored shells, that's a good sign that there are more scallops nearby. If you're in dark or deep water, you'll more than likely need to get a crewmember overboard to take a closer look before you commit to that particular spot.

Before you get your crew wet, follow a few rules—some official, some just based on good common sense. All scallopers, unless exempt, are required to have a Florida recreational saltwater fishing license. Scallops may only be taken by hand or with a hand-held net. Your boat must display a dive flag that is 20 by 24 inches or larger, with a stiffener, flown from the highest point of the boat. If you're wading from shore, each person must tow a 12-by-12-inch flag. When approaching the scallop fleet, keep an eye out for swimmers, divers, and snorkelers and keep a legal distance and speed: *Vessels approaching divers-down flags closer than 300 feet in open water and 100 feet in rivers, inlets, and navigation channels must slow to idle speed.* Keep a person aboard the boat at all times and instruct your scallopers that his or her word is law. Crowds of scallopers don't seem to scare away sharks, and the word from the captain to get out of the water should be taken seriously. Also, good common sense tells most people that cleaning scallops aboard and then throwing the offal into the water near snorkelers is well outside the range of good judgment. Most people, that is. Your lookout should also keep a head count of everyone in the water and alert folks, particularly children, lest they drift or swim too far from the boat.

If it's your first time scalloping, you'll need to make a trip to a local dive or tackle shop and pick up a few necessities. The aforementioned dive flag should be the first thing on your list, and mesh bags second. I'd advise getting bags in bright colors as dark ones tend to get lost on the bottom If dropped. If you think you'll be scalloping in waist-deep water you may not need anything other than a mask and comfortable wading shoes, but when the scallops get deeper where the tidal currents are strong you'll certainly want to consider investing in swim fins and snorkels for everyone in your party. Individuals are limited to two gallons of scallops in their shells. Boat limits are ten gallons total, even if you have more than five persons aboard. Take care to measure your catch carefully, as Fish and Wildlife patrols are out in force during scallop season, and they take bag limits of this precious resource very seriously. A two-gallon limit per individual will yield about a pint of cleaned meat. Unlike oysters, where you eat the entire animal, scallops are taken only for their adductor muscles, those which open and close the shell. Adductor sizes vary somewhat, and limits seem to have a higher yield toward the end of the season.

Scallop catching isn't hard once they're found. The hardest part for inexperienced snorkelers is using the equipment, but after a few minutes, even novices get the hang of timing their breaths and dives. While some scallops are easy to see, particularly if their light sides are facing upward and they're lying on top of the grass, many scallops are not immediately visible, and are snuggled down in the grass, dark side up. Finding an area with shorter grass and spotty white-sand areas is preferred, and if you find yourself in such an area, your catch rate will be faster. Look carefully along the edges of white sandy patches and you'll probably do better than if you are in grassy dark areas. If you do end up in an area of long turtle grass try approaching the grass with the tide running directly toward you. That way, you'll be able to look under the bending grass and will have a better chance of seeing the scallops. Midday times on sunny days help, too. Tides don't really make a difference as to whether the scallops are there, but picking them will be easier in slow-moving currents. You will notice that scallops move with the tides and that an area you scoured can be repopulated in a matter of an hour or so when there's current. Pick them up by hand or with a dip net as you find them and pop them into your dive bag, but be sure to pull the bag's drawstring, as scallops will occasionally swim and escape. Scallops don't bite so handling them is easy. Take them back to the boat frequently, measure your catch and get them on ice immediately. Cleaning scallops is not hard, but it's time consuming and smelly. A good reference is Dr. Charles Courtney's "An Illustrated Guide to Cleaning Scallops," found on the Web at http://tinyurl.com/6hqy97.

It's worth mentioning the hazards of scalloping. Scallopers should be aware of sea urchins and take care not to grab or step on one. Stingrays are plentiful but harmless unless stepped on, and late summer always brings hordes of stinging jellyfish. Be wary, but don't let these marine threats spoil your trip.

A more serious concern is the weather. Hot summer afternoons almost always fuel big thunderstorms. Keep your eyes open and keep listening to the radio. Be prepared to haul anchor and run toward safe waters should the sounds of thunder approach.

Scalloping is not big-game fishing, nor does it involve special skills, knowledge, or tackle. Scalloping is a fun day on the water for the entire family. The little kids can swim close to the boat, the bigger ones can pick scallops and look at starfish and small fish, and the adults can scallop, swim, or just enjoy each other's company. Followed by a dinner that night of freshly caught scallops, life ain't too bad.

18

. . . And How To Catch Them

Inshore Gear and Tackle

Learning to fish the inshore waters of the Gulf of Mexico from Citrus County westward to Pensacola is a complicated study of opposites. Nearshore water in the southern reaches of the Big Bend is measured in feet or inches, while that just past Cape San Blas beaches quickly falls off to many fathoms. And *bays* along the Big Bend relate in size to shallow *coves* on the Emerald Coast, where bays encompass vast bodies of water such as St. Andrew Bay and Pensacola Bay.

While offshore fishing is big-boat fishing, boats are not necessarily a requirement for the successful inshore angler. Inshore options include wading, beach, and pier fishing. There are boat options as well, including bay boats, flats skiffs, aluminum or fiberglass johnboats, airboats, kayaks, and canoes. No matter your budget, you have the ability to fish the gulf shoreline.

One of the biggest mistakes I see on inshore waters is the use of fishing tackle that outclasses the angler's prey. Yes, the occasional big jack crevalle, black drum, bull red, or tarpon will surprise an angler, but that's an exception. Most inshore fish can be taken easily with high quality, light- to medium-class spinning, casting, or fly tackle. I think many tackle retailers recommend line, leader, and terminal tackle based on weight, not on how appropriate it is for a particular fishing situation. Think about it. Not many fish are going to get near a shrimp pinned to the bottom by a 60-pound wire leader, two swivels, a 6/0 hook, and three ounces of lead sinker. Fish will attack a bait that swims naturally past his nose, but they're not interested in eating hardware. Heavy terminal tackle is necessary in some situations, but the lighter you can rig your tackle, the better chance you have of hooking up on inshore species. Inshore fishing *is* light-tackle fishing.

Your stock of good inshore tackle should include rods and reels—spinning, fly, or casting—that are comfortable to cast. Unlike offshore angling, inshore fishermen must make many more long and accurate casts on every outing. If you're throwing topwater plugs for sea trout on the flat, and expect to cast as many as 500 times a day, you might consider spinning tackle rather than a baitcasting outfit. On the other hand, if you're trolling for Spanish mackerel on a nearshore reef, baitcasters with quality drags are perfect. They're also good for creek fishing where short casts to banks and shorelines are needed. Fly rods should always be the lightest you can afford, as a fly rod's ability to cut through the air helps make longer, more accurate presentations to wary fish. For your first inshore spinning rod, you might consider a 6½- to 7-foot medium action graphite rod paired with a medium-light saltwater reel. If you're planning to wade or surf fish only, you might consider something longer, perhaps an 8-footer. A good casting rod choice would be something in the 6-foot range paired with a small saltwater reel, while 7- and 8-weight fly rods are favored by inshore fly fishermen.

Inshore Tackle Recommendations

Reels

Shimano Spheros 3000, 4000, and 6000, and Stradic 2500, 4000, and 5000 spinning reels. Shimano makes dependable light spinning reels that work well with monofilament as well as braided line. Both reels are designed for heavy use in salt water and require little care after a day on the water. The Spheros 6000 and Stradic 5000 are adequate for tarpon, sharks, and the bigger inshore species.

Shimano Calcutta 200 and 400 baitcasting reels. These are high-quality reels with heavy-duty drag systems. The Calcutta 200 works well with

10-pound-test braided line and is lightweight enough to comfortably cast all day.

Rods

Shimano and St. Croix casting and spinning rods. These rod makers offer a complete line of inshore casting and spinning rods to suit any budget. They are available at many full-service tackle shops.

Fly Fishing Tackle

G.Loomis and Sage fly rods; Tibor fly reels; Scientific Anglers and Cortland fly lines and backing. Quality fly tackle is very expensive, but it's worth every penny when casting all day or when fighting a big fish. Sage, Loomis, and Tibor are simply the best when it comes to rods and reels. Scientific Anglers and Cortland make complete selections of tropical-style lines appropriate for most gulf fly fishing. None are cheap. As depths can vary along any stretch of the Florida coast, many fly fishermen carry both floating and sinking lines, usually spooled onto separate reels or replacement reel spools.

Line, Leader, and Terminal Tackle

Daiichi hooks. If you're fishing live bait or replacing hooks on lures, Daiichi's super-sharp hooks are a good choice. Many inshore anglers replace the front hooks on lures with red Daiichi Bleeding Bait treble hooks to simulate the red gills of excited baitfish.

Triple Fish fluorocarbon leader material. Use 20-pound for trout and small inshore species and 25-pound for redfishing near oyster bars and sharp rocks. 80-pound is good for tarpon, and consider 40- to 50-pound-test for toothy Spanish mackerel and bluefish.

PowerPro Super Braid Spectra fiber line. PowerPro typically breaks at about twice its rated strength and has a much smaller diameter than comparable strength monofilament lines. The 10-pound-test line is popular for most light-tackle applications, but 30-pound should be considered for tarpon, snook, and nearshore cobia. Also, don't overlook the informative knot diagrams and line-winding devices included with spools of PowerPro.

Popping Corks

As the water temperatures rise in the gulf, brightly colored Paradise or Cajun Thunder popping corks rigged over live bait or jigs are popular. Easy to fish, especially for novice or young anglers, they provide lots of entertainment value as well as good catches. Expect to use lots of live shrimp if you put these below corks, as pinfish steal their fair share. However, anglers claim that by attracting pinfish to the shrimp, trout are attracted to the pinfish, and are caught in an attempt to steal back the shrimp. Other options to use beneath popping corks include D.O.A.s plastic shrimp, synthetic baits such as Gulp! or FishBites. Experienced guides all along the coast also count on trapped pinfish or pigfish as trout bait. Many big warmwater trout are caught with these small fish rigged under popping corks.

To effectively use a popping cork, you must *pop* or splash the cork with your rod tip occasionally, making the trout think other fish are striking bait.

Lures

D.O.A. TerrorEyz Jigs. One of the best all-round baits, the TerrorEyz is available in many colors and several sizes. The ¼-ounce version is most popular with inshore fishermen. Use light colors, such as chartreuse–silver glitter (#318), in clear water, and dark colors, such as root beer–gold glitter (#304), in muddy or stained water. Bounced slowly off the bottom near oyster and rock bars, these lures with upward-oriented hooks will produce good redfish and flounder action. They also work well in deeper water when slowly dragged in a swimming motion. Their soft bodies are relatively tough, but sometimes too fragile for toothy Spanish mackerel and bluefish, which eat them readily. The larger ⅜- and ½-ounce jigs are irresistible to tarpon.

D.O.A. Shrimp. This was the original true-to-life plastic shrimp, and it is still the best. The combination of its shape and balanced weight gives it a natural shrimp look when pulled steadily and slowly over grass tops for sea trout. Any species that eats shrimp will eat this lure. Use light colors, such as nite glow–fire tail (#329) in clear water, and dark colors such as avocado–red glitter (#371) in dark or stained water.

Mark Nichols, D.O.A.'s chief cook and bottle washer, recently developed a new method of making his shrimp easier to cast and to fish over rough bottom. After pulling out the factory hook, Mark trims off the tail fins and inserts a #3.5/0 wide gap hook (made exclusively for D.O.A.) through the tail, rigging it weedless by laying the barb along the shrimp's back. He then inserts a large glass rattle into the hole made by the original hook. This method makes the whole lure much more aerodynamic and actually more lifelike in the water, like a live shrimp rigged for bonefish. The rattles and 3.5/0 hooks are available at larger tackle shops and direct from www.doalures.com

D.O.A. Bait Buster. The Bait Buster is another lure built on an upward-oriented jig hook. It's design is very "mulletlike," with a single, very strong hook. Available in shallow-running, deep-running, and trolling versions, the version with the white body and green back (#372) will catch just about any inshore species. Swim the deep runner along jetties and docks and the shallow-runner on any flat where finger mullet hang out.

Corky Mullet and Corky Devils. The Corkys are the lures that catch record trout all along the gulf coast. These soft slow-suspending mullet imitations are one of the best coldwater lures for trout in shallow water. The pearl chartreuse (#01) and the chartreuse (#06) are both proven colors. They are available only from the manufacturer: www.corkybandl.com.

Brown Lures. Jason Brown, the grandson of the inventor of the Corky Mullet, makes his own line of soft-plastic tails. In many cases, and rigged with just the right amount of weight to allow slow sinking, they are as effective as the Corkys. They are available at: www.brownlures.com.

L&S MirrOlures. Every serious angler fishing the northern gulf should own at least one tackle box devoted solely to MirrOlures. Period. End of statement.

This line of readily available hard baits has evolved for the last seventy years into what many anglers consider their go-to lures for all species. They are so successful that it's hard to recommend just a few of their offerings. If you're new to fishing or new to MirrOlures, try these:

The 52M sinking twitchbait is the standard. The #18 color (greenback) is probably the all-time favorite of flats fishermen. The spotted STTR Series III holographic lure in red is used by thousands of wintertime trout fishermen. It can be trolled in creeks or fished slowly in deep river holes. The 17MR MirrOdine and the 19MR MirrOminnow, are new to the MirrOlure line, but very successful. Fished slowly, these small slow-suspending lures are good for all species. Green or black backs are good colors with which to start. Although small in size, many are eaten by large tarpon on the flats. Finally, don't overlook the Pups and Dogs. There are Top Dogs, She Dogs, Top Pups, She Pups, and Popa Dogs in a variety of sizes and colors. Each has a specific rattle or action and all are worth having. Many times fish will short strike a Top Dog yet hook up on either a smaller She Dog or a Top Pup. Good basic colors include none, hot pink, greenback, and black with a yellow head for early mornings or after the sun goes down.

Heddon Super Spook, Jr. Considered by many anglers their standard topwater lure, the Heddon Super Spook, Jr. is highly effective on most inshore species. Anything that eats a wounded mullet will eat one of these.

The noisy nickel color, walked in very shallow water will attract trout and reds from great distances, especially in very low light. Super Spook, Jr. lures come in freshwater as well as saltwater versions. The freshwater model works just fine in the salt but should be examined after catching a few big fish. Replacing the hooks may be necessary, and if so, replace them with 4X-strong #4 saltwater treble hooks, using a red Bleeding Bait Daiichi hook on the body and a more typical black hook on the tail. The science here is that the red hook emulates gill flash and attracts more strikes.

Other popular Super Spook, Jr. colors are the red head, bone, and chartreuse with a silver insert.

Rapala Skitterwalk. Rapala's Skitterwalk topwater lures come in two versions, both highly effective on any fish willing to hit a noisy bait on the surface. While the larger saltwater model, the SSW-11, is very effective, the freshwater model, SW-8, has been adopted by many anglers as their go-to lure for shallow-water gulf fishing. Hook replacement is usually necessary after catching a few big fish with the smaller Skitterwalk. The freshwater version comes in typical freshwater patterns, such as shad translucent and holographic silver. The larger model is available in hot pink, silver mullet, and bone. All these colors and patterns work well on saltwater fish.

Spoons. Dragging weedless spoons slowly over oyster bars and rock piles is a successful method of fishing for redfish all along the Gulf coast. Other versions of spoons are used to fish for pelagic species such as Spanish mackerel, bluefish, and even close-to-shore king mackerel.

Johnson's Silver Minnow (which now comes in many other colors than silver) and Mann's Tidewater Spoon are good choices for inshore use. Both can easily be used by kids and beginners, too, as it's simply a matter of casting them and making a slow, bottom-hugging retrieve.

The standard spoon for pelagics (mackerel and bluefish) is the silver Clarkspoon, and it's available in sizes up to #7/0 (4½ inches), but it's the #00 (2 inches) that's the real inshore killer. Rigged with a short wire leader and trolled or cast near fish striking bait schools on the flats, this diamond-shaped spoon is highly effective.

Flowering Floreos. In the 1960s, before soft-plastic tails became popular, the Flowering Floreo was the lure of choice on the flats for trout, reds, and all other species. A simple lead-head jig with a nylon skirt, the lure has taken a back seat to soft-plastics in recent years, but still holds its own when it comes to trolling for mackerel and bluefish or jigging for pompano.

The brightly colored ½-ounce version with the fluorescent orange head and yellow skirt is a popular model. Trimming the skirt back with scissors—an easy chore while the lure is still in the package—is an effective way to prevent short strikes while trolling. Leaving the skirt intact works fine when bouncing the jig along beaches or bars

for pompano. Many fishermen prefer to sweeten the hooks on Floreos, using strips of baitfish belly or FishBites when trolling or shrimp
pieces when pompano fishing.

Soft-plastics. There's no doubt that the use and development of soft-
plastic baits changed the dynamic of inshore fishing. Inexpensive,
easy-to-use, and highly adaptable to most terrains and depths, soft-
plastics are probably the most popular inshore bait.

Every angler seems to have a favorite soft-plastic bait and a favorite
way of rigging it. Soft-plastics are available in a multitude of shapes
and colors, many specific to certain manufacturers. Popular versions
are shad tails, split tail, and shrimp look-alikes. Most manufacturers
offer hooks and jig heads, sometimes paired to their plastic tails and
guaranteed to catch fish. Popular soft-plastics are made by D.O.A.
(www.doalures.com), Culprit/Riptide (www.culprit.com), Bass Assassin (www.bassassassin.com), Mann's (www.mannsbait.com), and
Stanley Lures (www.wedgetail.com). A look online will give you a
good idea of each product line, and its colors and configurations.

Rigging soft-plastics can range from simple to extreme. Anglers
fishing the deeper flats, sloughs, and holes seem to prefer ¼- or
⅜-ounce lead-head hooks. Those fishing in extreme shallow situations
prefer to rig weedless wide-gap hooks. Some fish soft-plastics on jig
heads exclusively under popping corks and others take their chances
with snags. And, there are a multitude of options in between. Exotic,
but successful, tools for fishing soft-plastics crowd the shelves at tackle
shops. Woodies Rattlers Rattl'n Hooks have rattle chambers attached;
D.O.A. makes pinch weights that attach to hook shanks; and Daiichi
offers ButtDragger hooks with the weights already attached.

Recently, the soft-plastics market has grown to include synthetic
flavors and smells. While D.O.A. products have some flavor enhance-
ment, they still rely on natural shape and action to attract fish. Fish-
Bites products were originally developed as simple sheets or strips
and were used by many anglers to sweeten soft-plastic rigs. This is
still a highly effective pheromone-based product and more lifelike
versions are now in the FishBites product line. Berkley's introduc-

tion of their GULP! baits marked a departure, in that shape, style, and smell all became important, although a truly realistic product was clearly not a goal. Bass Assassin also makes Blurp baits, most copying their popular line of shapes and colors, but with a smell factor included. All of these smell-enhanced baits have the advantage of drawing predators from afar. They are more expensive than their less-smelly counterparts, but still a bargain when compared to the cost of live shrimp or pinfish.

And, A Couple Things Every Inshore Fisherman Should Have

If you're serious about your inshore fishing, there are a couple of essential items I'd like to recommend for your kit.

The Boga Grip (www.bogagrip.com) is an excellent fish-gripping tool that ensures quick release of small fish, or big ones you intend to unhook, photograph, and release. They are available in 15-, 30-, and 60-pound versions and are amazingly durable. My ten-year old Boga Grip is rarely rinsed off and shows *no* signs of rust or deterioration. I do recommend attaching a large float to the lanyard, just in case you drop it overboard. In the same vein, and cheaper, is the Xtools Release Dehooker (www.xtools.us). This is great for quickly releasing fish caught on single hooks.

Waders and shore-bound fishermen will find the Wade Aid Belt (www.wadeaid.com) a valuable asset. It holds two extra rods behind you, has a pouch for extra tackle, a D-ring for a fish gripper, and a stringer. It also offers good back support and limited (but not U.S. Coast Guard approved) flotation.

For anglers needing a simpler rod holder for wading, boating, or kayaking, the Butt Rest (www.buttrestfishing.com) is a lanyard with a rod holder attached, allowing the rod to hang comfortably while rigging or paddling.

Finally, if you own an inshore powerboat and anchor frequently in shallow water, save your allowance for a Power-Pole shallow-water anchor (www.powerpole.com). Power-Poles come in 6- and 8-foot versions, and can be operated remotely from anywhere on your boat, allowing you to stop your drift immediately. This device, expensive as it is, can and will change your approach to shallow-water angling.

Offshore Gear and Tackle

Targeting offshore species in the gulf requires different equipment than that usually found at your local discount store. Offshore fish are big chunks of muscle, and your tackle should match the strength of a powerful fish doing his very best to get back home into a rocky crack, under a ledge or just as far away from the boat as possible. Even after coming up many feet from the bottom to attack a trolled lure, grouper instinctively speed back toward their hideouts. King mackerel, tuna, cobia, and barracudas are speedsters and easily strip hundreds of yards of line from a reel just seconds after the initial strike. The snapper clan bites lightly, so it's necessary to feel them on the line, but they can also dash quickly to cover. Specific species are best caught with specific tackle.

Bottom-fishing rods and reels need not be too sophisticated if you're targeting grouper or large snapper. Stout rods in 5- to 6-foot lengths and reels capable of handling 50- to 80-pound-test lines are just fine for bottom fishing. Longer more-flexible rods paired with reels sporting sophisticated quick-to-set drags work best for trolling deep-diving plugs for grouper. Reels for table-size snapper can be lighter, while that for kings, tuna, and cobia can be small too. They need drag systems capable not only of stopping long powerful runs but also withstanding ferocious initial strikes. A few small custom-rod makers are touting rods with spiral-guide rigging as an easier way to control fish, but depending on how deep your pockets are, less-expensive rods work just fine. Given the choice, put the bulk of your fishing budget toward a good reel. Also, spooling reels with modern braided line such as PowerPro will also give you an advantage in terms of feeling the fish bite. Unlike monofilament lines that stretch, braid has no stretch and telegraphs activity from below very well.

Many anglers who troll for king mackerel and tuna still prefer monofilament line, as its stretch softens hard strikes and its large diameter helps slow big fish making long runs. Braided lines are expensive, but it's not necessary to completely fill the spool of your bottom-fishing reel if you decide to use it. Bottom-dwelling fish such as grouper and snapper don't make long runs or take out lots of line, so 100 yards on a reel will prove adequate. Spooling 400 to 500 yards each of PowerPro on a boatload of kingfish reels can get very expensive. To compare fishing styles, understand that seasoned deepwater grouper and snapper anglers jam the star drags on their bottom-fishing reels by hitting them with a hammer, while trollers for trophy king mackerel usually fine-tune their drags, eliminating the slip caused by the drag on the lure or bait and line in the water, and adding a little extra resistance to accommodate the run and action of a hooked smoker.

Terminal tackle for fish on the bottom must be tough as well. Eighty- to 100-pound-test leader material, either monofilament or less-visible fluorocarbon, and big hooks are the rule for grouper. Forty- to 50-pound-test is fine for snapper, and light wire works well for trolling leaders.

There's a big argument as to which hook is better for bottom fishing: Is it circle hooks or traditional J-style hooks? Either will do, but conservation-minded anglers find that fewer undersize fish are gut-hooked with circle hooks. In fact, circle hooks are now required when fishing for reef fish in the gulf. Learning *not* to jerk a circle hook from a fish's mouth is difficult to some anglers, but killing fewer non-legal fish is worth the effort. A simple pull against a tugging fish is adequate to set a circle hook. Size 11/0 circle hooks are a good for grouper, while 4/0 is good for snappers. Look at the hook's gap from point to shank and assure yourself that there's enough distance to span the lips of your quarry. While sizes for J hooks are uniform among most manufacturers, sizes for circle hooks vary considerably. Use the right size for your targeted species regardless of its number. Trollers use a wide variety of hooks for live baits, but on stinger rigs, 4X strength, size 4 or 6 trebles are popular in the gulf.

Terminal-tackle recommendations for fishing live or cut bait are numerous. Two rigs stand out for bottom-fishing: the slip-sinker rig and the dropper rig. I prefer the slip-sinker rig for live baits and the dropper rig for cut bait. The dropper rig holds chunks of bait slightly above the bottom while the slip sinker allows live bait to swim more freely. Depth determines the weight of your sinker, but bank sinkers work best on dropper rigs and egg sinkers are appropriate as slip sinkers. For trolling live baits, learn to make and fish a stinger rig—it's a simple effective way to present baits to big fish.

Another method of hooking up on nice grouper and snapper is bouncing jigs off the bottom. Its a bit more work, but sometimes the action of a quick rising and falling brightly colored lure triggers a strike when even live bait doesn't work. Four- to 8-ounce bucktails are often used to reach extreme depths in the northern gulf. Vertical deep jigging with heavy and flashy metal jigs has recently become popular all over the gulf. The fluttering action of the jigs seems to be irresistible to bottom-dwellers.

I learned to troll large plugs using planers and hand lines. Times have changed—deep-diving plugs, thinner-yet-stronger lines, and sophisticated color depth sounders have made a huge difference in both the ease and success of trolling for offshore fish. First, you don't have to guess where to find the live or rocky bottom. Not only can you see a clear image of the bottom while trolling, but also with some training you can actually distinguish the air bladders of fish from the structure. Bait pods even make distinctive images on modern sounders. Strikes can be predicted in many instances.

Second, after determining the depth of the fish or bait, anglers are able to pick and choose big lures designed for specific depths. Early plugs generally ran deep, but with little information from the makers as to "how deep." Finally, high-tensile braided line has little resistance in the water. Pulling 30- pound-test braid for 20-pound-class grouper will easily get a thirty-foot-class lure to fifty-five or sixty feet with only 200 feet of line out at five knots of speed. Trolling live bait or smaller shallow-running plugs for kings requires less speed, as slow as one or two knots. Many anglers use downriggers or spool their reels with fishing wire to fish even deeper, and others use outriggers to fish a spread of lures near the surface. In the last twenty years, modern electronic equipment, line, and lures have changed the style of offshore fishing for many anglers.

Casting live bait or medium-size plugs to rocks in water as shallow as eight feet has become a popular pastime in recent years, especially in the Homosassa–Crystal River area. Using chum to pull the fish away from their hiding spots and setting baits into the chum line are a fun way to catch grouper without getting too far offshore. It's also a great way to pit your skills (and your rod) against some brutish fish. You'll need to use tackle you can cast. Big spinning outfits, spooled with 30-pound-test braid, work well here.

Offshore Tackle Recommendations

If you plan to bottom-fish, cast to, or troll for offshore species along Florida's Big Bend and Emerald Coast, you'll likely be confused by the selection of tackle and references available from catalogs and retail outlets. It's simpler than it seems, and what follows is a list of my recommendations.

Reels

Penn Special Senator 113H (4/0), 114H (6/0) reef reels. Penn makes these solid hard-working and reasonably priced reels mostly for bottom fishing.

Shimano TLD20 trolling reels (medium duty), Shimano Tekota 600 and 700 trolling reels. These reels feature level-wind mechanisms and very good drag systems.

Shimano Trinidad trolling reels. These finely built high-end reels are manufactured to take on almost any big and fast offshore fish. Consider the TN40 and TN50 if you plan to head off to deep blue water in search of tuna, big kings, wahoo, dolphin (mahi, dorado), sailfish, or marlin.

Shimano Spheros 8000FB or 12000FB, Shimano Bait Runner 4500, and Fin-Nor Offshore 85 or 95 spinning reels. These are not everyday discount-store spinning reels, but they are big saltwater tackle able to withstand a wide range of offshore species, except a few bottom dwellers such as gags and huge snapper.

Rods

Penn Slammer conventional and heavy spinning rods; Shakespeare Ugly Stik Big Water spinning and boat rods. Both Penn and Shakespeare make a complete line of heavy rods, suited for all types of offshore fishing.

SpiralStiX custom spiral guide boat and trolling rods. Spiral guides on these handmade rods keep rod torque to a minimum during big fights. See www.billystix.com for more details.

Shimano Tallus rods. Available in trolling and stand-up versions, these big-water rods cover the entire range of offshore needs. They are well-built with quality components and expensive but worth the price if a trophy fish is on the other end of the line. See www.shimano.com for more details.

Line, Leader, and Terminal Tackle

PowerPro braided Spectra fiber line. PowerPro typically breaks at twice its rated strength and has a much smaller diameter than comparable strength monofilament lines. It's available in multiple strengths suited to all offshore applications. Don't overlook the informative knot diagrams included with spools of PowerPro.

Triple Fish fluorocarbon leader. Use 80- to 100-pound-test for grouper, 40-pount for snapper. This virtually invisible leader has excellent knot-holding strength. In addition to the basic fluorocarbon, Triple Fish makes Chum Line, a scented leader, and Red Line, a disappearing leader for blue waters.

Daiichi Hooks. Use super-sharp Daiichi 10/0 to 13/0 circle hooks for grouper and 5/0 for snapper, cobia, and smaller amberjack. Make your king-mackerel stinger rigs using light fishing wire and 4X strong Daiichi Bleeding Bait treble hooks.

Mustad needle-eye J-hooks. Use 5/0 to 8/0 for stinger rigs or trolling feathers. They are made specifically for wire leaders.

Lures

Mann's Stretch Trolling Baits. Designed for fishing at different depths, these lures are very popular for grouper all along the gulf coast. While the Stretch 30+ seems to be the standard, the Imitator series has proven well on king mackerel, as has the smaller Stretch 25+. Every serious offshore angler who trolls should have at least one bucket of Stretch lures aboard. Different colors and versions attract fish differently, so many anglers change lures frequently until the action starts. Different speeds change the action of these lures, another option for getting more strikes while trolling.

L&S MirrOLures. The 111MR and 113MR MirrOLures are castable lures suited for fishing shallow rocks for grouper or for throwing at barracuda and amberjack over wrecks. MirrOlures such as the Top Dog and Popa Dog are also very good for any striking fish found offshore and are easy to cast with lighter tackle.

D.O.A. Lures. D.O.A.'s Swimming Mullet and larger TerrorEyz jigs are very realistic baits that are excellent for jigging over rocks or near shallow rocky channel edges for grouper. Their large plastic shrimp have proven good for grouper over shallow rocks, and for cobia and tripletail near markers.

Offshore Trolling Lures. If you think inshore fishermen can't decide exactly which lure to fish, just take a look inside the tackle locker on an offshore boat. Deep-water trolling can involve live bait, lures, or a combination of both. Some offshore trollers pull arrays of teasers along with live bait, and others use rigged ballyhoo in combination with big noisy feathers. Bright-color feathers, some noisy and some bubbling, are often used solo, rigged through the nose with size 7/0 or 8/0 hooks and 100-pound-test monofilament leaders. There are versions for dolphin, wahoo, tuna, kings, and billfish. They are available in all colors and sizes from a number of manufacturers, including C&H (www.candhlures.com), Boone (www.boonebait.com), Williamson (www.williamsonlures.com), and Iland (www.ilandlures.com)

Just Plain Ol Bucktail Jigs and Silver Spoons. Probably the most versatile lures any offshore fisherman can keep aboard his boat are heavy bucktail jigs and silver spoons. Either can be tossed at a passing cobia or school of marauding pelagics. Spoons can be trolled at various speeds and depths, using planers or downriggers. Big heavy jigs will attract grouper and snapper in 100-foot depths when even live bait won't work. And they're cheap. You can afford to keep several sizes of silver Clarkspoons aboard, rigged with a short wire leader and even a bucketful of 6-ounce bucktails doesn't cost a whole lot more than a fancy deep-diving plug or two.

Fishing Knots

"If you can't tie a knot, just tie a lot"—this is not good advice if you're a fisherman. Good knots are at the core of every successful fishing trip. No matter your tackle or bait, if you can't connect the two, you're in trouble.

Good fishing knots need to be strong. Some of that strength comes from the materials—line, leader, or both—involved, but following directions is important too. Recipes for knots, like those for baked bread, need to be followed to the letter. Good line material, whether monofilament or braided fiber, is only as good as the knots used to attach it to other line or to terminal tackle. Don't skimp by purchasing the cheap stuff, and remember that most monofilament and fluorocarbon lines weaken with age and direct exposure to sunlight. It's a good habit to change these lines at least yearly and more often if you fish frequently. Braided fiber lines cost more but seem to hold up longer.

Knot strength is measured as a percentage of the actual breaking strength of the line or leader; 100 percent is excellent, but few knots approach that strength.

Many successful anglers recommend the use of a loop in the tag end of the running line when attaching leader materials. Few fishermen, except trollers, use swivels or other devices, such as snaps or swivels, in the makeup of their leaders. There is little argument that the Bimini twist is the perfect loop to make when building a rig. And although it's a matter of honor and many anglers claim to be able to tie a Bimini twist in a few seconds, I think it's hard to do in a crowded, pitching boat. For that reason, I prefer the simple surgeon's loop, an ugly, but strong loop that works just fine in most conditions and with most tackle. I do use the Bimini twist for tarpon and other big-game applications, but many times tie up several rigs in the comfort of my family room. In the same vein, the Albright knot is beautiful, but a double surgeon's knot does a pretty effective (but usually ugly!) job of attaching leaders to running lines.

The knots that seem to be the most popular for a wide range of anglers are the Uni-knots. These simple strong knots are easy to tie and can be used to join lines together or to attach terminal tackle. They are easier to tie than blood knots for joining lines or improved clinch knots for attaching lures, jigs, and hooks. If you wish to fish with knots that are quick and effective, learn the system of Uni-knots.

Finally, a few tips for knot construction. One, when you're tightening a knot, it's best to apply some universal lubricant, otherwise known as spit. And, it never hurts to apply a small drop of cyanoacrylate, or super glue, to the finished knot.

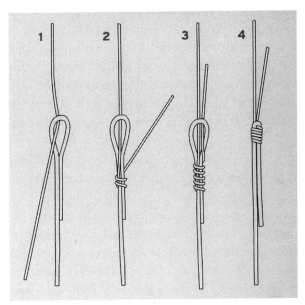

Albright Knot. Attach the backing to the fly line with an Albright knot. (1) Double up the last 2 inches of the fly line and pass the tag end of the backing through the loop. (2) Wind the backing over itself and the fly line at least five times. (3) Pass the backing through the loop as shown. (4) Tighten slowly; trim the ends closely.

All knot illustrations reproduced with the permission of Pure Fishing/Berkley.

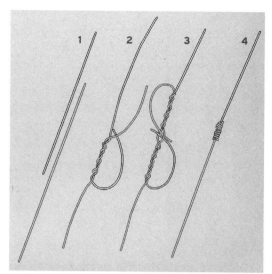

Blood Knot. The blood knot works great for splicing two lines of similar diameter. (1) Cross the two sections of line to be joined, and then wrap one tag end around the standing part of the other live five to seven times, depending on the line diameter. (2) Pass the tag end back between the two lines. (3) Wrap the other tag end in the same manner, and bring it back through the same opening. (4) Pull the stranding lines to tighten knot; trim.

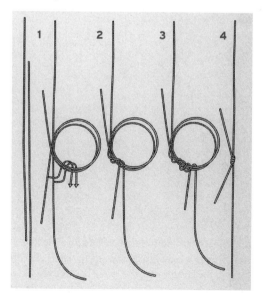

Double Surgeon's Knot. The double surgeon's knot is used for attaching tippet to leader. (1) Place the tippet next to the leader, then (2) form an overhand knot. (3) Form a double overhand knot by passing the same ends through the loop a second time. (4) Tighten by pulling all four ends slowly; trim the tags.

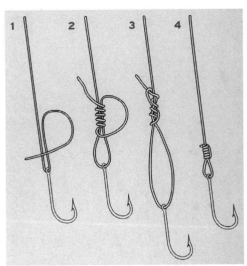

Duncan Loop. The Duncan loop allows a hook or crankbait to swing freely on a loop for maximum wobble. (1) Slide your line through the hook eye, and form a loop in the tag end as shown. (2) Pass the tag end through the loop, winding around the standing line and top section of the loop four or five times while moving away from the hook. (3) Moisten the line and pull the tag end to tighten the knot. (4) Slide the knot to the desired position by pulling on the standing line, and trim the tag end.

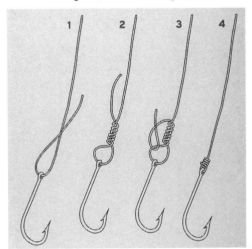

Improved Clinch Knot. Everyone should learn the improved clinch knot for attaching leaders and lines to hooks and swivels. The knot is easy to tie and retains nearly all of the line's original strength. (1) Pass the end of the line through the eye of hook or swivel. (2) Pull about 6 inches of the line through and double it back against itself. Twist the line five to seven times. (3) Pass the end of the line through the small loop formed just above the eye, then through the big loop just created. Be careful that the coils don't overlap. (4) Pull the tag end and main line so that the coiled line tightens against the eye. Again, be sure the coils haven't overlapped. Trim the excess.

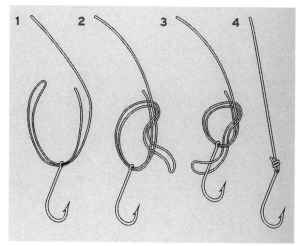

Palomar Knot. The palomar knot is easy and fast to tie, and handy for attaching hooks, swivels, and other terminal tackle to your fishing line. It is especially popular with anglers using braided fishing lines. (1) Double about 6 inches of line and pass it through the eye of the hook. (2) Tie a simple overhand knot in the doubled line, letting the hook hang loose. Avoid twisting the lines. (3) Pull the end of the loop down, passing it completely over the hook. (4) Pull both ends of the line to draw up the knot. Trim the excess.

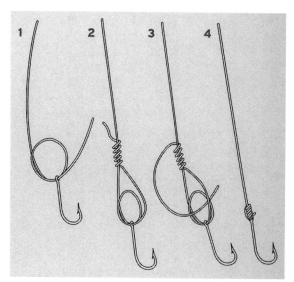

Trilene Knot. The Trilene knot is one of the easiest knots for novice anglers to learn how to tie. Experts also like the knot because it can be easily tied at night in complete darkness. (1) Slide your line through the hook eye and repeat, entering the line form the same direction and being sure to form a double loop at the hook eye, as shown. (2) Wrap the tag end around the standing line four or five times, moving away from the hook. (3) Pass the tag end back through the double loop at the hook eye, moisten, pull the knot tight against the hook eye, and trim the tag (4).

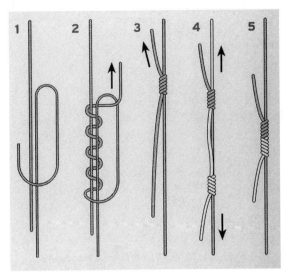

Joining Two Lines Uni-Knot. Used to join two lines of equal diameters. (1) Overlap line ends about 6 inches, forming loop in one line for Uni-knot. (2) Tie a Uni-knot with six wraps around the lines. (3) Pull the tag end to tighten the first knot around line. (4) Tie a second Uni-knot with the tag end of the other line. (5) Pull both main lines to tighten and bring the knots together. Trim the ends.

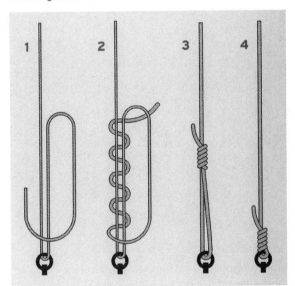

Terminal Tackle Uni-Knot. Used for attaching tackle to a line or mono leader. (1) Run the line through the eye and double it back, forming a circle. (2) Tie a Uni-knot by wrapping the tag end around the double line six turns and through the loop. Pull the tag end to tighten. (3) Pill the main line to tighten the knot. (4) Keep pulling tight in the main line and tackle until the knot slides tight against the eye.

Bait Your Own Hook—With Natural Bait

Fish bait comes two ways: real and fake. Natural, or real, bait can be either dead or alive, and while there's a group of anglers who proclaim that the use of artificial bait is more sporting, I don't think anyone will argue that natural bait won't catch more fish. After all, sport fish eat natural bait all their lives but seldom survive their last meal, no matter what it might be.

There are several categories of natural baits to consider when fishing the Gulf Coast of Florida. There's cut bait, usually chunks of fish, a favorite of anglers willing to anchor and wait for the predators to arrive. Another choice, small baitfish, can be fished live or dead and are widely distributed throughout the Gulf of Mexico. Shrimp are probably the most widely used coastal bait, either live or frozen. Even crabs, squid, miscellaneous crustaceans, and octopus have their places on the roster of baits used by gulf fishermen. Finally, using natural bait to chum or chunk is a popular method for attracting game fish, particularly when the fish are scattered. Chum can be homemade or purchased commercially and is generally used to attract small baitfish, which in turn attract larger predators. Chunks are typically used to create a feeding frenzy and to confuse larger fish. Almost any natural bait is suitable for chumming or chunking.

Cut bait can range from mullet heads to almost surgically "butterflied" pinfish. In the overall scheme of things, it's really pretty basic. Using cut bait is easy. Simply attach it to a circle hook, and either get it to the bottom or suspend it under a float. Its fish-attracting value is its smell, and many cut-bait fishermen are not so concerned with what species they cut but with the smell. Oily fish tend to smell fishier, and make the most effective cut bait. Mullet are almost always considered the universal choice for cut bait, but pinfish, squid, sardines, shrimp, ladyfish, and even lizardfish work well, too. Cut bait is also easy to obtain. Frozen mullet, squid, and shrimp can almost always be purchased at bait shops, or you can use the by-catch from a previous day's fishing. A supply of dead pinfish or ladyfish can speed up a hot afternoon of flats fishing when you're just looking for action, even if it's in the form of small sharks or rays.

Bottom and grass dwellers, such as pinfish, pigfish, as well as other porgies, are excellent inshore and offshore live baits. The sight of any of these small baitfish struggling against a cork on the flats or a sinker on a rock pile is enough to attract ferocious strikes from trout, redfish, grouper, and snapper. Hooked through the nose or tail and freelined, they do the same for cobia, tarpon, and king mackerel. They are generally hardy and survive in aerated live wells so long as the water is not too hot. There are a number of ways of catching these baits. Most can be caught on grass flats or over live bottom. Size 16 hooks baited with cut shrimp, FishBites, or leftover Gulp! bait work well, and it gives the kids something to do while the grownups fish. Live-bait fishermen wishing to quickly fill their live wells often use pinfish traps baited with fish scraps, set on the grass flats the night before the big day. Others use cast nets after chumming baitfish close to the boat. I recommend ½-inch mesh for a pinfish cast net and a mixture of canned cat food or jack mackerel mixed with whole wheat bread as chum. Chum slowly, and the little guys will come steadily to the boat.

The schooling-baitfish group, generally classified as white bait, includes scaled sardines (pilchards), Atlantic thread herring, gulf menhaden (pogies or alewives), cigar minnows (round scad), and bay anchovies (glass minnows). Usually seen in huge numbers boiling the water's surface, they can also be found in lesser numbers around structure such as channel markers and small inshore rock piles and bars. They can be used either live or dead, and many of these small fish are available frozen from bait shops. All can be chummed-up and cast-netted for live bait, but care should be taken to choose the right net mesh size. A mesh that is too fine can result in gilled fish, making a mess of dead baits. I recommend a ⅜-inch cast net for most species of white bait. Also, as you'll likely be chumming in water over 10 feet deep, use the largest diameter net you can comfortably throw. As well as being chummed up and used as live bait, dead white bait can also make darn good chum for larger species, either ground up or "chunked."

Bigger white baits can also be caught on hooks. The Sabiki rig has become a popular method of catching baitfish all over the gulf. They feature an array of natural-looking tiny jigs, and are weighted and dropped into schools of baitfish. Some anglers sweeten the small hooks with live or synthetic baits for more hookups. These rigs are highly effective for cigar minnows around markers and at night under lights when snapper fishing offshore.

All of the white baits make excellent offshore baits, but sometimes are difficult to keep lively. Considerable aeration is needed in live wells, and special care should be made not to overcrowd the baits.

I've been told that the most prevalent fish species anywhere is the bay anchovy, or glass minnow, but represents only one of many species of white bait in the gulf. White bait, just by numbers alone, is a significant part of the gulf's food chain and an always-excellent bait.

While on the subject of offshore fishing with live bait, I'd be remiss not to mention the blue runner, a member of the jack family, and the ballyhoo. Blue runners are often found in schools or over flats in the warmer months. These feisty "hard tails" make excellent bait for most offshore game fish, in particular grouper and pelagic species. They are easily caught with Sabiki rigs or small jigs and keep well with good aeration. A popular method of preparing blue runners as bait is to trim the tips off of their tails, making them more active than usual, and more attractive to predators. Stinger rigs, made using two hooks and a short piece of wire, are popular with king-mackerel fishermen who use large baits such as blue runners. One hook, usually a J-hook, is put through the bait's lips and the other, a treble, is inserted near the bait's tail. Short-striking predators have little chance.

Ballyhoo are a version of needlefish and are usually found in bait stores, sometimes pre-rigged for offshore trolling. They, along with big mackerel, are the natural bait of choice for big-game anglers fishing the deep canyons of the upper Gulf of Mexico.

Shrimp are as close to a universal saltwater bait as exists. Found over grassy bottom in various sizes, shrimp are the candy of the gulf. Many anglers will attest to game fish eating shrimp and paying no attention to hordes of small bait fish or mullet. Try it sometime. If you see fish striking mullet or white bait, throw a live shrimp or a shrimp

Ballyhoo usually are rigged in advance for offshore trolling.

imitation, into the melee. Shrimp will turn heads and mouths. Most fishermen prefer to buy live shrimp from bait houses, and depending on location and supply, shrimp are sold by the dozen or in hundred-count. Some anglers prefer to keep their shrimp frisky in a live well, but others simply put them in plastic bags and lay them in their coolers, insulated from the ice itself by a piece of newspaper. Amazingly, shrimp keep fresh for many hours using this method, and fresh-dead shrimp work fine for many applications, particularly inshore under popping corks or for spawning sheepshead.

Shrimp are also effective offshore when bottom fishing but tend to attract small fish such as Key West grunts and black sea bass. These smaller snappers and grouper are also perfectly happy to eat frozen shrimp—a good thing, as their larger cousins are usually not quick enough to get to the hook.

Shrimp is always a popular Gulf bait. Rigging one with a simple jig head is an excellent way to fish deeper water.

Another almost-universal bait is the lowly mullet. Found everywhere along the Gulf Coast and in varying sizes, they work well dead or alive. Juvenile finger mullet are excellent live baits for any species, offshore and inshore, and are easily cast-netted. Larger mullet, cut into chunks, are highly fragrant and make very good cut bait for tarpon, redfish, trout, and even grouper. Avoid freshwater mullet caught up coastal rivers, though. While they are the same species as coastal mullet, their diet of algae affects their taste and appeal to predators.

And, speaking of taste, many native Floridians (like me) prefer a fried freshly caught coastal mullet over fried grouper any day.

Other baits are by no means lesser baits. Fiddler crabs make excellent sheepshead bait, and sand fleas are certainly much more tasty to beachside pompano than nylon jigs. Both are available at bait shops gulf-wide, especially when the sheepshead are spawning in late winter and the pompano are active from spring through fall. Small blue crabs (or chunks of larger ones) will stop tarpon and cobia in their tracks, and are always in demand during the warmer months. Try a small blue crab the next time you go grouper fishing too. Fiddlers, sand fleas, and blue crabs all keep well in a covered bucket with a bed of wet seaweed. Mud minnows, or killifish, are those small minnows you see swimming along gulf shores, usually in very shallow water and in small schools. When nothing else is working for redfish or trout, many inshore anglers will free-line mud minnows. They are

Sand fleas, the preferred bait of pompano fishermen, are caught by straining sand in the rolling surf.

hardy and easy to catch with either cast nets or small hooks baited with scraps of shrimp.

Finally, resist the urge to pickle the next octopus you bring aboard. They do make a great meal when doused with olive oil, lime juice, salt, and pepper, but they make even better grouper and snapper bait. It's a tough choice, whether to eat octopus ceviche or broiled grouper? I usually can't decide whether to fish or eat bait.

Hire Your Very Own Captain

Why hire a guide? Why not?

You've trailered your boat a zillion miles to a destination you don't know, expecting to fish every day. On the first day of your visit, it makes good sense to hire a professional who regularly fishes the area. He likely fished there yesterday, and the day before, and the day before that. He knows what's biting and where. Most guides don't mind showing visiting anglers around and giving them tips, so long as the information isn't abused. If you hire a guide for a scouting trip, be

It takes a big, specialized boat to fish the blue water in the northern Gulf of Mexico. Big boats mean not only big bucks but also big fish!

sure to let him know your intentions. He may not show you his honey holes, but I can assure you that you'll take home more knowledge from one day with him than you would from a month on your own.

Another reason to hire a guide may be that you're not equipped to do the type of fishing he offers. Inshore fishermen can enjoy a day offshore in a boat that's safer offshore. And many avowed beach and shore fishermen hire guides for boat trips, fully understanding the amortized cost of owning an infrequently used yet expensive boat. A perfect example is tarpon fishing. Great sport, but not necessarily something you want to do every day. Hiring a professional guide for a tarpon trip makes perfect sense. He has the right tackle, boat, baits, and skills for the job, allowing you to concentrate on landing what could be the fish of a lifetime.

Professional fishing guides are professional people, and they should run professional businesses. Be sure to hire a guide who holds at least a U.S. Coast Guard 6-Pack or Operator of Uninspected Vessels license. Holders of this license have passed USCG scrutiny and tests, and are also trained in First Aid and CPR. He or she should also have liability insurance and hold a Florida fishing license covering all the fishermen on his boat. If a guide asks you to purchase your own fishing license—start asking questions. I've listed many local guides in this book and all have claimed to be insured and licensed, but ask them individually and directly to be sure. Other good sources for information about professional guides are the Florida Guides Association (www.florida-guides.com) and the Coastal Conservation Association (www.ccaflorida.org) Web sites.

Expect to pay your guide a fee, which will likely include use of his skills, his boat, tackle, ice, and bait. It may or may not include soft drinks, a shore lunch, a bag lunch, or fish cleaning. Offshore boats typically have at least one mate aboard who works mostly for tips, so be generous if he works hard. Inshore and offshore captains also deserve tips, based not necessarily on the number of fish caught, but on the effort put into the day. Fifteen to twenty percent of the basic charter fee is reasonable, with a higher percentage in order for a big boat with a crew.

Charter boats, like this one from the fleet at Destin, are a good way to get offshore and have a successful day with a professional captain leading the way.

There's nothing worse than coming home with no fish or tales of no action. Hiring a guide can improve your chances for catching, and you'll likely have a good time. But remember that even guides are subject to the foibles of bad weather, muddy water, and moody fish.

To quote the cliché, "I'm a fishing guide, not a catching guide."

Party Boats, Head Boats, and Pukers

An alternative to chartering an individual boat and captain for you and a few friends or family members is to sign on to a fishing boat outfitted to fish offshore with as many as 100 anglers aboard. And, much like Ishmael coming aboard the *Pequod*, captained by Captain Ahab in the novel *Moby Dick*, you might find yourself fishing alongside a modern-day version of Queequeg, with tattoos, scars, and an ugly sneer.

This sort of fishing is not for everyone, but it's perfect if you enjoy catching potluck and the camaraderie of a big crowd.

Essentially, you pay a fee to fish, and the fee usually includes tackle and bait. Tackle isn't great, but it's sturdy, and bait can range from frozen fish to squid. You can take your own gear, but why buck the system? And, besides, free is good. This is very basic bottom-fishing. Some boats fish half days, usually in winter, but some fleets offer full-day trips. Some offer multiday and overnight excursions too. Expect to spend about 25 percent of your time in transit to the fishing if you're leaving from one of the Emerald Coast's deep-water ports for a day trip.

The *Apollo* fishes out of Crystal River and the Captain Anderson fleet sails from Panama City Beach. One of the best examples of party-boat operations is Capt. Jim Westbrook's *American Spirit*, which departs Destin Harbor. An air-conditioned 80-footer, this boat is well-staffed by a courteous crew, dedicated to making the trips fun for everyone aboard.

A typical day aboard the *American Spirit* involves as much as a two-hour trip to a fishing area selected by the captain. On the ride, the mates stay busy rigging rods and preparing bait, while the galley doles out coffee and breakfast. Galley food, though good and reason-

Party boats are often crowded but offer an excellent value for anglers wishing to try their hand at deep-sea fishing.

ably priced, is not included in the cost of the trip, and many anglers bring coolers with their own supplies, if the boat allows them. Call ahead or check the operator's Web site for boat rules.

On arrival at the fishing spot, there's no anchoring involved; anchoring one of these big boats is not easy. Party boats usually fish in water that's 100-plus feet deep (not so deep for the *Apollo*), and with engines running, the captain simply holds the boat over the selected spot and orders, "Lines in, folks."

Standard fishing gear is Penn 4/0 reels on very short rods, rigged with 80-pound-test monofilament line, double-hook dropper rigs, 3/0 hooks, and as much as 12 ounces of lead. There's a lot of hard reeling involved in bottom fishing, even with no fish on the end of the line, and lots of anglers whine toward day's end. Once you're hooked up, don't worry about playing the fish. The main goal is to get your catch to the surface without getting tangled in the other anglers' lines. Mates are standing by and will help you get your fish aboard, tagged, and iced.

Most of the catch aboard party boats is grouper, snapper (American red, vermillion, Lane) and a variety of bottom fish. Amberjacks, Spanish and king mackerel, cobia, and even wahoo appear during the summer months, depending on the depth and bottom structure. And, there's always a buzz when a big shark is hooked up or a trophy grouper or snapper comes aboard.

An 80-foot boat can handle big, wallowing seas, but can you? Jokingly called *pukers* by captains, crew, and regular customers, these big boats can pitch and roll in even the calmest seas, causing seasickness for even experienced head boaters. Preparing yourself with over-the-counter remedies (Dramamine, Bonine) or prescriptions (transdermal scopolamine patches) is a good idea. Avoid going below to cure queasiness; stay on deck, breathe fresh air, stay away from the engine's exhaust, and keep your eyes focused on the horizon. Watch what you eat too. If you're prone to seasickness, keep your food intake light, and for sure avoid a hearty, greasy breakfast or a late night of drinking before the trip. But if you get sick, go ahead and get it over with. No one will make fun of you, as most have been in your shoes before.

If you're lucky enough to get aboard during a slow business day, you'll probably have plenty of room to stretch out. However, most of the party or head boats fishing from gulf ports are crowded much of the year. Actually, some cancel trips if the number of reservations is low, finding it not profitable to take just a few anglers. With anglers shoulder-to-shoulder along the gunnels, lines can tangle easily, so it's best to pay attention to what you're doing and the location of your own line. Certain fish, bonito and cobia in particular, are famous for tangling line. Snapper and grouper just get tugged to the surface, but these speedsters can really make a mess. Should you tangle with your neighbor, ask a mate to help, and keep your cool.

Finally, a word about money, specifically tips. At the end of the day, a tip jar will be passed around, and the take is usually distributed among the mates and the galley crew. These folks, sometimes students, count on your gratuities to supplement their wages. A $20 donation to the tip jar is not much to pay for the crew's putting up with you. And, if there's a crewmember that was especially helpful or cheerful, slip him a fiver at the end of the day.

Party Boat Operators

Destin and Fort Walton Beach

American Spirit Deep Sea Fishing, (850) 837-1293, www.newflorida girl.com, newflagirl2000@aol.com.

Crystal River

Apollo Deep Sea Fishing, (352) 795-3757.

Panama City Beach

Capt. Anderson's Deep Sea Fishing, 1-800-874-2415, www.capt andersonsmarina.com, captanders@aol.com.

Jubilee Deep Sea Fishing, (850) 236-2111, www.jubileefishing.com, deepseafishing_2000@yahoo.com.

Don't Have a Boat? Take a Walk!

Having access to a fishing boat certainly is an advantage, but it's not an absolute necessity in many areas along Florida's Big Bend and Emerald Coast. In fact, *not* having a boat is an advantage in many situations.

There are places you just can't fish easily with a boat. Beaches with rough-breaking surf are sometimes perfect habitat for pompano, but boaters must avoid getting too close to the shore. Some shallow shorelines within bays and estuaries are too shallow to approach by boat, or even by kayak or canoe, yet they offer excellent shallow-water trout and redfish action. Public fishing piers offer structure and habitat for game fish underneath, sometimes along barren coastline, that's accessible only to the anglers on the pier. And, even if you have a boat, you'll probably find areas, such as oyster and shell bars, that you'll just want to fish quietly and efficiently by wading.

Surf and shoreline wade fishing is very democratic. Anyone can walk along a public beach and throw heavy jigs or sand fleas into the trough behind the first set of breakers. Pompano feed in these troughs as sand fleas and other crustaceans wash away with the waves receding action. Other options for surf fishing are live shrimp under corks fished outside the breaking waves for mackerel, trout, and even whopper reds along the shoreline. Artificial lures such as noisy top-water plugs work well but usually when there's a run of baitfish and predators along the beaches. Beach and surf fishing is more prevalent on the Emerald Coast, as the Big Bend of Florida is relatively beach-free. Wading a shoreline is sometimes as simple as parking your car and unloading your gear. There are many public landings and parks all along Florida's Gulf Coast that allow fishermen to get their feet wet. And you'll often see folks stopped along the western stretches of US Highway 98 getting their wading gear ready or just loading a stringer of nice fish into their cooler.

There are two types of public piers along the Gulf Coast. One is the long pier that juts into the gulf; the other is the pier that runs alongside big bridges, typically the byproduct of an older demolished bridge. Both are natural traps for bait and predators, including off-shore species such as grouper and pelagics such as king mackerel. Long piers are usually constructed along a beach and offer refuge to fish from the miles and miles of white-sand bottom. Bridge piers are usually in the path of waterways, and the natural tidal action provides a constant flow of bait beneath the structure. Both are fun places to fish, but there may be rules restricting certain types of tackle. Other-wise, it's usually a free-for-all when the schools of striking fish start to hit or someone hooks up a trophy-size cobia, tangling up lines and heating tempers.

All along the Gulf Coast, you'll find areas in bays and coves where you could easily edge your boat up to a bar or deep shoreline, clatter around, splash an anchor, and generally run all the fish off to Mexico. Stalking fish, particularly redfish, black drum, and big sea trout, by foot is akin to turkey hunting. It's just you and the fish, but they know their habitat better than you and can sense you coming toward them at great distances. After you've learned how to shuffle along a bar top and make long casts to attentive game fish, you'll be hooked. Fishing by foot takes a different skill set than boat fishing. It also takes special and sometimes specialized gear.

Beach fishing can be as simple as a single rod and reel and a pock-etful of bait. Or it can involve a modified wheelbarrow with rod holders, a tackle box, a cooler, chest waders, and a supply of snacks for the day. Most surf fishermen use longer rods capable of getting the lure or bait well offshore, but that's not necessary all the time. Remember that many game-fish species run so close to the shore that they are pitched, rolled, and confused by the wave action. Don't buy a special rod and reel for your first trip to the surf; just bring one of your medium-size spinning outfits.

Pier and bridge fishing usually involve tackle heavy enough to handle the weighty rigs needed to get the baits to the bottom and to pull fish away from pilings. Many fishermen use gear carts, as there's usually a fair walk from the pier's entrance to the end, where all the pros congregate. Remember to try the close-to-shore trough, and you may not have to walk all the way out to the end of the pier. And fish landing nets or hooks are always a good idea on these higher structures, as fishing line is not really ideal for hoisting flopping fish once they're out of the water.

In general, wade fishing on flats and bars is easier if you have some specialized gear. Longer rods, even those of light- to medium-action, are helpful to make long casts. Wading belts offer the convenience of extra rods, tackle storage, and stringers at close hand. The Wade Aid

Pier fishing is a great way to wet a hook without a boat.

Belt (www.wadeaid.com) is excellent, and despite not being able to claim the feature, offers some flotation should you trip and fall. The Butt Rest rod holder (www.buttrestfishing.com) is also handy, at a lower cost. High-top wading shoes are also good, as oysters, sharp rocks, and stingrays are not easy on the feet or ankles. Stringers with breakaway features are also popular among many wade fishermen, but I'm not among that crowd. I'm six feet tall, and if I'm wading to my armpits in 4½ feet of water towing a stringer of trout, I'm an easy target for a cruising bull shark. Nope. No stringers for me!

Pier, beach, and wade fishing all deserve attention from anglers wishing to experience the full range of gulf fishing in Florida. They're generally less expensive, and in many instances, more productive, than boat fishing. And, for the landlubbers—or those with delicate stomachs—who want to fish, it's the only way to go.

Artificial Reefs and Wrecks, Big Bend and Emerald Coast

Woods 'N Water magazine obtained this information primarily, but not exclusively, from the Florida Fish and Wildlife Conservation (FWC). The FWC, *Woods 'N Water*, and I cannot guarantee accuracy, as some reef materials can be displaced or completely removed by storms or other natural causes.

The GPS or LORAN C entries in the GPS field indicate in which format the original coordinates were obtained. The original source of some coordinates is unknown. The other set was mathematically calculated and may not be as accurate as the original coordinates.

The latitude–longitude format is shown in decimal–minute (DDMM. MMM) format.

Reef information is listed alphabetically by county and has been abbreviated to the most recently deployed reef materials.

Information is listed for: Bay County (Panama City), Citrus County (Crystal River, Homosassa), Escambia County (Pensacola), Franklin County (Carrabelle, Apalachicola), Levy County (Yankeetown, Cedar Key), Okaloosa County (Destin, Fort Walton Beach), Santa Rosa County (Pensacola), Taylor County (Steinhatchee), Wakulla (St. Marks, Panacea), and Walton County (Destin, Fort Walton Beach).

Table 1. Reefs of Citrus County (Crystal River, Homosassa)

Deploy	Reef Name	Material 1	Loran 1	Loran 2	Latitude	Long.	Depth	Relief	GPS
4/19/2005	Phase 3, Drop 3, South	Con. Logs (4)			2847.355	8303.429	31	10	DGPS
4/19/2005	Phase 3, Drop 2, NE	Con. Logs (3)			2847.386	8303.431	31	10	DGPS
4/19/2005	Phase 3, Drop 1, NW	Con. Logs (3)			2847.39	8303.441	31	10	DGPS
4/15/2003	Phase 1, Drop 2	Con. Poles (300)			2847.304	8303.497	31	8	DGPS
5/31/2001	Phase 2, Fish Haven #1	Con. Logs (10)			2847.352	8303.491	31	10	DGPS
6/14/2000	Phase 1, Fish Haven #1	Con. Culverts (221)			2847.274	8303.501	31	9	DGPS
6/2/2000	Phase 1, Fish Haven #1	Con. Culverts (230)			28-7.314	8303.476	31	9	DGPS

Table 2. Reefs of Levy County (Yankeetown, Cedar Key)

Deploy	Reef Name	Material 1	Loran 1	Loran 2	Latitude	Long.	Depth	Relief	GPS
6/22/1995	Levy #1 Big Bend Reefs	Con. Cubes (24)	14417.6	45378.4	2904.96	8254.73	21	3	
6/22/1995	Levy #2 Big Bend Reefs	Con. Cubes (96)	14418.9	45378.6	2904.67	8255.02	18	3	
10/1/1991	White City Bridge	Bridge Rubble	14359.1	45770.2	2910.011	8338.978	55	9	DGPS
10/30/1990	Suwannee Regional Reefs	Con. Cubes	14363.1	45525.4	2859.18	8319.11	40	3	Loran
12/31/1989	Betty Castor Reef	Modules Concrete	14410.4	45699.9	2916.5	8323	22		Loran
4/18/1989	Cedar Key Reef Site 2	Concrete Culverts	14375	45467	2858.91	8312	26		Loran
1/30/1989	Cedar Key Reef Site 3	Concrete Culverts	14375.2	45639.5	2906.83	8325.52	36		Loran
1/10/1989	Cedar Key Reef Site 3	Concrete Culverts	14375.1	45641.3	2906.92	8325.72	36		Loran
12/7/1988	Cedar Key Reef Site 2	Concrete Culverts	14375.2	45466.5	2858.93	8311.91	26		Loran
11/10/1988	Cedar Key Reef Site 3	Concrete Culverts	14375.3	45639.7	2906.87	8325.5	36		Loran
10/28/1988	Cedar Key Reef Site 3	Concrete Culverts	14375	45639.7	2906.84	8325.57	36		Loran
9/23/1988	Cedar Key Reef Site 2	Concrete Culverts	14375.1	45467.4	2858.95	8312.01	26	4	Loran
8/30/1988	Cedar Key Reef Site 3	Concrete Culverts	14374.9	45641.3	2906.629	8325.892	36		Loran
8/19/1988	Cedar Key Reef Site 2	Concrete Culverts	14375.3	45467	2858.712	8312.099	26		Loran
7/21/1988	Cedar Key Reef Site 3	Concrete Culverts	14375	45640.7	2906.621	8325.824	36		Loran

Table 3. Reefs of Taylor County (Steinhatchee)

Deploy	Reef Name	Material 1	Loran I	Loran 2	Latitude	Long.	Depth	Relief	GPS
6/26/2002	Buckeye Reef Addition #2	CC Fish Havens (50)			2938.4	8354.31	48	4	DGPS
6/27/1998	Steinhatchee Reef	Concrete Cubes (112)	14461.4	46011.1	2939.867	8337.646	20	3	GPS
6/29/1996	Buckeye Reef	Steel Scrap	14430.3	46133.8	2939.003	8354.245	47	15	GPS
7/27/1995	Taylor #1 Big Bend Reefs	Concrete Cubes (24)	14471.5	46108.9	2945.89	8343.64	27	3	Loran
7/27/1995	Taylor #2 Big Bend Reefs	Concrete Cubes (96)	14473.7	46105.6	2945.66	8343.92	27	3	Loran
5/18/1993	Bird Rack #2	Concrete Culverts	14482.5	63271.5	2947.076	8337.129	5		Loran
5/17/1993	Bird Rack #1	Concrete Culverts	14489.7	63283.4	2950.091	8338.642	4		Loran
5/12/1993	Bird Rack #3	Concrete Culverts	14475.1	63249.9	2943.438	8334.373	5		Loran
5/11/1993	Steinhatchee Reef	Concrete Culverts	14460.2	46009.9	2940.017	8337.426	22		Loran
6/24/1992	Steinhatchee Reef	Concrete Culverts	14459.9	46011.2	2940.005	8337.602	22		Loran
4/16/1990	Steinhatchee Reef	Steel Scrap	14460	46011	2940.018	8337.564	22		Loran
12/31/1965	Steinhatchee Reef	Steel Scrap	14460.6	46011.6	2939.48	8337.49	20		Loran

Table 4. Reefs of Wakulla County (St. Marks, Panacea)

Deploy	Reef Name	Material 1	Loran l	Loran 2	Latitude	Long.	Depth	Relief	GPS
6/22/2000	Oar-2K Reef	CC Fish Havens (42)			2953.605	8407.669	27	6	GPS
6/30/1999	Marker 24 Barge No. & So.	CC Culverts (65)	14441.5	46345.8	2953.411	8409.408	29	5	DGPS
6/28/1999	Marker 24 Barge South	CC Culverts (80)	14441.4	46345.3	2953.358	8409.401	31	5	DGPS
6/16/1999	Marker 24 Barge North	CC Culverts (93)	14441.5	46345.8	2950.411	8409.408	29	5	DGPS
5/20/1997	Oar/Wakulla DZ#I (4)	CC Culverts	14395.3	46350.6	2943.825	8417.854	52		GPS
5/14/1997	Oar/Wakulla DZ#I (3)	CC Culverts	14395	46350.2	2943.763	8417.874	53		GPS
5/6/1997	Oar/Wakulla DZ#I (2)	CC Culverts	14396.3	46352.2	2943.725	8418.101	52		GPS
6/18/1996	Dog Ballard Phase 3	CC Cubes (108)	14475	46368.1	2957.053	8404.817	26		GPS
8/17/1995	Wakulla #1 Big Bend Reef	CC Cubes (24)	14473.9	46401.8	2958.16	8407.92	27		GPS
8/17/1995	Wakulla #2 Big Bend Reef	CC Cubes (96)	14473.7	46405.7	2958.14	8408.377	27		GPS
8/8/1994	Dog Ballard Phase 1	CC Culverts	14476.3	46359.1	2957.051	8404.852	26		GPS
8/8/1994	Dog Ballard Phase 2	CC Poles	14475.6	46369	2957.112	8404.819	25		GPS
6/4/1994	Oar/Wakulla DZ#I (1)	CC Culverts	14394.6	46350	2943.609	8418.031	65		GPS
6/1/1993	Oar/Wakulla DZ#3 (8)	CC Culverts	14397.5	46348.8	2944.043	8417.333	56		GPS
6/21/1992	Oar/Wakulla DZ#3 (7)	CC Culverts	14394.6	45350	2944.01	8417.28	55		GPS
1/26/1991	Oar/Wakulla DZ#2 (2)	FG Boat Molds	14393.6	46353.8	2943.719	8418.5	58		GPS
12/6/1990	Oar/Wakulla DZ#2 (1)	FG Boat Molds	14393.6	46353.4	2943.679	8418.311	58		GPS
7/3/1990	Oar/Wakulla DZ#3 (6)	CC Rubble	14397.5	46346.4	2943.926	8417.142	65		Loran
7/2/1990	Oar/Wakulla DZ#3 (5)	CC Culverts	14397.5	46346.4	2943.926	8417.142	65		Loran
7/1/1990	Oar/Wakulla DZ#3 (4)	CC Culverts	14397.5	46346.4	2943.926	8417.142	65		Loran
6/30/1990	Oar/Wakulla DZ#3 (3)	CC Culverts	14397.5	46346.4	2943.926	8417.142	65		Loran
6/29/1990	Oar/Wakulla DZ#3 (2)	CC Culverts	14397.5	46346.4	2943.926	8417.142	65		Loran
6/28/1990	Oar/Wakulla DZ#3 (1)	CC Culverts	14397.5	46346.4	2943.926	8417.142	65		Loran

Table 5. Reefs of Franklin County (Carrabelle, Apalachicola)

Deploy	Reef Name	Material 1	Loran I	Loran 2	Latitude	Long.	Depth	Relief	GPS
6/3/2004	St. George Is. Brg Rf-West	Con. Pilings (40)			2930.052	8449.937	75	10	DGPS
5/13/2004	St. George Is. Brg Rf-W Cen	Con. Bridge Span			2929.995	8449.426	75	10	DGPS
4/23/2004	St. George Is. Brg Rf-E Cen	Con. Bridge Span			2929.955	8448.656	75	10	DGPS
4/9/2004	St. George Is. Brg Rf-Cen	Con. Bridge Span			2930	8449.068	75	10	DGPS
3/28/2004	St. George Is. Brg Rf-East	Con. Bridge Span			2930.014	8448.178	75	10	DGPS
5/25/2003	Rose City Reef	Con. Fish Haven (50)			2940	8430	50	6	DGPS
6/21/2001	Yamaha Reef -South Add.	Con. L Beams (52)			2934.355	8432.192	76	20	DGPS
6/18/2001	Yamaha Reef -South Add.	Con. L Beams (42)			2934.355	8432.192	76	20	DGPS
6/22/2000	One More Time Addition	Con. L Beams			2942.36	8437.38	40	3	DGPS
1/6/2000	FL Gas Transmission Rf (B)	Con. Rubble			2949.868	8430.249	21	6	DGPS
6/24/1999	Two Dogs Culverts	Con. Culverts (130)	14365.7	46464.6	2945.92	8431.685	37	2	DGPS
6/14/1999	Two Dogs Reefballs	Con. Reefballs (130)	14367	46464.6	2946.072	8431.478	37	4	DGPS
6/26/1998	Bryson Additions	Concrete Rubble	14326.1	46286.6	2931.329	8424.562	79	6	GPS
6/18/1998	Bryson Additions	Concrete Culverts	14326	46286.4	2931.312	8424.558	79	6	GPS
2/11/1997	Bryson Memorial Reef	Ship Steel Tug 85'	14325.4	46285.8	2931.327	8424.523	79	22	GPS
2/11/1997	Bryson Memorial Reef	Ship Steel Tug 108'	14325.1	46285.4	2931.244	8424.526	75	29	GPS
5/4/1995	Yamaha Reef Addition	Concrete Pilings	14313.6	46364.8	2934.45	8432.26	85	12	GPS
5/2/1995	Yamaha Site Addition	Concrete Pilings	14313.6	46364.8	2934.42	8432.26	85	10	GPS
12/27/1993	Yamaha Reef	Barge Steel	14313.6	46364.8	2934.42	8432.26	85	15	GPS

Table 6. Reefs of Bay County (Panama City)

Deploy	Reef Name	Material 1	Loran I	Loran 2	Latitude	Long.	Depth	Relief	GPS
4/25/2006	MB-84	CC Modules Walters (3)			2945.329	8553.724	124	10	
4/25/2006	MB-82	CC Modules Walters (1)			2946.176	8551.192	124	10	
4/25/2006	Don Ard Memorial Reef	CC Modules Walters (3)			2945.339	8552.367	124	10	
4/25/2006	G Merrill Clift Reef	CC Modules Walters (1)			2944.445	8552.388	128	10	
4/25/2006	MB-88-HI	CC Modules Walters (5)			2947.485	8551.980	115	10	
4/25/2006	MB-88-G1	CC Modules Walters (5)			2947.484	8551.985	115	10	
4/25/2006	MB-88-D1	CC Modules Walters (5)			2947.482	8551.996	115	10	
4/25/2006	MB-88-C1	CC Modules Walters (5)			2947.480	8552.001	115	10	
4/25/2006	MB-88-B1	CC Modules Walters (5)			2947.509	8551.989	115	10	
4/25/2006	MB-88-A1	CC Modules Walters (5)			2947.484	8552.033	115	10	
1/11/2005	Carbody-mbara	CC Modules Walters (4)	14113.9	46847.4	2954.139	8532.39	60	10	DGPS
1/112005	Mbara-laars-l	CC Modules Walters (4)	13955.7	46834.7	2946.994	8550.002	115	10	DGPS
1/11/2005	Mbara-laars-2	CC Modules Walters (2)	13946.7	46837.7	2946.986	8551.189	115	10	DGPS
1/11/2005	Mbara-laars-5	CC Modules Walters (3)	13939.6	46823.8	2945.332	8551.208	115	10	DGPS
1/11/2005	Mbara-laars-4	CC Modules Walters (1)	13943.2	46831.1	2946.194	8551.209	115	10	Dgp5
1/11/2005	Mbara-laars-3	CC Modules Walters (4)	13937.3	46840.5	2946.976	8552.412	115	10	DGPS
1/112005	Mbara-laars-6	CC Modules Walters (3)	13920.8	46830.2	2945.35	8553.734	115	10	DGPS
1/11/2005	Mbara-laars-7	CC Modules Walters (2)	13916.7	46822.7	2944.441	8553.762	115	10	DGPS
8/9/2004	Bobby Guilford Site	CC Pilings			2953.235	8532.62	65	8	DGPS
6/8/2004	Carbody	CC Reefballs (38)			2953.874	8532.573	60	6	DGPS
5/14/2004	Hathaway Bridge 2 Start	Bridge CC Beams			2959.1	8551.2			DGPS
5/14/2004	Hathaway Bridge 2 Finish	Bridge CC Beams			2958.3	8551.5			DGPS
5/6/2004	Hathaway Bridge 1 Start	Bridge CC Beams			3004.6	8558.2			DGPS
5/6/2004	Hathaway Bridge 1 Finish	Bridge CC Beams			3003.2	8558.4			DGPS

Date	Name	Description							
4/22/2004	Carbody	CC Reefballs (37)			2953.884	8532.6	60	6	DGPS
4/17/2004	Steel Dredge Boat	Steel Dredge Boat 50'			2946.72	8550.03	115	10	DGPS
7/11/2003	Fami Tug #2	Steel Tugboat 95'	13992.3	46930.8	2958.123	8551.261	100	30	DGPS
7/10/2003	Fami Tug #I	Steel Tugboat 85'	13992.2	46930.8	2958.123	8551.274	100	20	DGPS
6/26/2003	Carbody	CC Reefballs (105)			2953.635	8532.635	60	5	DGPS
2/12/2003	Fish America Foundation	CC Reefballs (100)	14109.5	46843.5	2953.628	8532.634	67	8	DGPS
10/25/2002	Smurfit-stone #5	Steel Cylinders (2)	14118.6	46845.2	2954.15	8531.65	60	12	DGPS
10/25/2002	Smurfit-stone #6	Steel Cylinders (4)	14114.6	46839	2953.44	8531.73	65	12	DGPS
9/19/2002	Smurfit-stone #1	Steel Cylinders (4)	14115.6	46843.1	2954.741	8532.51	60	12	DGPS
9/19/2002	Smurfit-stone #3	Steel Cylinders (2)	14111	46845.1	2953.829	8532.56	65	12	DGPS
9/18/2002	Smurfit-stone #4	Steel Cylinders (2)	14114.7	46843.3	2953.826	8532.01	60	12	DGPS
9/18/2002	Smurfit-stone #2	Steel Cylinders (4)	14109	46839.2	2953.23	8532.426	65	12	DGPS
6/21/2002	Beanie and Hosehead Reef	CC Reefballs (10)			2953.835	8528.155	23	6	DGPS
6/21/2002	Brian Moeller Reef	CC Reefballs (10)			2953.948	8528.268	22	6	DGPS
6/21/2002	Phinizy Reef	CC Reefballs (10)			2954.155	8528.44	25	6	DGPS
6/21/2002	Charles House Reef	CC Reefballs (10)			2953.15	8532.605	68	6	DGPS
6/21/2002	Mbara Barge Addition	CC Reefballs (10)			2953.145	8532.792	68	6	DGPS
6/12/2002	Carbody	CC Reefballs (95)			2953.791	8532.009	60	5	DGPS
6/28/2001	Unnamed	CC Precast (117)	14118.2	46839.9	2953.692	8531.281	52	8	DGPS
6/2612001	Unnamed	CC Precast (112)	14118.2	46839.9	2953.692	8531.281	52	8	DGPS
6/19/2001	Mbara Barge	Barge Steel 195'	14106.5	46840.5	2953.145	8532.792	71	12	DGPS
6/14/2001	Car Body Site	CC Reefballs (98)	14116.4	46842.9	2953.878	8531.791	54	8	DGPS
7/9/2000	Accokeek	Navy Tugboat 143'	13988.7	46935	2958.475	8551.915	100	37	DGPS
7/1/2000	Dan Barge	Barge Steel 100'	14079.3	46971.9	3004.838	8543.843	60	5	DGPS
6/14/2000	Bell Shoal	CC Reefballs (36)	14140.7	46837.7	2954.486	8528.461	21	6	DGPS
6/14/2000	Bell Shoal	CC Reefballs (37)	14141.8	46847.8	2955.354	8529.094	21	6	DGPS
5/30/2000	Arizona Chemical	Steel Heat Exch.	14112.5	46839.2	2953.355	8532.004	66	4	Both

Table 7. Reefs of Walton County (Destin, Ft. Walton Beach)

Deploy	Reef Name	Material 1	Loran l	Loran 2	Latitude	Long.	Depth	Relief	GPS
6/18/2001	Frangista Beach	CC Culverts (52)	13783.2	47123	3019.752	8622.91	77	6	DGPS
6/30/1999	Walton Hopper Barge	Barge Steel 195'	13783.3	47122.4	3019.686	8622.899	77	12	DGPS
6/5/1997	Seagrove Reef	CC Culverts	13934.4	47101.8	3017.447	8606.497	70		Loran
11/15/1995	Walton #1	CC Ghettos (65)	13973.9	47087.3	3015.052	8601.605	58	6	DGPS

Table 8. Reefs of Okaloosa County (Destin, Ft. Walton Beach)

Deploy	Reef Name	Material 1	Loran l	Loran 2	Latitude	Long.	Depth	Relief	GPS
6/21/2005	Urchin Reef, Drop #11	Con. Walters FL (70)			3021.805	8627.846	70	10	WAAS
6/8/2004	Starfish Reef, Patch #4	CC Modules Walters Special (15)			3008.699	8637.529	100	10	WAAS
6/8/2004	Starfish Reef, Patch #3	CC Walters FL Special (15)			3008.795	8637.474	100	10	WAAS
6/8/2004	Starfish Reef, Patch #2	CC Walters FL Special (15)			3008.923	8637.526	100	10	WAAS
6/8/2004	Starfish Reef, Patch #1	CC Walters FL Special (15)			3008.969	8637.67	100	10	WAAS
4/22/2004	Starfish Reef, Patch #8	CC Walters FL Special (15)			3008.92	8637.807	103	10	WAAS
4/22/2004	Starfish Reef, Patch #7	CC Walters FL Special (15)			3008.795	8637.867	103	10	WAAS
4/20/2004	Starfish Reef, Patch #6	CC Walters FL Special (15)			3008.674	8637.807	103	10	WAAS

Date	Site	Description							Fix
4/20/2004	Starfish Reef, Patch #5	CC Walters FL Special (15)			3008.625	8637.67	103	10	WAAS
6/17/2003	Sand Dollar Reef	CC Culverts (110)			3008.75	8642.875	120	10	DGPS
6/17/2003	Sand Dollar Reef	CC Culverts (110)			3008.98	8643.01	120	10	DGPS
6/11/2003	Sand Dollar Reef	CC Fish Havens (34)			3008.845	8643.103	123	6	DGPS
6/11/2003	Sand Dollar Reef #28	CC Fish Havens (34)			3008.845	8643.117	119	6	DGPS
6/9/2003	Sand Dollar Reef	CC Fish Havens (31)			3008.639	8643.016	120	6	DGPS
6/9/2003	Sand Dollar Reef	CC Fish Havens (31)			3008.745	8642.935	120	6	DGPS
6/26/2002	Okaloosa Reef Odyssey	Ship Steel "Seabarb" (85')			3008.93	8640.608	110	22	DGPS
6/7/2002	Destin Reef "02"	Modules CC Fish Havens (57)			3009	8633.33	110	6	DGPS
5/8/2002	Valparaiso #8	CC Culverts (188)			3008.993	8633.269	101	10	DGPS
5/30/2001	Valparaiso #7	CC Culverts (109)			3008.78	8640.785	105	5	DGPS
5/30/2001	Bob Reay Reef "Belize Qn"	Steel Tugboat 85'	13585.1	47058.5	3008.802	8640.376	112	35	Both
4/20/2001	Destin Deepwater CC #2	CC Culverts (116)	13582.3	47058.7	3008.796	8640.684	108	8	Both
11/29/2000	Eglin Reef #1	Ship Steel 74'	13770.3	47097.9	3015.917	8623.16	94	22	Both
6/20/2000	Okaloosa Co. Lap Site C	CC Fish Havens (18)			3008.381	8648.968	134	6	DGPS
6/20/2000	Okaloosa Co. Lap Site C	CC Fish Havens (18)			3008.308	8648.959	134	6	DGPS
6/15/2000	Okaloosa Co. Lap Site C	CC Fish Havens (18)			3008.375	8649.064	134	6	DGPS
6/15/2000	Okaloosa Co. Lap Site C	CC Fish Havens (27)			3008.513	8649.13	134	6	DGPS
6/12/2000	Valparaiso 6-A	CC Culverts (30)			3008.55	8648.975	130	4	DGPS
6/12/2000	Valparaiso 6-B	CC Culverts (30)			3008.49	8649.046	133	4	DGPS
6/12/2000	Valparaiso 6-C	CC Culverts (30)			3008.569	8648.948	131	4	DGPS
5/25/2000	Okaloosa Co. Lap Site B	CC Fish Havens (16)			2958.402	8631.241	244	6	DGPS

Table 9. Reefs of Santa Rosa County (Pensacola)

Deploy	Reef Name	Material 1	Loran I	Loran 2	Latitude	Long.	Depth	Relief	GPS
5/26/2006	Santa Rosa Mar. Resort IV	15 Walters Sides			3004.514	8711.429	85	10	
5/26/2006	Santa Rosa Mar. Resort IV	15 Walters Sides			3004.474	8711.223	85	10	
6/30/200%	Santa Rosa Mar. Resort III	Con. Fish Havens (55)			3004.935	8710.423	85	6	WAAS
7/12/2004	Santa Rosa Mar. Resort II	Con. Reefballs (35)			3004.9	8711.7	85	5	DGPS
6/30/2004	Santa Rosa Mar. Resort II	Con. Reefballs (36)			3004.899	8711.683	85	5	DGPS
6/2/2003	Santa Rosa Marine Resort	CC Fish Havens (64)			3003.452	8711.933	97	6	DGPS
10/24/1996	East Lap Chemical Courier	Ship Steel Tug 80'	13276.9	47048.3	3005.95	8710.95	95		DGPS
6/27/1996	East Lap Reefballs	CC Reefballs (15)	13288.3	47044.8	3005.71	8709.54	94		Both
6/26/1996	East Lap Reefballs	CC Reefballs (15)	13285.8	47048.2	3005.938	8710.052	94		DGPS
6/25/1996	East Lap Reefballs	CC Reefballs (15)	13284.1	47048.6	3006.4	8710.07	94		Both
6/20/1996	East Lap Reefballs	CC Reefballs (15)	13284.6	47050.9	3006.82	8710.08	94		Both
6/19/1996	East Lap Reefballs	CC Reefballs (15)	13271.1	47050.3	3006.68	8711.41	94		Both
12/31/1987	Woodburn Reef	Steel Truck Cabs	13300.4	47010.1	2920	8704	138		Loran
12/31/1987	McKay Reef	Tires	13348.2	47028	3004	8704	156		Loran
12/31/1980	J. Brown–Liberty Ship	Ship Steel	13515.2	47083.9	3012.783	8648.35	85		Loran

Table 10. Reefs of Escambia County (Pensacola)

Deploy	Reef Name	Material 1	Loran I	Loran 2	Latitude	Long.	Depth	Relief	GPS
6/1/2006	Admiral Fetterman	Reefballs & Rubble			3004.682	8711.878	93	5	
6/1/2006	Mayor Whibbs Reef	Con. Reefballs (18)			3004.637	8711.633	90	5	
5/17/2006	USS Oriskany Reef	Navy Aircraft Carrier			3002.555	8700.397	212	134	

Date	Name	Description							
2/1/2006	Bay Bridge #2	Brdge Rubble Con.			3005.900	8709.000	100		WAAS
1/19/2006	Bay Bridge #1	Brdge Rubble Con.			3005.880	8709.050	100		WAAS
6/24/2005	Ray Jones Reef	Con. Reefballs (15)			3005.36	8710.53	90	5	DGPS
6/24/2005	George Wilkins Reef	Con. Reefballs (19)			3005.41	8710.856	90	5	DGPS
1/9/2005	Don Phillips Barge & Parks	Barge Steel 120'			3005.75	8710.6	100	8	DGPS
6/28/2004	Pat Donnelly Reef	Con. Reefballs (27)			3004.686	8711.142	90	5	DGPS
6/22/2004	Rusty B Reef	Con. Reefballs (20)			3004.756	8711.37	89	5	DGPS
6/2/2004	Brown Barge Mid School	Con. Reefballs (5)			3006.512	8711.638	91	5	DGPS
6/28/200	Penhall II Reef	Brdge Rubble Con.	13275	47043.3	3005	8711	94	10	DGPS
6/14/2003	Mara	Con. Walters FL (16)	13267.3	47046.2	3005.465	8711.85	95	10	DGPS
6/14/2003	Celia Reef	Con. Walters FL (15)	13266.7	47045	3005.235	8711.895	92	10	DGPS
2/12/2003	Knicklebine Barge	Barge Steel 117'			3001.97	8711.495	122	11	DGPS
2/9/2002	Penhall Reef	Brdge Rubble Con.	13270.8	47046.3	3005.523	8711.497	92	12	DGPS
6/20/2000	Concrete Fish Havens	Con. Fish Havens (21)	13303.9	47045.4	3005.916	8707.95	96	6	DGPS
6/20/2000	Concrete Fish Havens	Con. Fish Havens (21)	13289.9	47044.7	3006.257	8707.964	95	6	DGPS
6/20/2000	Concrete Fish Havens	Con. Fish Havens (21)	13289.2	47045	3005.831	8708.149	96	6	DGPS
4/1/2000	Navy Dive Tender Ydt-15	Ship Steel 132'			3005.267	8709.55	90	28	DGPS
4/1/2000	Navy Dive Tender Ydt-14	Ship Steel 132'			3005.33	8709.64	90	28	Both
	FWC-EE-1	Special Module			3003.006	8704.880			
	FWC-EE-2	Special Module			3005.255	8706.781			
	FWC-EE-3	Special Module			3004.598	8708.657			
	FWC-EE-4	Fish Haven Towers (2)			3001.419	8710.195			
	FWC-EE-5	Fish Haven Towers (2)			3005.129	8706.402			
	FWC-EE-6	Fish Haven Towers (2)			3003.278	8705.557			
	FWC-EE-7	Goliath Reefballs (2)			3001.462	8709.373			
	FWC-EE-8	Goliath Reefballs (2)			3002.931	8705.101			
	FWC-EE-9	Goliath Reefballs (2)			3005.404	8707.126			

On-The-Water Etiquette

What does etiquette have to do with a successful fishing trip? I'm not talking about your mom making you remove your fishing cap at the dinner table, but I'm talking good-sense on-the-water, fishing manners. Knowing the rules of the road, understanding proper radio procedures, and using common courtesies may not put more fish in the boat but will certainly make the trip safer and stress-free for you and for others.

Rules Of The Road

Many boat captains licensed by the United States Coast Guard (USCG) will agree that the most difficult questions on the Captain's Examination deal with Rules of the Road. Not unlike highway rules, these boating rules are complicated but can be distilled to a few basic components.

First, motor on the right side of *any* channel or navigable waterway and always pass oncoming traffic with them on your port (left) side, just like in your car. You may pass a boat ahead of you on either side, provided there is ample channel width to do it safely and not to impede his travel. Remember, too, in channels marked "Intracoastal Waterway" in western Florida, that red channel markers will be on your starboard (right) side when you're traveling north or west. Also, in most cases, red markers will be on your starboard side when you're coming toward port, or shore—*Red, Right, Returning.* It's also important to pay attention to local signs and informational markers pointing out shoals, manatee, no-motor, and idle-speed zones. When the sign says "Slow Down" or "Be Careful," obey it.

Second, always assume that any boat approaching you is under the command of an operator who does not know the rules nor has he read the previous paragraph. Be cautious, slow down if necessary, make your intentions clear, and then proceed. When it comes down to the bottom line, only you are responsible for the safety of your passengers and your vessel. If you have time, I recommend you take a look at either *Chapman's Piloting, Seamanship & Small Boat Handling* (ISBN 0-688-14892-1) or *Boater's Bowditch* (ISBN 0-07-136136-7), both excellent references. Florida also requires residents born after September 30, 1980, to take a boater education course before operating a vessel powered by a motor of 10 horsepower or more. The FWC publishes *How to Boat Smart*, a book containing the course information and test materials. Whether you need to take the course or not, I highly recommend you read the book. It's available at many marinas and tackle shops, or by calling the FWC's Boater Safety Section at (850) 488-5600.

Communications Etiquette

Depending on your style of fishing and the size of your boat, you should have at least one marine-band VHF radio aboard. It should also be on, monitoring at least channel 16, while you're underway. Many marinas monitor other channels (channel 9, for example) and local boaters sometime monitor specific channels (68 or 73 are good ones) for boat-to-boat communications. Channel 16 is for hailing only. Once you contact your party, switch to another channel to complete the conversation. Channel 22A is the Coast Guard's private channel—use it only in case of an emergency and only if they instruct you to do so. Always hail the USCG on Channel 16.

Handheld VHF radios are fine for close-to-shore use or for emergency backups to larger permanently mounted units, but their transmitting power is limited. VHF radios are more public, in that everyone on the channel you're working is listening, but that can be good in times of peril. And don't encourage children (or childlike adults) to play with VHF radios while aboard your boat. There are serious safety considerations that require the channels be kept free of idle chatter.

Finally, cell phones are good, but coverage can be limited in some offshore areas of the gulf and non-existent in desolate Big Bend areas. They're also no use in areas where you don't have your little black book aboard the boat.

Boat-Ramp Etiquette

Just the thought of a busy Saturday at a boat ramp is enough to raise a boater's blood pressure. A little bit of planning can go a long way

Crowded boat ramps can mean heated tempers. Plan your launch before you get your trailer wet.

to make the experience of launching your boat a smooth seamless operation.

First, stop a good distance away from the ramp and remove your tie-downs, put in your drain plug, prime your engine, turn on your batteries, unhook your trailer-light connections, and load the cooler and tackle. Then, attach enough line to your boat's front cleat so that your boat will be under control by your assistant standing alongside the launch ramp or on the dock. Or, if you're launching solo, tie the line to the winch post of your trailer.

Then, slowly and without becoming flustered, wait your turn and back down the ramp. It's okay to stop part of the way down the ramp to remove your safety chain and winch snap. *Don't* try backing on a busy weekend day if you've never done it before. Bring a friend who knows how to back a trailer, or even better, practice backing at home during the week.

Third, get the boat into the water and float it away from the ramp so that the next person in line can quickly launch. If you're powering the boat off the trailer, be sure to have whomever is driving the trailer know exactly where they are to park your rig.

Finally, on your return, keep your boat as far away from the ramp to unload your crew. Your gear can wait until the boat is up on the trailer. Get your trailer and get in line. Be sure to attach your safety chain and winch strap before coming up the incline. Then, pull to a not-so-busy area to finish readying the boat for travel.

No Wake and Idle Zones

"No Wake" means no wake and "Idle Speed" means idle speed. It's plain and simple.

Both are slow-speed zones with the interest of docks, moored boats, and sea life in mind. There are usually good reasons these zones exist along Florida's Gulf Coast and most are strictly enforced.

Keeping your wake to a minimum generally means running slow enough to keep your bow down and your wake flat behind your boat. Idle speed usually means running at 1,000 rpms or less, or at the speed your motor typically runs when out of gear. Idle speed is sometimes much slower than no wake. Pay close attention to regulatory signage, as many of these zones apply to areas outside of marked channels only.

Fishing Etiquette

This is a fishing book, and it would be unfair not to mention a couple of pet peeves passed along to me by several experienced gulf anglers. All involve good common sense, good manners, and the Golden Rule.

Never, never motor over to another boat that's fishing an area and ask, "How's the fishin'?" This is the ultimate sin. In certain areas, the unwritten rule is that if you can tell the color of the angler's shirt, you're too close. Also, don't run close to a boat that's on an obvious drift. You can easily tell which way he's fishing by paying attention to the wind, tide phase, or just the direction he's casting. One thousand feet or one-quarter mile is a reasonable distance on the flats, and as much as a mile between offshore boats is common.

On the same subject, don't creep toward another boat while he's fishing a particular spot—even if it's your favorite spot. It's first-come, first-served on the water. You'll just have to wait for him to leave—or come back another time. Don't even think about fishing *next* to him.

The same general concept applies to trolling. Experienced trollers understand that effective trolling involves making overlapping courses and wide turns. If another boat is trolling, be aware that he might be working an area as big as a square mile, and that he needs several hundred yards to make a turn. The exception to this rule might be trolling for Spanish mackerel nearshore or within bays, where boats tend to troll on parallel courses close together. Still, you should never crowd another boat, particularly when trolling.

Fishing near and around residential docks is more popular in the backwaters of the Emerald Coast than on the Big Bend, mostly a result of larger populations. Docks with boats generally have deeper water than residential docks and sunlit pilings hold heat—both good bait and fish attractors. In addition, electric lights on docks make them great spots for night fishing. If you plan to fish residential docks, take time to practice your casting so that you can accurately cast your lure under a dock. There's nothing that riles a homeowner more than hearing a heavy lure slap the side of his boat, safely hung on the dock from davits. And if the homeowner asks you to leave, be courteous, and move on down the shoreline.

Finally, certain areas along the Gulf Coast are home to commercial fishermen, trying their best to eek a living from clam leases, oyster beds, and crab traps. Take care not to run through lease areas or over active oyster beds. And *never* pull a crab trap just to see what's inside—it's illegal to interfere with traps, and besides, crabs pinch.

When fishing from a dock, be sure to ask permission from the owner.

Acknowledgments

While I'd love to take credit for every little bit of information in this guide, I can't. The truth is I am fortunate to know a group of fishing guides and serious fishermen along the Big Bend and Emerald Coast who were more than willing to give their opinions on various subjects.

Listed by location, south to north, I thank them all:

Capt. Mike Locklear, Homosassa
Capt. Earl Waters, Back Country Concepts, Homosassa
Capt. Cade Burgdorf, Outcast Fly Shop, Homosassa
Capt. Billy Henderson, Ozello
Daryl Seaton, Nature Coast Fly Shop, Crystal River
John Patrick, Crystal River
Capt. Matt Fleming, Yankeetown
Capt. Brian Kiel, Cedar Key
Bernie Fowler, Cedar Key and Suwannee
Richard Bowles, Suwannee
Capt. Wiley Horton, Steinhatchee
Rick Davidson, Steinhatchee
Joey Landreneau, Keaton Beach
Capt. Rusty Jenkins, St. Marks
Capt. Jody Campbell, Shell Point and St. Marks
Capt. Adam Hudson, Lanark/Carrabelle/Apalachicola
Capt. Kamen Miller, Carrabelle
Capt. Alex Crawford, Carrabelle

Capt. Pat Dineen, Panama City and Destin
Jim Wilson, Panama City
Capt. Rob Cochran, Destin and Navarre
Capt. Wes Rozier, Pensacola Area

Also, for their help with logistics, I'd like to thank the following:
Citrus County Visitors Bureau, (www.visitcitrus.com)
Emerald Coast Convention and Visitors Bureau (www.destin-fwb.com)
Apalachicola Bay Chamber of Commerce, Anita Grove (www.apalachicolabay.org)
Taylor County Tourism Development Council, Dawn Taylor (www.taylorcountychamber.com)
Southern Resorts, Destin/Ft. Walton Beach /St. Joe (www.southernresorts.com)
American Spirit Deep Sea Fishing, Capt. Jim Westbrook, Destin (www.newfloridagirl.com)
Sea Hag Marina, Charlie and Danielle Norwood and all the "hags," Steinhatchee (www.seahag.com)
Woods 'n Water magazine, Aaron Portwood (www.woodsnwater.net)
DeLorme, Charlie Conley (www.delorme.com)
Maptech, Martin Fox (www.maptech.com)
Pure Fishing/Berkley, Eric Naig (www.purefishing.com)

And to my Dad, Tom Thompson, Yankeetown, who advised me, "Not to sell the movie rights (to this book) too cheap!"

Recommended Reading

Sport Fish of the Gulf of Mexico, Vic Dunaway, ISBN 0-936240-18-0, www.florida sportsman.com.

Sportsman's Best Book and DVD Series, Snapper & Grouper, ISBN 0-936240-31-8, www.floridasportsman.com.

The Cobia Bible, Joe Richard, ISBN 0-9649317-2-9, available from the author at rich2735@bellsouth.net.

Maptech Chartkit, Region 8 (Florida West Coast and the Keys), Maptech Chart Navigator Software, www.maptech.com.

DeLorme Florida Atlas and Gazetteer, www.delorme.com.

Saltwater Directions Fishing Charts, Florida Series, www.saltwaterdirections.com.

Waterproof Charts, www.waterproofcharts.com.

Florida Boating and Angling Guides, Florida Fish and Wildlife Conservation Commission (FWC), Florida Marine Research Institute (available at tackle shops, visitors bureaus).

How to Boat Smart, Florida Boating Safety Course, FWC, www.myfwc.com, (850) 488-5600.

The Florida Boater's Guide, A Handbook of Boating Laws and Responsibilities, FWC, www.myfwc.com, (850) 488-5600.

Federal Requirements & Safety Tips for Recreational Boats, (available at tackle shops and marine dealers, or from the U.S. Coast Guard at uscgboating.org).

Back to the Basics, DVD Series, Omega Media Group, www.nutsandboltsfishing.com.

Redfish on the Fly, A Comprehensive Guide, Capt. John Kumiski, www.spottedtail.com, ISBN 0-963-51186-6.

Catching Made Easy, Capt. Rodney Smith, www.catchingmadeeasy.com.

Chapman Piloting: Seamanship & Small Boat Handling, Hearst Marine Books, ISBN 0-688-14892-1.

Boater's Bowditch, The Small-Craft American Practical Navigator, Richard K. Hubbard, International Marine/McGraw-Hill, ISBN 0-07-136136-7.

Practical Fishing Knots II, Mark Sosin and Lefty Kreh, The Lyons Press, ISBN 1-55821-102-0. This is a well-illustrated, complete guide to many popular fishing knots.

Know Your Knots, Pure Fishing, Inc. A pocket-size guide to popular knots. Reproduced in this book with the permission of Pure Fishing/Berkley.

Knots To Know, Innovative Textiles/PowerPro. Included with every PowerPro line purchase. Knots shown work well with braided fiber lines.

Animated Knots by Grog, Grog LLC, www.animatedknots.com. Helpful Web site featuring animated instructions for tying fishing and boating knots.

South Australia's Ultimate Fishing Resource Guide, www.fishsa.com/kntesbi.php.

Hatteras Outfitters, www.hatterasoutfitters.com/bimini.htm. Illustrated and animated instructions for tying a Bimini twist.

Index

Executive Director of the Florida Outdoor Writers Association, Tommy L. Thompson is a writer and photographer specializing in saltwater fishing and a frequent contributor to *Florida Sportsman* and *Shallow Water Angler* magazines. Thompson is a licensed U.S. Coast Guard charter-boat captain and active saltwater fishing guide on Florida's Gulf Coast.